PROFILES OF KAD RELATIONS WITH THE BLACK COMMUNITY

'92 - '20 PROFILES OF KAD RELATIONS WITH THE BLACK COMMUNITY

by Yi Woo Ae (이 우 애), formerly Ame Ai (雨 愛)
a Korean adoptee

LitPrime Solutions
21250 Hawthorne Blvd
Suite 500, Torrance, CA 90503
www.litprime.com
Phone: 1 (209) 788-3500

Cover by Janine Vance.

Published by LitPrime Solutions 10/28/2020

ISBN: 978-1-953397-21-8(sc)
ISBN: 978-1-953397-22-5(e)

DEDICATION

"He is how a lot of poets get to know each other."
—Kojo Nnamdi

I dedicate this to my dear friend E. Ethelbert Miller, longtime director of the Afro-American Studies Resource Center at Howard University, as he is a bridge between two worlds: the Black community and the Korean adoptee community. Though not an adoptee himself, he is sympathetic to Korean adoptees and introduced me to many Korean adoptees when I moved to Minneapolis, for both me and my ex at the time. He has also connected me to the Korean-American poetry community as well.

"If any of your people—Hebrew men or women—sell themselves to you and serve you six years, in the seventh year you must let them go free. And when you release them, do not send them away empty-handed. Supply them liberally from your flock, your threshing floor and your winepress. Give to them as the Lord your God has blessed you. Remember that you were slaves in Egypt and the Lord your God redeemed you. That is why I give you this command today."
—Deuteronomy 15:12-15, New International Version (NIV)

"Not everything that is faced can be changed; but nothing can be changed until it is faced."
-James Baldwin

"'Build houses and settle down; plant gardens and eat what they produce. Marry and have sons and daughters; find wives for your sons and give your daughters in marriage, so that they too may have sons and daughters. Increase in number there; do not decrease.'"
—Jeremiah 29, NIV

TABLE OF CONTENTS

INTRODUCTION: THE PURPOSE OF THIS BOOK

Disclaimer: I use the racial terms preferred by that race, and I do not censor curse words.

Black Lives Matter is meant to highlight that currently Black lives mean less than white lives to the criminal justice system and the government of the United States of America. Even though Black Lives Matter is about the Black community, I need to first establish that our lives are connected and even intertwined. In terms of action, the focus of this book is how Korean adoptees can talk with their adoptive parents, or other white people and non-Black people of color (NBPOCs) in their circles if they are no longer communicating with adoptive parents, in a way that supports Black Lives Matter, the movement. All the other races fall in a spectrum between the Black and white races. This book looks specifically at the relations between Blacks and Asians through the lens of the 1992 LA uprising, with the perspective of an Asian adoptee.

This is a non-academic work based primarily on my personal experiences and perspectives on race/racism involving Korean adoptees (KADs). This book is *not* about the history of the LA riots as there is already a plethora of information available about that; it is a starting point for speaking about race relations between Blacks and KADs. In 1992 I was nine years old and in the DC area. I did not experience the LA riots myself. My husband was in LA a week after the riots to be shipped out as a merchant marine but asked to be flown out the next day to Washington state, as the tensions were palpable.

I want to clarify that I would consider myself at the 101-level of anti-racism, so I know a little, but I'm in no ways an expert. Unfortunately, a lot of people at the 101-level are more interested in virtue signaling and boosting their own ego, seeking forgiveness, than actively part of the work to change things and seek to soothe their conscience while still keeping to their assumptions about both Black people and what's appropriate. Both KADs and other Asians who are activists around racial issues tend to be those who had relations with Black people. Otherwise, pardon the pun, they don't have as much skin in the victim game, and it is sometimes painfully obvious how little they relate and understand, even if they are Black-adjacent.

Just as Starr Carter, the lead character from *The Hate U Give*, has to balance between two worlds, KADs often feel like they have a foot in two (or more) worlds themselves. If KADs think that Koreans do not face similar experiences to Black Americans, they should read more about Korean history in Japan.

Since Minnesota is the KAD capital of the United States (having more KADs than lakes), I used Minneapolis, a major city in Minnesota, as a metaphor for KADs in general. I wrote this in 2007, far before I knew that the next major riots would originate in Minneapolis in 2020. Please keep this in mind when reading this book.

I chose the year 1992 because it was a significant year for both the Black community and the KAD community. The year 2020 is a significant year for both communities as well, and under the same Saturn in Aquarius astrological configuration. I also chose to abbreviate it to '92 because 93 is the number of love, according to Thelema, as well as angel numbers. If we can remember that we are all One then we can add our Oneness to 92 to get the number of love. In addition, '20, for the year 2020, numerologically represents 2, the number of compassion. Despite all the protests and riots, I want to remind the reader to always come back to love and compassion.

However, there is a difference between uniting with love versus believing that love is enough. My parents did not mind if they had a child with disabilities, a Black child, a boy, or whatever because they had enough love to go around, they said. Dad told me it was nearly impossible to adopt a Black child at that time, due to controversy over the child losing his heritage. They chose me in the end.

In the process of researching and writing this book, I conducted a literature search and interviewed adult KADs who have had time to understand their life in a larger perspective. Some have more credentials to speak on this topic and others represent the vast majority.

The purpose of this book is not to highlight racism between Blacks and KADs, the purpose of this book is first to highlight that the relationship between the two is better than the media portrays, without downplaying the negative parts. I showcase a variety of experiences with varying levels of significant and repeated exposure to the other race. This book is divided into three parts: profiles, background history, a how-to, and a call to action. In terms of another focus of this book, I argue later for the inclusion of adoption-based and race-based trauma into the Diagnostic and Statistical Manual of Mental Disorders (DSM). I also need to share with you the importance of acknowledging that trauma as defined in the DSM is not currently all-inclusive. Whether we believe we chose our present life or not, we are the bridge between worlds.

The effect that Black-Korean relations have on KADs is strong. I already know four or five other KADs who have taken the ideas of "Black power" to heart and have ridden on the shoulders of Black organizations for lack of a similar KAD organization.

I need to share what you can do as a KAD (or Asian adoptee) and how you can do it to support, not co-opt, the Black Lives Matter movement.

KOREAN AND KAD RELATIONS WITH THE BLACK COMMUNITY

1636:	***Night Watch created***
3/5/1770:	***Crispus Attucks***
12/1791:	***2nd Amendment***
8/11/1965:	***Watts Rebellion***
1986-1990:	***83 Lawsuits Against Los Angeles Police Department***
3/3/1991:	***Rodney King beaten***
3/15/1991:	***Officers charged in beating***
3/16/1991:	***Latasha Harlins killed***
11/15/1991:	***Soon Ja Du sentenced to 5 yrs probation***
4/21/1992:	***State appeals court upholds decision***
4/29/1992:	***'92 LA uprising***
4/1992:	***Adoption from China begins***
5/1992:	***Asian-Pacific American Heritage Month***
1992:	***Karen Bass passes City Charter***
7/1992:	***Harlins family receives $300K settlement***
5/1993:	***Rodney King's mentor creates Colorful Flags***
1993:	***Tupac releases a song about Latasha***
7/27/1998:	***National Korean War Veteran Armistice Day***
2015:	***Jamar Clark shot in Minneapolis***
2016:	***Philando Castile shot in Minneapolis***
2017:	***Black officer sentenced to 12.5 yrs for shooting white woman***
5/25/2020:	***Korean Consulate sends face masks to KADs***
5/26/2020:	***George Floyd is killed***
6/11/2020:	***Breonna Taylor Act***
6/12/2020:	***Kara Bos wins landmark case in Korea for KADs worldwide***
6/25/2020:	***Karen Bass passes The Justice in Policing Act***
6/25/2020:	***The 70th Anniversary of the Korean War***

Table 1: Timeline

SA-I-GU (LA UPRISING OF 1992[1])

The craziness began before Rodney King's verdict. In 1990, tensions were already escalating between Korean-American merchants and the Black community. Due to this racial tension, editor James Ryu of *KoreAm Journal* reprinted articles from the Black media because Korean-Americans wanted to know what was being said about them.

Sa-i-gu literally means "April 29th," which was the day of the LA uprising. The anger arose from a convergence of two news stories: one about the acquittal of the policemen who beat Rodney King and another about the murder of Latasha Harlins by Soon Ja Du of Empire Liquor, over a $1.79 bottle of orange juice.

Her grandmother Ruth, who was raising her, warned her not to entire Empire Liquor because her Uncle Richard used to work there and found them to be suspicious that people were stealing from them and left when he refused to work unpaid overtime. After being dropped off by a friend who wasn't welcome in the store, Latasha Harlins was shot by a woman, just like her mother was in 1985, a few blocks from her home (Stransky). She was buried beside her mother. This was all witnessed by Asmail Ali who saw her raise two dollars to pay for the juice when accused of stealing, and she was still holding those two dollars when she killed (McKennett). Mrs. Du was sentenced to five years of probation, 400 hours of community service, and a $500 fine instead of the maximum of 16 years of imprisonment decided on by the jury because the Judge Joyce Karlin believed Mrs. Du's ability to act with reason was compromised by three past robberies, a drive-by shooting, and the fact that her son had been threatened by Crips unless they hired them. She is a clear example of why people with trauma should not own guns but are the most likely to buy them. She was like the older man in the movie *Gook*, a movie about two Korean brothers who befriend a Black girl, which was set on April 29, 1992 in Paramount, CA (Chon).

---

[1] The best song about the LA uprising is "April 29, 1992" by Sublime.

Astonished at the result, Latasha's aunt, Denise, led protests outside the judge's home, and the Harlins family led vigils outside Mrs. Du's house every year after her sentencing. Denise also interrupted an awards ceremony for Charles Lloyd, Mrs. Du's defense attorney, on behalf of her niece who was a pillar of the community.

After Latasha's death, the Korean community leaders, who had been working to build rapport with Black community leaders for five years prior, issued a "Merchants Code of Ethics" alongside Brotherhood Crusade and many contributed "Gifts of Love" to the Harlins family (Stransky).

Officer Kim witnessed one of the few moments of hope during the uprising. Despite Koreans talking about how it's in their blood to be unable to compromise and negotiate, what he saw during the uprising was 40,000 Koreans united in an effort to clean up the city (Kim and Yu 208).

The 1992 LA uprising, as well as the 2020 George Floyd protests, both began as a result of police brutality. The Los Angeles Police Department (LAPD) Chief at the time of the 1992 LA uprising was Daryl Gates, and before that was Chief Parker. Gates even said that Blacks die from chokeholds because they do not respond to them the way "normal people" do. He died in 2010 from bladder cancer (KFSN-TV and Radar Staff).

Rodney King died two years later, found suspiciously dead in his pool at the age of 47. Before his death, he had written *The Riot Within: From Rebellion to Redemption*.

Gates is known for introducing the Special Weapons and Tactics (SWAT) teams to the world and for using an armored battering ram on a suspected crack house but using it on the wrong house. SWAT teams have proliferated due to the Pentagon's excess property program, also known as the weapons giveaway program, and no-knock raids are most often performed against families suspected to have marijuana (62%), with or without babies, young children, pets, and elders, which is imaginably quite traumatizing (ACLU Foundation). There have also been raids on graffiti artists, pet neglecters, poker games, and moonshine brewers. In 1993, the LA SWAT team was taken over by Director Phil Hansen (Sack).

William Bratton, who replaced Daryl Gates as the LAPD Chief, transformed the LAPD for the better by bringing down the murder rate to the lowest they had been in over 40 years (M. Taylor).

Not every looter was Black[2] and not every shopkeeper was Korean-American. No two Black or Korean-American people are alike, and their identity is far more complex than the media would have us believe. To banish the media-perpetuated myth that only Korean stores were burned by Blacks, even stores with Black-owned signs were burned (Kim and Yu 184), which is the same thing that happened during the Minneapolis protests about George Floyd. There was too much media emphasis on Korean stores being burned, when any store in the area was at risk. Despite most of the citizens in Koreatown and Hollywood being Latino, not Black or Asian, U.S. citizens not from that area concluded that the Black-Korean conflict drove the uprising.

In nonfiction true life story *A Single Square Picture*, Katy Robinson, a KAD, recalls how "[l]ater, the program turned into a tabloid-style exposé of racism in America. The camera followed a teenage girl, a Korean adoptee who had grown up in a white family in a Chicago suburb. [...] "The program then turned to stock footage of Korean shopkeepers whose stores had been looted and destroyed during the riots in Los Angeles after the Rodney King verdict". Once Robinson understood the dynamics she was working within it became clear why "some Koreans look at me with pity when they discovered where I lived. [...] I didn't need anyone's pity, and besides, Korea seemed to have its own racist views of neighboring Asian countries, Blacks, and darker-skinned people in general" (Robinson 178). What Lee imagined and Robinson

[2] In fact, most rioters during the Minneapolis protests about George Floyd were white, probably from the Boogaloi Bois, a conglomeration of various, but similarly violent ideologies.

lived is a reality that survives in Korea to this day. Let this be a warning to adoptees; may they understand the dynamics in the situations in which they find themselves, and that is part of why I wrote this book.

In Koreatown was a blend of extremes. It was a mix of *sokch'ima* (literally underskirt) older conservative women and young Koreans, some of whom were in gangs and/or distributed cocaine (Kim and Yu 167 and 211). Despite these differences, Koreans tend to stick together for better or worse. Even though Motown and LA's Chinatown both had white people mixed in, Koreatown was purely Korean. Even in my experience in the DC area, there were more Blacks than Chinese in that Chinatown. Paul Kim said, "[T]hey come back to Koreatown and become more Korean than the people born and raised in Korea!" (Kim and Yu 217). Flabbergasted, Kim describes in "Getting Real" the time when he asked a Korean who graduated from Yale why he was still in Koreatown. The answer was that it was his cultural heritage. This stick-togetherness did not jive with Kim, because he had noticed that the Koreans there worried too much about themselves and not the others who live in the area. "I can't make it safer for Koreans here and not care about the Mexicans who live next door," says Kim (Kim and Yu 217). Koreatown is an experience to say the least, but might not necessarily be the perfect permanent solution for KADs attempting to reconcile their American self with their Korean self.

LA has the highest population of Koreans outside of Korea, but it is one tough city (Kim and Yu xxi). L.A. has a large rate of crime and violence, which is perpetuated by the media. Members from each neighborhood are afraid of the neighborhood next door (Kim and Yu 321). Neighborhoods are segregated and people tend to stick to their own kind, even though things used to be different (Kim and Yu 136, 141, and 149).

Korean gangs there go by names like the Korean Killers, Koreatown Crazies, and Satanas (meaning "Satan") (Kim and Yu 142). Kyu Min Lee used to belong to the Korean Killers, but by now, "[m]ost of the original Korean Killers, or the KK[3], are dead or in state prison," says LAPD Officer Paul Kim about the disappearance of the Killers, "[T]hey got into burglarizing other Korean people's homes. Once they were making money, they started going to Las Vegas" (Kim and Yu 212). Officer Paul Kim was the first LAPD Korean officer who could speak English and Korean fluently (Kim and Yu 215). Some Korean gangs got involved with selling ice and using weapons. Gangsters, who had to do community service at the Korean Youth Center a decade ago, dressed in a unique way, either like a spiky-haired *cholo* or like Bruce Lee (Kim and Yu 132). Paul Kim wants to make clear how a Korean gang is different: "What is called a Korean gang is really not a gang. Most of the time, it's a business group or just groups of free-spirited entrepreneurs, except that they use illegal methods," so think white-collar crime with a tough façade (Kim and Yu 211).

Many Koreans also chose to be in the Wah Ching, a Chinese gang, mostly female, because they were better dressers, had better cars, and treated women better (Kim and Yu 144). "The Korean kids were very rough; they looked like hillbillies compared to the Wah Chings," says Paul Kim. The Tai Hong murder, the murder of the Chinese, was over a beautiful Korean woman who wouldn't date Korean men (Kim and Yu 212). "Chol Soo Lee was charged with murdering a fellow prison inmate while he was serving a term for the famous San Fransisco Chinatown killing of a Wah Ching leader [...] Eleven Asian American lawyers volunteered their services free. It was obvious that Chol Soo Lee had been politically framed," says Jay Kun Yoo, "We organized the Chol Soo Lee Defense Committee on July 17, 1978" (the South Korean Constitution Day) (Kim and Yu 287). Dredge Kang, a gay man from the DC area said that he used to romanticize the city, but that everything had been a disappointment (Kim and Yu 88). It is not the type of city to romanticize.

[3] What a horrible acronym!

The demographics have been constantly changing since 1967, when there was only one Korean restaurant and grocery store (Kim and Yu 196). On a side note, I was one of five minorities in my high school only to find out that the museum for that city said many years later that the city is now 20% Korean. Another demographic shift could be due to the influx of Latino/a and Latinx households, transforming majority Black neighborhoods to half-Black neighborhoods.

Sunny Jo, creator of the largest worldwide web group, K@D, has noticed that adult KADs tend to congregate in large cities where they can find other Koreans (but as I mention in another section though, they tend to grow up in white neighborhoods). In "Making of KAD Nation" she says,"This has created a number of geographic anchors for the KAD community, among them Los Angeles, San Francisco, the Minnesota Twin Cities, New York, and Toronto in North America; Seoul in Korea; and Stockholm, Amsterdam, and Brussels in Europe. A few majority languages are used to tie the community together, such as English, French, and 'Scandinavian,'" (Oparah, Shin, and Trenka 289).

"I had never heard a good story from adoptees until after I went to Korea. There was always sexual abuse, verbal abuse, mental abuse, all kinds of abuse. In one case, a family had four biological sons and one daughter who was adopted from Korea and she had to do all the chores. I have a one-sided view of adoption. Even Korean adoptees in Korea didn't have good experiences. When I got back was the first time I heard good stories. They mostly came from urban areas like Los Angeles or Detroit" (Nabiya).

In 2019, LA had the largest Asian, Indigenous, Latino/a or Latinx, and white population of all counties in the United States, with LA having also the largest increase from 2010 to 2019 (U.S. Census Bureau).

The part of LA that people witnessed on the media during the 1992 LA uprising was the part that had already experienced enough white flight (10-20% initially) until minorities constituted at least 80% of the neighborhood, property price reduction due to lower demand, higher taxes to compensate for fewer public services that are funded by citizens, and the loss of grocery stores and banks, leaving behind liquor stores and highways (PBS).

Over 200 Korean liquor stores were burned in the 1992 uprising. I believe that alcohol dependence was a large part of the problem during the LA uprising of '92 and not necessarily race alone. Bong Hwan Kim said that after the Korean liquor stores had been burned, he, and others, set up a liquor store conversion project to help Korean merchants start other businesses that would help the community; however, there are still several Korean liquor stores in existence today. During this project the city council decided to waive sewage hookup fees if a store owner wanted the store to be converted to a laundromat, not necessarily a huge moneymaker, but better for the community.

Perhaps LA is also where Koreans get the stereotype that they own stores that require menial work. Y. Chang and Young Kim, the first Korean to start a sewing company and laundromat respectively, knew that the Korean garment business peaked between 1976 to 1979 (Kim and Yu 201).

Not everyone was fond of the idea of the conversion project because one still needed an additional business to afford a business that wouldn't turn much of a profit. Store owners who did not want to convert their store had the option to improve the sales of non-alcoholic beverages (Kim and Yu 350). This great idea was, unfortunately, not successful because they ran into the problem that the customers kept asking for beer, which could have pointed to rampant alcoholism that kept race relations at subpar levels (Kim and Yu 185). After the uprising, Small Business Association (SBA) loans did not send Korean store owners, who were trying to get their stores back up, the money for expensive liquor licenses (Kim and Yu 249). So, despite the great intentions, many Korean store owners ended up worse off, which did not do much for race relations.

After the uprising, some Korean store owners were interviewed. Readers would have been astonished to know that, with poor understanding of English, a Korean store owner Young Soon Han bought a liquor store by accident. In “Second Homeland” she said she didn’t even know the word “liquor” and that no one in her family drank. If the family knew that the stores themselves were creating such huge problems with health, mental health, and race relations, they would not have bought it (Kim and Yu 245). Even though alcohol sales averaged only 30-35 percent of total liquor store sales before the uprising, since they sold grocery items as well, that percentage is too large. A lesson that should have been learned from the uprising is that it is detrimental to a community to burn down a store where you can buy food, cash checks, and send mail. The town without a grocery store is like a person without a head.

If the argument against the Korean liquor stores was that they were monopolizing the market, that argument can soon be put away. In “Second Homeland” by Young Soon Han said that Black entrepreneurs and business owners were not able to start businesses, so taking away Korean businesses hurt the community, rather than helped it (Kim and Yu 246). In order to prevent the uprising from reoccurring, it seems that many LA citizens had to go to Alcoholics Anonymous meetings and learn how to become businessmen and women. And who could have taught them that had experience? Koreans.

MEDIA PORTRAYAL OF KOREANS

Korean-Americans have not been portrayed very positively in the media for a while now, when there was any news portrayal at all. First it was the LA uprising over the death of a Black teen, then it was the LA Rodney King uprising which put Korean-Americans on the map, though not necessarily in a good way, and, in what was current news when I first wrote this: Cho Seung Hui, the Virginia Tech killer of 2007. The news portrayal of Koreans played on preconceived notions that Korean immigrants have strong accents. The media is what creates and perpetuates stereotypes (a.k.a. "stereotype tattoos"), so, for example, Blacks might not trust Korean store owners because their preconceived notions of them as selfish and greedy and there's little that the Korean store owner can do, or does, to change that opinion. However, there was actual price gouging and Korean store owners refused to hire Black employees. Part of that was because Koreans might not have trusted Blacks because of the pervasive negative stereotyping in the media (Wing).

People remember seeing the picture of Korean business owners standing on roofs holding guns. They say this is not because they put profits over people, but because they had put in about 80-100 hours a week for at least 10 years. In this case, the picture was *not* worth 1,000 words. Our voices are literally hushed as well as figuratively hushed. Elaine H. Kim, co-editor of *East to America*, received a massive amount of hate mail telling her to side with white people over Blacks (Kim and Yu xvii).

Asians are considered the invisible minority, and the media generally does not solicit their opinions unless it matches up to the stereotyped narrative it wishes to convey in the conversation about race relations. Koreans, as with other non-Black minorities, are not the enemy of Black people, but are stuck in the middle of this centuries-long conflict. Black congressmen and Koreans living in Korea routinely know very little about Black-Korean race relations. Basically, our successes are used to banish affirmative action and our failures make xenophobic natives believe that we don't deserve to be here, the same sentiment used toward Latinos/as and the Latinx[4] community. Korean-Americans just do what they would do were they in Korea, which is to fulfill parental expectations to get into a good college and get a good job, but in America such culture clashes with other cultures. By just doing what they've always done, they become resented and feared by white people and resented by Black and brown people because white people conveniently pit them against each other. If Koreans accept the rules of engagement of only their Korean culture, they are doomed in America.

Another negative assumption perpetuated from the media was that LA was getting plenty of government help to rebuild, but, in reality, the Federal Emergency Management Agency (FEMA) stopped supporting the city and the Employment Development Department (EDD) of the Small Business Administration (SBA) stopped supporting the city as well (Kim and Yu 249).

LA's Koreatown from the eyes of its members during 1992 considered it to be one of the most violent places in the United States of America (Kim and Yu 16). Those outside of Koreatown see it as a symbol for Korean-Americans throughout the nation (Kim and Yu xxi). What a difference are those opinions! Aren't Koreans supposed to be humble and subdued? Ha! Just watch Korean action and horror movies.

Speaking of news portrayal, movie portrayal of Koreans is moving toward portraying Korean and Korean adoptee women, as thieves, particularly jewel thieves, because they are already seen as mysterious and nimble, e.g., Cassandra Cain in *Birds of Prey*, Constance in *Oceans 8*, Ming Fleetfoot in *Jumanji* (including a Korean adoptee stunt double), and arguably Nagini from *Harry Potter*. This is ironic

[4] A 2019 poll found that only 2% of United States Americans who were of Latin-American descent preferred to use Latinx as it is used exclusively in the United States of America (McWhorter). However, this word is kept for those who are transgender readers.

since Korea as a country is very safe; you can leave things out in the open (bags, phones, etc.). There's even a Korean movie called *The Thieves*. Some people see this as a good thing because it's different from past movie portrayals, but it's not actually a good thing. The thief stereotype is one of the worst stereotypes, which has plagued both the Black community and the gypsy community.

KOREANS WITH THE BLACK COMMUNITY

There has been over a century of scholarship by Black, Caribbean, and African authors regarding the significance of place throughout the African Diaspora. However, one thing a friend pointed out was that the Black race is the only race that is not connected to a place (to which I replied that the white race isn't either). And maybe that's the point. It could mean that the descendants of slaves who came to America unwillingly are severed from their homeland and that the European immigrants who came to America willingly severed themselves from their homeland to assimilate. It could be that way so that the politics of Black vs. White is so severed from it's actual purpose that it's like environmentalists who never visit the park. Or we could see it as that way to unite all Africans, Caribbeans, and descendants of slavery under one umbrella so that there's power in numbers. But who knows?

Koreans are different in each U.S. locale, so it is difficult to put a stereotype on them or say that Korean-Black relations are the same throughout the United States. On the West Coast they're more likely to be in the movie industry, but on the East Coast they're more likely to be in the government or financial industry. According to my friend, Erykah Soleil, there was never any animosity between Korean and Black vendors in Newport News in the 90s. Howevever, in LA, the perception of Korean-Americans is that they are owners of liquor stores or members of gangs, which, unfortunately, hasn't changed much since 1992. Bong Hwan Kim has noticed this disparity between stereotypes. Outside of LA, he says, "When I tell them I work with Korean American gangsters in Los Angeles, they get this blank look of total bewilderment on their faces" (Kim and Yu 343). Maeun Koch'u says that in Virginia, where I grew up, Koreans were all teachers, doctors, and valedictorians, but in New Orleans they were just refugees.

One of the possible causes for all the anger between the races had to do with cars. Koreans would buy expensive luxury cars that were far too large and had amenities they didn't even use. This should not be too surprising. My mother told me that L.A. is a "car culture" and that in some areas, freeways are 16 lanes across, full of traffic. Officer Kim says Blacks would ask him why Jewish business owners park their old Toyotas and pickup trucks in the back while wearing casual clothing, but Koreans park Cadillacs in the front while wearing large gold rings, "We start to think about where the heck they made that money. And we figure they made it from us" (Kim and Yu 211).

I see how this could be a cultural misinterpretation. I know that even potential male suitors have to prove their economic standing before most Korean women will even consider dating them, which is similar to white men buying expensive sports cars to attract white women.

Part of what can explain the attitudes against the Koreans during the violence of '92, is their attitude towards "bling." Officer Kim found out, through interrogating some Korean kids, that the kids could afford to drive Cadillacs because their parents did not teach them discipline and let them live at home for free (Kim and Yu 212).

However, I can also see this as something that is common to all cultures, as it could be a matter of ego and not culture. I have a hard time believing that Blacks think the only people showing off "bling," or expensive tastes, are Koreans. LA is near Hollywood. I've seen the Black music videos with Flava Flav chain necklaces. I've seen the Black culture with their "grillz," or gold-plated fake teeth. At home, I'm well aware of the Latinos/as who go drag racing with cars designed to making popping noises whenever I want to sleep. And in the white culture, even the current president as of 2020, who I decline to name, has gold toilets.

Just as Koreans don't judge Blacks for being Black, Blacks don't judge Koreans for being Korean. They judge each other on how each other acts. But, unfortunately, things that are totally normal in one culture is completely rude in another. For example, Koreans greet people by asking for your age or if you've eaten, which would be considered rude in America.

"Koreans, lacking in language and street manners, behave just as if they were in Myongdong," says K.W. Lee. Myongdong is a very crowded shopping district in Seoul where people push and shove each other on the sidewalks. Koreans, without meaning intentional ill-will have offended Blacks deeply, partly because they are used to places like Seoul and Myongdong, which are too crowded to even care. In Korea, adoptee Janine Bishop observed that people often shove and push without smiling or talking just so they can get to their destination in one piece. Not only might it be that it's crowded and that they're private people, but, much like their Russian neighbors, they don't even smile when taking pictures of themselves, which was something I distinctly remember when being given a picture of my birthmom (Kim and Yu 311). However, I hear that this tradition is changing.

And, of course, some Koreans hate Blacks too. Part of the reason why Koreans may be racist toward Blacks is because Confucianism puts a lot of emphasis on class, as with Hinduism. As a result, Koreans would rather associate with the race associated with the higher class ranking. "Some Koreans think that poor people in America are lazy. Ah, lazy, my foot! If those Koreans were in the exact same situation, do you think they'd do any better? I doubt it," says Officer Kim, wishing people would stop pointing fingers. He says, "I ask myself, if I was them, would I be any better? And you know what? I would be a lot worse. I would be much more violent and less patient. I would be more 'give me, give me, give me'" (Kim and Yu 217).

Asians who hate Black people hate at least half of America, black Native Americans, most of Africa, Black Muslims, aboriginals from many countries, and also quite a bit of Europe. In the same way, Black people who hate Asians hate East Asians, South Asians, Asians in America, Asians in Hawaii, Indians in England, Indians in Trinidad, Asian Native Americans, technology companies that dominate American life, and most American doctors. Unfortunately, Black people who fear white policeman and conclude they hate all white people must also logically be anti-Semetic and hate Russians,

Germans, Italians, Irish, Spanish, French, Celts, and other Europeans. Not only that but they must logically also hate Black people who are partially white, white Native Americans, and even themselves in past lives. Does anyone else see how ridiculous it is to be bigoted and racially prejudiced and how much it can hurt your individual cause? We all started out speaking the same language prior to the Tower of Babel and we can speak the same language again if we all spoke the language of love.

When one visits LA, it is a common understanding that Koreans don't like Blacks. However, they will respond well to perceived good manners. So what has happened, perhaps, is that some African countries are louder than others, like Nigeria, for example. Being raised to be quiet, Korean see loudness as rude. Being raised to be loud and extroverted, Africans see quietness as aloof and shoving as rude. In fact, it took quite some time before my roommate who led the Student for Minority Outreach realized I actually liked her.

Korean-Americans are generally not sociable or expressive because they were told to be quiet, be obedient, and not to rock the boat, so many think they are angry. This is something I relate to myself. When I had depression in high school, no one could tell, and to this day I worry about coming off as too aloof to my coworkers. Korean-Americans think it's desirable to be quiet because, in Korea, men who are quiet are seen as intelligent gentlemen.

The conclusion most people took away from the LA uprising is that Blacks and Asian people do not get along. *Au contraire*, I think there are many similarities between the cultures. For example, In the same way that Blacks fought against segregation, Koreans and Korean adoptees fought for reunification. It is actually police and the Black community that do not get along.

Despite general racism, such as the belief that Asians carry diseases or the practice of fetishizing Asian women, Blacks and Asians get along better than some people think. Grace Lee Boggs, wife of James Boggs, her Black husband, is an award-winning activist labor organizer, filmmaker, and author well known in the support of the Black community (Nguyen). The Korean community in America and abroad has finally accepted Hines Ward, half-Black, half-Korean football superstar. He teaches Koreans to look beyond stereotypes.

They do not understand that some of us respect them and that many have been part of #Asians4Black Lives. Many POCs benefitted from what Blacks have done in their own struggles. "In high school, I saw Blacks as role models," said one 1999 Gathering participant (Freundlich and Lieberthal). "I decided I wanted to be just like him [the Black gardener]," said Elizabeth Kim, "Grandmother was horrified and told my parents, who explained that certain proprieties must be maintained in a nice society" (Kim, Elizabeth 97).

Much to many Blacks' surprise, some Korean Americans admire them. "I have always identified with the people who reminded me of Korean peasants, hardworking, honest, decent, poor, with something spiritual about them, whether they were Appalachian mountaineers, Del Paso Heights blacks, or Filipino migrant farm workers," says K.W. Lee. K.W. Lee, was actually assigned to report on news relevant to the Black community, despite his Asian face (Kim and Lee 13-14).

Not all Koreans hate Blacks, as the media would lead us to believe, but instead feel a kinship to them. Bong Hwan Kim, who has a professional and personal affinity to Blacks says, "My current work on behalf of poor and immigrant communities often pits me against homeowners' association, which are predominantly white" (Kim and Yu 343).

Kyu Min Lee is an example of someone who has embraced Black culture. He is in charge of a show on the largest rap music station in Los Angeles (Kim and Yu 114). He is unique. He wore a zoot suit at his ninth-grade graduation and always had a passion for Black music. In 1988, he did not finish school because he wanted to open a hip hop music store in a Black neighborhood and was hired as the national rap music promotional director a year later (Kim and Yu 119 and 122). He was someone who could have been a great representative of 88 Rising before 88 Rising was a thing. For those who don't know, 88 Rising is a record label that hires on Asian rappers.

He teaches Koreans to look beyond stereotypes of what Black music is or is not. Kyu Min Lee expresses his feelings by saying that hip-hop is not just music or fashion, but is rather about authenticity, morality, and self-motivation. He adds that hip-hop is not about gangs either, but is for those who want to quit the gang lifestyle and who really want to analyze the music. Lee is attuned to culture in America that many people do not see or see only as negative (Kim and Yu 124). His mother regrets that she brought him to Korea, where he embraced rap, but Lee reminds her that he was glad that she did and that not all of what she thinks is bad necessarily is bad. His next project is to paint a Crip. He feels bad that the average Black person cannot have the things he has, cannot achieve the things he has achieved, and cannot have the job he has because hiring managers don't want to hire them (Kim and Yu 125).

K-pop, K-rap, and K-R&B are all old news by now. Now the latest thing is K-reggae, but that is South Korean, not American. NST & the Soul Sauce has been studying the Jamaican roots of reggae from the 1970s and the 1980s. Their song, "Swallow Knows," honors both reggae and Korean pansori, a 17th century musical style. Skull of RGP (Reggae Peace like a River), formerly of Skull and Haha, performed "Love Inside" with Stephen Marley, and it's popular in Jamaica. I feel that he's earned the right from the Black community to have dreads. There are also K-reggae bands that produce lovers rock, a subgenre of reggae (Dunbar).

Much to many Koreans' surprise, some Blacks admire them. "There are about 500 black Buddhists in South Central, mostly as a result of Japanese American Buddhist activities in the past," says Abbot Doh-an Kim, "There are several black members of the kung fu training program in our gym, and three Blacks have joined our temple" (Kim and Yu 94). This reminds me of the Black man who trained me in Jujitsu in college. Another Black man also taught me capoiera, but that is a Brazilian martial arts. My ex was a huge fan of Bruce Lee, though Lee was from Hong Kong.

In American history, Blacks were here first. And Koreans were grouped with them, being non-white, particularly when seeking a home or an occupation, such as on the assembly line. The various schools there were majority Asian or majority Black schools. Bravo Medical was a majority Asian school in East LA (Kim and Yu 141), but for half-Korean, half-Black Kook Kim Dean, his school was majority Black.

For some people, the majority demographics are Black and Asian so it is necessary to get along. Alexander Hull, in L.A. and Sandy Lee, in Las Vegas, have experienced this (Kim and Yu 222 and 237).

Many Koreans and Blacks grew up together. In the early 1950s, Koreans were required to go to elementary school through high school with Blacks. Due to this requirement many Koreans who went to school with Blacks during the mid-century were very close with Black kids. What are they doing hating their childhood friends? The pressure to do so tends to come from their parents, forcing Korean children to either drop their friends or keep their friendship a secret from their parents.

My ex and I had talked about the fact that were I living during the middle of the century, as an Asian, I would have had to go to the schools designated for Blacks and would have been considered "colored" and would have had to sit at the back of the bus. Only white people have the privilege of asking and contemplating which time period they would have rather experienced without race being a concern.

In the world of Black vs. white dynamics, Asians may be more accepted by the Black community because they do not fall under either category. In Virginia and LA, there were laws forbidding interracial marriage until the *Loving v. Virginia* case, which started Loving Day. Kook Kim Dean's parents found a loophole, even though his Black father married outside of his race, his wife wasn't white, so people let it go. Dean's Korean mother often fixed African-American meals (Kim and Yu 316). He is proud of his parents for staying married for 40 years. He realizes that they love each other very much. Dean's father went all the way back to Korea to see Dean's mother when he had finished his tour of duty in Germany in 1954.

I had a Black coworker who told me that the "in" thing is Asian people, in the Black community. This could have been as equally true for men as it was for women.

Kun Soo Kang's aunt came to America because she had married a Black soldier, and it was through her that her family was able to come in 1987 (Kim and Yu 325). Racism was prevalent when U.S. soldiers were stationed in Korea, but mostly from the white Americans. Character Sarah said, "I saw some Korean ladies who'd transformed their straight hair—somehow—into cottony Afros. Doug told me that if a woman so much as accepted a single dance with a black soldier, that was it for her. She would have to start working the black clubs because white soldiers would reject her" (Lee, Marie 112). Just writing about this reminds me of *Miss Saigon*, a musical play about the Vietnam War.

Since Korean-Americans did not participate in the learning process, they don't see that they share common challenges with their Black brothers and sisters. Korean and Southern Black cultures both respect family, religion, and education. Just as African churches praise passionately with repeated phrases and loud shouts, Asian churches are just as passionate with violins. Smith also said that she learned to speak more like African Americans than Koreans. This racial hatred seems to make no sense since in LA, many Koreans were raised in Black culture.

Dong Hwan Ku argues that we are similar in sad things too: As with Korean adoptees, many Korean-Americans just live and die in the area where they grew up, particularly in the countryside. The Asian-American community is well-aware that despite the "model minority" myth, many Asians live in poverty, are uneducated, lack company benefits, and are sometimes with large families sharing a room and working multiple jobs. The lack of life insurance is also common among D.C. metro area Koreans. Blacks and Koreans both understand being colonized or dominated by another culture. Korea is the Poland of Asia. (Poland was taken over by their more powerful neighbors.) It has been taken over many times throughout history and is what gives rise to the uniquely Korean *han*, simplified to mean a cultural mental depression.

Koreans and Blacks are much more similar than either side could realize in both good ways and bad ways. They are both direct. According to interviewee Monica Kim, "corporal punishment of kids is seemingly more accepted in both Korean and black communities than in the white community. I also think individuals from both communities are more likely than white people to be considered traitors to their people if they date outside of the Korean or black communities" (M. Kim).

I think the main reason why things are slow to change within this race-to-race hatred is due to race-to-same-race hatred, which prevails in both Black and Korean communities. As I mention elsewhere, Black communities are divided by the darkness of their skin, and Koreans are divided by how well they speak English, both being measures of how white we are or are not. (In the same way, the LGBTQ community is measured by their masculinity, whether it is extreme masculinity in the gay community, the idea that transmasculine people are traitors to feminists, or that transfeminine people used to have male privilege.) We could both change things, but are not doing it when our own community is divided between those who can fit in with white society and those who cannot.

Koreans in America are like Blacks in America by the way that they divide themselves. Light-skinned Blacks are pitted against dark-skinned Blacks, whereas Korean-speaking Koreans are pitted against English-speaking Koreans. The reason why this division does not exist for white people is because Asians and Blacks measure themselves by each other's degree of whiteness. Hatred among Koreans is similar to the expression used for Black people: "If you're brown, stick around; if you're white, you're right; and if you're black, get back" (Roorda and Simon 309).

The same was true on the East side during that time: In Landover, Maryland, and Southeast DC, the neighborhood was Black and Korean, with some Southeast Asian refugees mixed in. Anyone who has ever been to Southeast DC knows that it was and is predominantly Black (at least to the right of the Anacostia River where it has not been gentrified). When I was in a job interview in 2011, my manager told me that the area in which I would be employed (where I was a few blocks from the Navy Yard shooting) used to have drive-by shootings and methadone clinics before the baseball stadium and Starbucks were installed. I am probably the only non-Black person to have visited Southeast DC to the right of the Anacostia River, and it's a shame that white people are too afraid to visit because they should really see the conditions that Black people live in. I was there because I was dating someone in a maximum penitentiary at the time, on paper, and he told me about his positive experiences there. The bus ride was rather awkward... I still keep in touch with his mom.

This means that yes, Koreans hate Koreans too and blame them for the uprising. Some Korean parents saw missionary work as more valuable than community work because they did not see Koreans as grateful or worth it due to all the hierarchy in Korean systems. "I didn't donate a penny for the riot victims. They dug their own grave. Koreans are killing the California economy. They don't pay insurance and they cheat on taxes," says Y. Chang, especially harsh toward her own race. "If you order pulgogi [barbecued beef] at a Korean restaurant, the dish is filled with water," says Y. Chang, "These stories must be told so that people can find out how bad Koreans are. They have to know how bad they are so that they can change. Korean businesses are corrupt. Korean media are corrupt. Korean scholars are corrupt" (Kim and Yu 206).

To provide an example of the Korean-American image problem in LA, Officer Kim says, "Why is it that when you go to Korean bars, the guys are all drunk? Why are ninety percent of the massage parlors in Los Angeles—most of them being nothing but fronts for prostitution—owned by Koreans, with the husbands manning the front desks and wives inside?" (Kim and Yu 211).

The greatest divide I see between these race groups is education, but, in my opinion, the thing Koreans do not understand is that it is not about wanting education, but the ability to get an education, a real education. In my opinion, the thing Blacks do not understand is that it is not about the ability to learn, but the competition and pressure to raise one's social standing in a Confucian framework.

Even though Blacks, at the time of the uprising, were strong politically but weak financially, the Korean-Americans were strong financially and weak politically[5]. (Both were strong culturally, but they weren't respecting each other's cultures.) Both groups at the time were generally ignorant about the other because what they knew about each other was from the media or very superficial and transactional encounters, agrees Kook Kim Dean who is half-Black, half-Korean (Kim and Yu 319).

Korean-Americans there have changed the economy, but have not made as many strides in politics (Kim and Yu xxi). In terms of politics, the Asian-American minority myth has been used as a wedge and rationale to remove affirmative action for Blacks and Latinos/as and the Latinx community. It's possible that Korean adoptees contributed to this myth since they were raised within mostly middle class white families. Instead of allowing this to happen, we need to be assertive about our own public policy opinions.

Also, keep in mind that race and culture are as different as gender and sex. Just as it would be rude for a KAD to tell a Korean waitress, "thank you" in Korean, it would also be rude and/or inappropriate to wear baggy jeans to Africa. I wonder if they already believe that is the American beauty ideal.

Generally, I'm optimistic that America will eventually turn this around. We've done amazing things in the past and can do amazing things in the future, particularly with the younger generations who are ideally less prejudiced. It's important to visualize success in this arena of race relations. The exciting possibilities for change are endless.

---

[5] Asian-American millenials are less likely to vote even though they're the most highly educated ethnic group per capita (NowThis News).

GEORGE FLOYD PROTESTS IN MINNEAPOLIS IN 2020

Despite the inherent challenges of comparing racial relations between two states, because different industries are prevalent in different states[6], it is something I will attempt to do if only as a metaphor or starting point for discussion.

Minnesota is the #1 KAD state. Minnesota itself holds more than 15,000 KADs (Swanson) out of the 150,000 KADs in the United States of America (E. Kim). This is even more than the 11,000-12,000 KADs on Facebook (The Gide Foundation). By the way, there are 167,000 Korean adoptees not living in Korea, with many living in Sweden, Australia, Denmark, France, and the United Kingdom (Kim and Dobson). Adoptee poet Nabiya asserted in 2007 that statistics showed that the number of KADs residing there was close to 30,000, but the numbers have gone down. Prior to that, in the early 90s, which is when this book begins, it was over 12,000, but the State of Minnesota stopped tracking all international adoptions in 1999. In addition 85% of the Asian-American and Pacific Islander (AAPI) Minnesotan community lives in the Twin Cities, to include Minneapolis (Minnesota Department of Health). The closest thing KADs have to a KADtown is Minneapolis, Minnesota. A large number are also in St. Paul, Minnesota.

Cheri Register, adoptive mother, has noted this among adoptees in Korea. " 'Are you from anywhere other than Minnesota?' American adoptees in Seoul ask each other," says Register (Register 9). I was also asked this question by the only interviewee who was living in Korea in 2007, Jane Jeong Trenka. Jennifer Arndt-John built an adoptee

[6] In LA, the major industries are agriculture, talent suppliers for the film industry, logistics networks, research and development, the services sector (including tourism), and entrepreneurs, the latter being mostly represented by the Asian community. Manufacturing is the primary industry in Minneapolis.

organization called Rainbow World in Minnesota because the area is rich in adoptee resources (Vickery 71). Her organization has already worked with Kim Dalros, co-creator of the Here photography project, and the International Adoptee Congress (International Adoptee Congress).

I even moved to Minneapolis, Minnesota in 2008, after I wrote the first draft of this book. Unfortunately, I moved from that location after my first winter there, and I remembered how much I hate the snow.

However, the dark underside of this area is that the Twin Cities had 30 thousand racially restrictive property deeds dating back to 1910. The racial divide between the Black and white community is the largest in the country by the measures of poverty, unemployment, homeownership, and at-risk youth, making it an unsurprising location for Derek Chauvin's murder of George Floyd in 2020 (Olitzky). There's a $47,000 difference between a Black family's combined income and a white family's there. According to "Mapping Police Violence, Minneapolis police are 13 times more likely to kill black residents" than white residents and 99% of cops who murdered did not face charges (Kendi).

Most of the conflict in Minneapolis might appear to be a white vs. Black matter. And truly most Black people do not even consider KADs if they don't know one personally. However, for those who are aware of KADs, they might not resonate with them just for the fact that the majority of KADs may lack awareness of their own ethnicity or lack a healthy perception of themselves as Koreans.

Darnella Frazier, a junior in high school, was part of a large group of onlookers who saw Derek Chauvin knee George Floyd in the back of the neck for about eight minutes outside of Cup Foods while Hmong Tou Thou and half-Nigerian Alex Kueng let it happen (Nevett). The Insurrection Act was invoked with regard to the uprising, which were instigated by out-of-town white people, as in the case of the majority arrested in Minneapolis, with several eyewitness acounts suggesting that the Boogaloo Bois (a diverse conglomerate of anarchists), Identity

Evropa (the American Identity Movement)[7] disguised as Antifa[8] (a loosely organized network of anti-fascists), or even law enforcement themselves. The infamous "Umbrella Man," who broke AutoZone windows with a sledgehammer, was identified as a member of Hell's Angels (Treisman). The police officers were a mix of white, Asian, and even Black. It wasn't the first time something similar had happened, as Minneapolis protests also happened after the shooting of Jamar Clark in 2015, but it was the one that made the biggest headlines (Fletcher). The resulting damage was 70 businesses burned to the ground and 500 businesses damaged or looted (Treisman). Since then Reclaim the Block asked the city council to reinvest $45 million in communities that would othersie have gone into the police budget (Bates and Villa).

[7] Remember that Identity Evropa recruited Kiyomi Brewer. They also were behind the fatalities in Charlottesville, Virginia.

[8] The Twitter account ANTIFA_US tweeted "Tonight's the night, Comrades. Tonight we say 'Fuck The City' and we move into the residential area… the white hoods… and we take what's ours" (Collins, Zadrozny and Saliba)

The Ku Klux Klan created my high school, and only five Black people attended at any one time. I chose the college I would attend because I wanted to be in a college with more diversity than I ever witnessed in my high school. When I chose it for its diversity, my parents were nothing less than shocked because I had never displayed to them that I was racially aware. To me it was the most diverse place I had ever attended, but to my white friend, Erykah Soleil, who had been in a Black high school, it was the least. I will be displaying my privilege here, but when I continued my college education, my second college was the most diverse college in the nation, and yet I had never had a single Asian teacher throughout all of my official schooling, though I did have one Black teacher in high school and one in college, even though the teacher who taught me Krio, the language spoken in Sierra Leone, was white.

In college during my undergraduate studies, I wrote a thesis about *Furious Flower: An African-American Poetry Conference*. Even though I was the only Asian attending the conference, I was also the only one interested enough to focus a year's worth of research on it. I was most interested in Toi Derricotte, an African American who is so light-skinned that she often passes for white. I felt that a "White Rat"[9] would best understand the situation of an adopted Korean. The two communities that should accept us do not accept us. But, unlike Toi, I could never pass for a white person because I still *look* Asian.

Cave Canem was first introduced to me through *Furious Flower* held at James Madison University. It is a group of African-American poets started in 1996 by Toi Derricotte and Cornelius Eady and is headquartered in New York. Lori Tsang, who I was unable to interview, was deeply disappointed that she was not able to enter Cave Canem despite the fact that many of the members were her friends for the sole reason that she was not Black. Eventually, Kundiman was

[9] This is the title of a short story by Gayl Jones.

founded as Cave Canem's offspring and caters to Asian-American poets.

It meant nothing to me to be the token Asian as I had always been among white people. When I was a senior in college, I then started to be invited to all-Black gatherings because my roommate was the leader of the Students for Minority Outreach. Since then I've been invited to witness traditional African dance, been on a bus trip to Pittsburgh, been to all-Black Christmas parties, and more recently was invited to the National Moorish Science Temple, in which I felt more singled out because I wasn't wearing a turban, not because I was Asian. I have also translated the communications from someone with a strong Trinidadian accent to an African-American coworker, which I'm sure wasn't appreciated. One of my friends even gave me an Ghanaian name, or nickname.

I originally wrote this in the spring of 2007 when I was dating a Black man. This book is as relevant then as it is now. In fact, it might be even more relevant now.

The ex I was with in 2007, when I wrote this, was not my first long-term Black ex-boyfriend[10] or even the first Black man I wanted to marry. The one big thing that differentiated me from most other Korean adoptees at the time was the fact that I want to marry a Black man and have Black children and learn how to do his/her/their hair.

Korean adoptees are the most likely to marry white spouses, but if one were to analyze by gender, it's mostly the women that marry white spouses, and the men are somewhat more likely to marry another Asian (Yam).

It might not be uncommon for an Asian to date or marry a Black man nowadays, as Asian-Americans are the race most likely to marry interracially, but it is rare to find a KAD with a Black significant other. The proof is in the 1999 survey results from the premier KAD research institute in America, the Evan B. Donaldson Institute, as well as from survey results from the International Korean Adoptee

[10] That was a four-year relationship.

Association (IKAA) and research from Sweden, the KAD capital of the world.

My ex, who I will not name for our privacy purposes, understood my desire to know more about my family tree because he happens to be Black and many of his family's records are untraceable as well. He received a "D" in school because he was unable to trace his heritage for a family tree assignment.

I trimmed his hair, and he stroked mine. One of the times I was most jealous was when I saw him allow a white woman to touch his hair after we had broken up, as it was an act of intimacy, not curiosity.

That particular relationship in 2007, actually starting 2002, had us both feeling Racism (with a capital R) louder than we had experienced racism in the past, mainly because he wasn't afraid of my father. As an Asian adoptee, my father often implored me to embrace whiteness and reject blackness despite the fact that most of my friends were Black. Being born an adoptee (adopted before birth) in itself is an exercise in cultural appropriation as a way of life, an "expected and appropriate" white way of life. When I am told to stick with my own kind, "kind" signifies all people White Anglo-Saxon Protestant (WASP). My father told me not to marry outside my culture and does not approve of the majority of my friends because they happen to be Black. However, he adopted outside his culture. Hmm. My dad said that his prejudice against him stemmed from the fact that he worked at a gas station in college and did not take off his hat indoors, not due to the color of his skin. I'll let the reader come to their own conclusions. It's likely that part of his visceral response to my ex was related to past lives as well.

My Korean surrogate birthmother, appeared devastated that I wanted to marry a Black man, without knowing anything about him, my father called me racist names, and I thought I would never see my parents again. The one tactic I have learned for dealing with Koreans is by telling them that my ex was "American." I know that the Korean community uses that term to mean white, but my ex was technically American. The most socially comfortable I have ever been in a job was at Macy's at Tyson's Corner because most of my colleagues dated interracially.

If it were not for my premature journey through the nuances of racism against Blacks, I would not have understood the nuances of racism against Asian people because in order to understand the nuances, one must understand the history. In fact, I studied African-American poetry when my ex studied Korean history and *chaebols*, so we could teach each other about each other's own history. When we went to Hong Kong, everyone assumed that I was visiting my family rather than his.

We were together when I wrote this, and we were together years later (we were together six years total) as we watched Baltimore[11] burn on the television screen. Eight years later, after we had gotten back together, in the summer of 2015, racial relations had gotten worse between the Black and white races and racism was at the forefront of everyone's mind in the news, but it never dawned on either of us that it affected our lives in particular. We heard stories of a white man shooting the original Black church in America, and we heard stories of a white National Association for the Advancement of Colored People (NAACP) leader who had been posing as a Black woman, Rachel Dolezal. All this comes on the heels of story after story of police brutality against Blacks and the Baltimore uprising, which is closer to the home in which I was raised.

Our relationship began with defying stereotypes as his family was more affluent than mine and he went to a more affluent school than I did, but none of that mattered in the face of racism. He experienced the worst of American exceptionalism, meaning the ability to move between classes. In Northern Virginia, he started off in a bigger house, went to a private elementary school, and went to a richer high school than I did in the richest county in the country and ended up making

[11] My first longterm Black ex-boyfriend loved the city so much that he visited it practically every weekend, so it's sad that his favorite city went through this.

an average of $13,000 per year when all was said and done in one of the most racist states, Minnesota. His fall from the upper middle class was as common as the fall of a middle class Korean in South Korea. He was shielded from reality in a profoundly white neighborhood and had no idea that three-fourths of Black men in DC have been in prison. He and his sister dated white people with few exceptions, me being one of them. It didn't occur to him that visiting a white neighborhood, in possibly a red shirt, would be his downfall. It wasn't until 2020 that my eyes were open to the extent of the problem.

We never did marry, though it was not from lack of trying. We tried living together, we tried dating long-distance, we tried meeting each other's families. I integrated myself into his family more than he was able to integrate himself into mine. It's true that we weren't perfect. He enjoyed showing me off as it made him appear more intelligent, and I enjoyed showing him off as it made me appear more cool. He saw himself as intelligent, and I thought of myself as cool and loved it when he vouched for me and said, "She's with me; she's cool," but no one seemed to see it until we were together, so being together, in some ways, helped us feel more like ourselves. He was my mouthpiece to my father, but my father preferred to think I had been "brainwashed" because the way I saw myself was not the way he saw me. It was an exhausting and tumultuous relationship filled with mini-breakups, as we had to deal with the recession after we graduated, his criminal record, a preponderance of evictions, constant drama, and personality conflicts before even knowing how to manage personal finances and live on our own. The way the traumas of racism affected our ability to be together was just too great, both externally and internalized, blatantly and culturally. despite our love for each other. For example, I could not understand the trauma response to police and prison. I had no idea there was so much police brutality or that there was so much sexual violence in prisons. I don't know if he sheltered me as much as I had sheltered my parents. And if he wished to hurt me, after we had broken up, he could imply that I was a Trumper, which I'm not.

Worst of all was the subtle, unconscious racism that we experienced from each other. He, as well as other close Black male relations I've had romantically or platonically, held prejudiced beliefs about me. In our relationship that spanned six years together and six years apart, we became caricatures of our own stereotypes and subconsciously loved each other for it and hated each other for it. Other Black men have used me as a fetish, a math tutor (even though my major was in English), an unofficial mentor, a source of money, a pushover that could be bossed around, or a reminder of the past. As with Black people, Asians do not have the luxury of being unique and standing on our own merits. The person I thought had best friend potential cut ties because I reminded him of his ex-wife. This is not unique to Black men either; because I reminded a white boss of his Korean wife, the racism was so bad that I brought it up to the Equal Employment Opportunity Commission (EEOC). I've experienced one bit of prejudice from a Black female roommate because she thought I didn't like her because I was shy. However, Black women, in my experience have treated me without prejudice and as part of their inner circle. I suspect this is because they have a shared invisibility with Asians, whereas Black men are most feared. They also have more to lose if they expressed racism. I've also experienced different preconceptions from a Chinese boss, but my Vietnamese boss was sympathetic to me, as I remember. I'm sure I'm guilty of microaggressions too. Of course, white men can be much more racist. A white coworker once told me to my face that he wanted his nephew to travel to Korea to get a good Korean wife because they were "non-aggressive."

I eventually married someone who was more palatable to my family and friends who I love dearly, who is progressive and open-minded, and who is understanding as I have worked on finalizing this project. But just as a bisexual does not want her same sex experiences and identity erased after marrying someone of the opposite sex, I still wanted to assert that anyone's ability to marry or even platonically love should not be dictated by the color of their skin.

Even though it is rare to see a marriage between an adopted Korean and a Black person, there do exist at least many friendships between them. Of course, romantic relationships are different from platonic relationships.

Even though my parents are white, my facial features and ability to speak English fluently make me less threatening to the Black community. Since I am an adoptee, others will consider me the ethnicity of my friends. When I dated white men, people called me "White," and when I dated Black men, people called me "Black." In this sense, I saw "colorblindness" coming from Black people as acceptance.

Janine Bishof said that in her freshman year of college she wanted to date a Black guy, but her dad told her that the world wasn't ready and that she would get hurt (Kim and Yu 309). Non-adoptee Kyong-Ae Price said that her father considered her dead just when she married a white man (Kim and Yu 75). These are the words that I lived by, that I would be considered dead and twice abandoned. I wanted to highlight that even the most common interracial marriage combination of Asian female with a white male is still not always looked upon favorably.

PROFILES

Seven '07 Bios

1. Hollee McGinnis: A KAD adopted into a white family
2. Jennifer Arndt-Johns: A KAD adopted into a white family
3. Nabiya: A KAD poet adopted into a white family
4. Rhonda Roorda: A Black adoptee and author adopted into a white family who has researched on the Black and Korean adoptee experience
5. SooJin Pate: Dr. SooJin Pate is a professor, DEI (Diversity, Equity, and Inclusion) practitioner, and writer dedicated to centering the lives and experiences of historically marginalized communities. As a professor, she teaches courses on U.S. history and culture through the lens of race, class, gender, and sexuality in the Twin Cities area. As a DEI professional, she helps companies and organizations embed racial equity into their systems and processes. And as a self-care practitioner, SooJin has led workshops on how to take care of yourself when taking care of others.
6. Tabetha Jones: A KAD adopted into a white family
7. Thomas Park-Clement: A first-generation KAD adopted into a white family

‘07 Interviews

Disclaimer: Interview opinions do not necessarily represent my opinions.

LOS ANGELES AND THE BLACK ADOPTEE EXPERIENCE

Are you familiar with the uprising that happened in 1992 in Los Angeles between Blacks and Korean people?

Rhonda Roorda (a Black adoptee): “What is your opinion of what caused it and how this incident might still be affecting the relations between Blacks and Koreans? No. Can you explain it? [After I explain it:] See, that also happens in New York and movies, like *Do the Right Thing* with Spike Lee between Blacks and Korean store owners. The country has a long way to go, but I think things are moving in the right direction”.

In the book *In Their Own Voices* you tell a story about how the simple act of a Black man saying “Hi” to you made you run home crying. Tell me how you went from a Black adoptee who was afraid of other Black people to writing *In Their Own Voices*?

Rhonda Roorda: “D.C. is diverse but it is still segregated. I grew up in private schools. The Black kids there fit in my bubble because they conformed to white and Christian rules. When my parents moved to a predominantly Black neighborhood I was still in this bubble. While on my paper route, I was thinking ‘I could not control what happens.’ This Black man invaded my space, invaded my bubble. That situation called me to deal with my issues if I wanted to breathe.”

Do you feel that living in the diverse D.C. metro area has been beneficial to you as an interracial adoptee?

Rhonda Roorda: "It was a benefit. I am the only one in the family who is adopted and the only one who is Black. D.C. is diverse ethnically, racially, and socially. I could see all walks of life and people who looked like me in the 1970s and 1980s. People were very curious about me living in a white family. I received lots of bold looks. People didn't care about etiquette and asked me questions bluntly. I was forced to deal with adoption issues head on instead of avoiding the issue."

You have a Korean cousin who married a Black woman and now lives by Andrews Air Force Base. This is rare in the Korean adoptee community where many people marry white people or other Asians. Why do you think there are not more of these types of interracial marriages among Korean adoptees?

Rhonda Roorda: "My cousin was raised in an all white community and feels more comfortable with the Black community. He came out about it after he left home and joined the military. To him it was natural and comfortable to marry a Black woman. He was not part of a community of color in New Hampshire. I think it doesn't happen more often because there are cultural differences that make it challenging, but in general there are not nearly as many interracial couples as compared to homogeneous couples, but the numbers are increasing. A lot of military Black men and women have relations with Asian men and women and are creating Amerasian children, but not nearly as much as same race children".

You said that you are friends with Hollee McGinnis, cofounder of AKA[12] [Adopted Korean Association] and currently employed

[12] Interestingly, these are the same initials as Alpha Kappa Alpha, which is a well-known Black sorority.

at the Evan B. Donaldson Institute, and that you think Korean adoptees share many similarities with Black adoptees. Can you elaborate what you mean?

Rhonda Roorda: "We are trying to address what you are talking about. We want to cross the color and cultural line. Domestic and international transracial[13] adoptees are in two different groups, not because we don't like each other, but because we think our issues are different. There is a great power in coming together. Everyone is on their own journey and are just now finding each other. It takes more effort. Our commonalities that we share are that we understand abandonment, loss. We are all going through navigating who we are in family versus society and trying to find healthy ways to express ourselves. We can be supportive of each other. Hollee is very supportive of crossing this seemingly large gap".

Have you read any books about adoption? If yes, which books have you read? How did that book affect you?

Hollee McGinnis: "Actually, I've never really read any books about adoption! The core for AKA was *New People*, a history on the intermixing of Africans and Caucasians[14]. I learned that the discourse of Black versus white was not always that way. It used to be that mulatto could be an identity and had been so before. A lot of my adoption stuff is through people, through physical contact."

[13] I learned that this term is not readily understood by non-adoptees. It means adoptees that do not share the race of their adoptive parents.

[14] The term "Caucasian," coined by Johann Blumenbach in 1776, and referring to Caucasus Mountain region, inspired the term "Caucasoid" in the 1780s from the Göttingen School of History, which referred to a time when they were trying to prove that white people had bigger cranial diameters, and thus more intelligence (Show Up for Racial Justice and PBS). Can you think of anything else that happened in 1776?

Rhonda Roorda: "Have you read *Outsiders Within*? I'm 2/3 through. I had a friend, John Raible, who contributed to that book. It is very good. I also read *Black Baby, White Hand* and *Voices of Korean Adoptees*. I've read memoirs, academic books, poetry, books by and about adoptive parents, documentaries, films, pamphlets, and magazines."

What advice would you give to adoptive parents thinking about adopting?

Rhonda Roorda: "Love is absolutely essential and should never ever be compromised. But it takes more than love. It takes understanding. This is lifelong commitment. It needs lots of forgiveness and reconciliation and love to support children into adulthood. Adoptees are not perpetual children; we spend the majority of our life in adulthood. Adoptive parents should prepare their minds to get ready about having a child of color. They should ask themselves: Do I have a network in place that will be supportive of my future blended family? Parents should raise their child instead of the child helping them to understand. Too many children are raising their parents and that's unacceptable. Too many kids are not able to navigate when they come out to society. They don't know who they are and some are starting to figure it out at ages of thirty and that's unacceptable. Parents need to have a comprehensive plan and must be committed."

What advice would you give to other transracial adoptees?

Rhonda Roorda: "In the same way that 'parents can't prop their feet in idle' about cultural and racial issues, 'adoptees can't prop their feet in idle' in a coccoon. If they are not prepared they are gonna be stuck psychologically, emotionally, physically. We need people who will hold us accountable to be the best we can be, which may be different than how we were raised. While parents love us, we can be harmed because we're different. Case in point: My parents may have loved me; however, early on they didn't know how to care for my hair. They thought I could jump in the ocean, jump back out, and dry my hair off. Well, my hair got dry and broke off. My skin got ashy. My skin and hair were harmed because they did not know how to care for it. You can't treat everyone the same. It's not about equal or not equal; it's about difference. And adoptees can't sit idly by and self-sacrifice to the point of not causing waves. That is unacceptable. At the end of the day it's about how we live our lives. If we are not appropriately taught we can't blame our parents. I've seen too many adoptees self-sacrifice and those who do die a slow and painful death. When I die and talk to God, and He asks me what I have done with all the gifts he has given me, I want to tell him that I've done what I can to be the best I can be with those gifts. *To say 'Oh, I didn't want to make waves,' as many adoptees do, is unacceptable*[15]. You only have one life to live."

So you are saying that neither parents nor adoptees know how to deal with race?

Rhonda Roorda: "Yes, and it is detrimental. *Kids are teaching parents and kids are protecting parents because they don't want to hurt their parents*[16]. Parents need to be parents and kids need to be kids. Parents need to understand race issues. They need to be models, be leaders in the household. I saw this one white parent ask her very young child 'Do you want us to teach you about Martin Luther King Jr.?' It's not for the child to decide. Parents need to have a plan.

In what ways have you explored your Korean side?

[15] Emphasis added

[16] Emphasis added

Tabetha Jones (a KAD): "I am curious about stuff in general. I dated one Korean who was also discovering his Korean side. Danny was born out of wedlock. Her mom remarried a white man and his sister is half and half. We went to Koreatown in Los Angeles. It was amazing. I like to listen to people speaking Korean. It sounds calming and melodious. I think it's interesting that in Los Angeles, Koreans tend to live next to Latinos. When we were there his cousins said, 'Don't stay out late. Come home early' because Chinese, Japanese, and Latinos all have gangs and they all want to kill Koreans who don't have gangs. There is a huge gambling problem in the Korean community. A Korean chef at a Japanese restaurant almost gambled everything away".

MINNEAPOLIS AND THE KOREAN ADOPTEE EXPERIENCE

Tell me what you know about Korean adoptee history.

Thomas Park Clement: "International adoption started from exporting half and half babies from war zone. It was a social conscious thing. What has happened in many countries is that half and half babies are usually exterminated. Some people I know personally have dyed their baby's hair super Black and hid them. Half and half's are looked down on because their pure blood is contaminated. It made sense then that they were adopted because, "What chance would they have?" But the adoptions never stopped. The question now becomes, "Why should they be exported when they become instantly a minority?" To muck up the system, everyone poor over in Asia is trying to immigrate through marriage due to overpopulation. From the Asian mentality they think, "What's your problem? You have a free ticket." There is a lot of jealousy. Adoption is complex socially and morally. I understand all components, but I'm overwhelmed and keep hearing about more components."

Tell me about Minneapolis.

Jennifer Arndt-Johns: 'It boils my Korean blood a bit when I see that so many people know Minnesota from Lake Wobegone, a place that doesn't even exist" (Vickery 67).

Your poem "yellow" says that yellow people make others anxious. Who is more anxious? You or them?

Nabiya: "I wouldn't call it anxiety, but disgust. I didn't want to be in that environment where people were narrow-minded. But I would say that I am anxious around Korean-Americans because of the social stigma of being adopted. At home, white guys weren't attracted to me because everyone saw *Karate Kid II,* and I wasn't like that. I normally dated Black guys because I feel more historical parallels with them because we were brought against our will. My first boyfriend was a Malcolm X-like Black Muslim named Malik.

How did you meet author Jane Jeong Trenka?

Thomas Park Clement: "Jane emailed me saying, "First, I'm not a stalker, but I'm doing research and your name repeatedly pops up. I have some information you might want to know. Some of my original records are at ISS [International Social Service] along with yours. We met there. The guy wasn't supposed to show us the records, but he did. They weren't records about our family, but were from the orphanage. For adoptees everything in your past is a mystery, and you can only dig so far. I learned that my orphanage name was Tommy Park, but there were two Tommy Parks. One was half Black/half yellow and I was half white/half yellow. That explained why there was so much confusion in my early records. My parents are from North Carolina where there is a lot of prejudice. My parents wanted a baby who was half and half. I used to have all the correspondence. The agency told them, 'We have the perfect boy for you. He is half Black.' They said,

'Oh no, we live in North Carolina.' So the orphanage rolled back and said, 'We have a baby who is half white and is 6-7 years old.' They said that was too old and wanted someone closer to four. The orphanage told them, 'No Tommy is 5-6,' then, 'No, Tommy Park is 4-5.' On the back of my picture, it said in Korean (I had a friend translate), 'Used to be Tommy Lee.' Under that it said '6-7' with a line through it then '5-6' with a line through it. The orphanage changed my name and age to get me out of there".

Is there anything else you would like to add?[17]

Nabiya: "I have been active in the Korean adoptee community for a long time. Minnesota is the hotbed of Korean adoption since 1998. It was a big embarrassment for Korea. Minnesota alone has 30,000 adoptees[18]. I am a fourth generation Korean adoptee. You would be fifth generation. The first generation was 'really fucked up, really really fucked up.' The European adoptees' suicide rate in the first generation was 50%. The Korean adoptees couldn't deal with it. The adoptive parents couldn't either. 'Not only do you have Asian babies, but then they grow up to be Asian adults. White people can't deal with race. They understand blatant racism, not the nuances of racism. To them, subtle racism isn't racism.' For the first generation there was no support".

---

[17] The reason this question seems too early was because it was part of my college thesis that was cut out so that the focus could be strictly on the Korean adoptee experience.

[18] I don't know where Nabiya got this number, but the Adoption Medicine Clinic from the University of Minnesota Masonic Children's Hospital has completed more than 30,000 pre-adoption reviews for children in over 40 countries (University of Minnesota).

SUMMARY

I found your contact information through Rhonda Roorda. She said that Korean adoptees and Black adoptees have similar experiences, issues, and concerns. How do you envision what it will take to make people see that we should join forces?

Hollee McGinnis: We are already starting to through network connections. Domestic and transnational adoptees have always been separated in practice even though many domestic adoptees may be transracial and transnational adoptees may not be. Transcultural means same race, different ethnicity. For example, an Irish person in an adoptive family. Domestic and transnational adoptees may have similar and parallel transracial aspects to their experiences. I am not sure if a Russian adoptee in a white home has the same experience as a Colombian adoptee in a white home. Their race is not so conspicuous. The question is 'Who do we involve or not involve?' Indians and Colombians have already formed groups, but I don't know of any Russian groups (perhaps they haven't come of age?) Is our shared experience transcultural or transracial? What about the fact that some Colombians look more white and some look more Black?

Twenty '20 Bios

1. Amy Elizabeth: A KAD psychologist and therapist adopted into a white family
2. Bree Davis: A KAD adopted into a white family with a half-Black child and quarter-Black/quarter-Latino child
3. David Taylor: A KAD adopted into a white family and married to Enetty Taylor
4. Enetty Taylor: A Zimbabwean adopted into an Austrian family and married to David Taylor
5. Hayley Hoffman: A KAD adopted into a white family who is related to Helsen Valdes, an Ethiopian adoptee
6. Helsen Valdes: Ethiopian adoptee who was adopted at an older age by a white family and who is related to Hayley Hoffman, a KAD
7. Holly Choon Hyang Bachman: The owner of Mixed Roots Foundation and a KAD adopted into a white family
8. JaeHee Melanie Chung-Sherman: A KAD psychologist and therapist adopted into a white family
9. Jessica Farrell: Half-Korean and quarter-Black adoptee adopted into a white family
10. Jordan Davis: The only domestic Black adoptee featured here who was adopted into a white family. Even though he does not have significant and repeated experiences with Koreans and Korean adoptees, I want these profiles to reflect the diverse range of experience or lack of experience with the other race.
11. Lisa A. Quaites: Lisa A. Quaites was born to a Barbadian father and Korean mother in post-war South Korea. Her single mother cared for her mixed-race child for as long as she could. Lisa was adopted to the United States in

1969 and raised by a Black military family. Lisa's memoir, *Faith & Favor: Discovering Family at Fifty*, delves into her quest to find her birth mother, and reveals how she unexpectedly found her biological father on her journey. Lisa and her husband, James, raised their two daughters in the Midwest where they continue to call the heartland their home.

12. Matthew Goodman: A KAD adopted into a white family who works with Black business partners
13. Milton Washington: A half-Korean and half-Black KAD adopted into a Black family
14. Monica Kim: Monica was born in Busan, South Korea and was adopted as a baby by a family just outside of Baltimore. Volunteering in Baltimore exposed her to a different life and opened her eyes to the educational disparities. Her interest in the Black community increased when she started working with predominantly Black Division I student-athletes. She has long felt an affinity with the Black community since she knew more Black than Asian individuals growing up. She has also seen how students of color gravitated towards her in academia, which is still predominantly white in many areas of the country. Since then, she has been involved with diversity and inclusion initiatives in education, such as implicit bias training of search committees. She is grateful to share this learning journey with her partner where they can exchange information about their respective cultures. Monica believes her eclectic background has given her unique insight, but she continues to learn about all cultures.
15. Rachel Kavanagh Baldwin: A half-Korean and half-Black KAD raised in a white family.
16. Renford Reese: The mentor to Rodney King, KAD ally, and a Black man who lived in LA and can speak on his experience with the Korean community

17. Rutledge: Black fiancé to Young-wha, a KAD adopted into a white family
18. SooJin Pate[19]: Dr. SooJin Pate is a professor, DEI (Diversity, Equity, and Inclusion) practitioner, and writer dedicated to centering the lives and experiences of historically marginalized communities. As a professor, she teaches courses on U.S. history and culture through the lens of race, class, gender, and sexuality in the Twin Cities area. As a DEI professional, she helps companies and organizations embed racial equity into their systems and processes. And as a self-care practitioner, SooJin has led workshops on how to take care of yourself when taking care of others. She is the author of *From Orphan to Adoptee: U.S. Empire and Genealogies of Korean Adoption* (University of Minnesota Press, 2014) and co-host of the Antiracist Parenting Podcast.
19. Yoon-Sook Kim: A social justice anti-racist KAD adopted into a white family and former fiancée to a Black man
20. Young-wha: A KAD adopted into a white family and fiancée to Rutledge, a Black man

[19] She's also a graduate of Howard University, a historically black college or university (HBCU).

Disclaimer: Interview opinions do not necessarily represent my opinions. Many interviewees used pronouns interchangeably, not in an LGBTQ[20] way, but in a way where "you" often means the objective "one." In addition, a couple of interviews were self-censured.

Tell me what you know about transracial adoptee history.

Hayley Hoffman: I don't know much. What I've learned in the past week after joining the KAD community is that we're a special group that was formed or made available (I don't know the word) out of the Korean War.

JaeHee Melanie Chung-Sherman: I know a pretty significant portion. Going back to World War I and II and the Korean War. I've been working in the field for 21 years. I was also in placement in child welfare for 10 of the 20 years in international and private and public foster care placement.

What's been fascinating is that in 1953, when Harry Holt[21] placed racial Korean adoptees, these are Koreans that are predominantly black, white, and Latinx. The diaspora was grounded in racism or racial divisions. When we talk about Korean adoptees, the second wave happened toward the '60s due to the profession establishing

---

[20] "Lesbian, gay, bisexual, transgender, and questioning" and preferred by 71% of those surveyed who fall under that umbrella over LGBTQIA, per Community Marketing, Inc. (Community Marketing & Insights).

[21] According to SooJin Pate, Henry Holt already had six kids and was in retirement age when he was rejected by an adoption agency, so he decided to start his own agency.

a pipeline of children. The vast majority of the 1st generation were multiracial, as a treatise in terms of the Americans losing the war. The diaspora into American homes were biracial.

[There was the idea of] "We're doing a good thing" grounded in saviorism and white guilt, westernized guilt. In terms of immigration law, Asians weren't allowed to immigrate, but there were special visas given to Asian kids, separated from their family systems and brought on an immigrant visa finding what it means to be American. They are still being deported. These waves—when we think of adoption—what's truly baked into the system is racial oppression for a "better life." The pipeline and establishment had been established between Holt and KSS. So for parents who didn't want to wait or didn't qualify due to restrictions or didn't want a Black or Latinx child, they went to Korea. It's the proliferation of the white-adjacent child because it's more acceptable to a white system.

I think about the LA riots in terms of community system, in terms of even the opportunities. Koreans were co-opting the space but weren't allowed to move outside due to redlining, all the way back to Jim Crow. [There was a] dichotomy of who gets opportunity [and a] stratosphere of race and opportunity. Segued into the LA riots were Koreans moving into communities with their own ideals, anti-Blackness, and lack of historical knowledge of grief, oppression, etc. and treating Black Americans pretty horribly. And also the Black Americans had no understanding of Korean history. It was a tinderbox. The Black and Asian model minority myth pits us against blacks. We've all been played. And you'll find that in adoption. It's like a whole book that could be written.

[There is a] stratosphere between adoption and the wealth distribution and who gets to define whiteness as a property and not identity. And Blacks are always left on the bottom, and it pisses me off. And I'm going to think about African-identity adoptees from Ghana, Ethiopia, Liberia integrating, hating, integrating into families in the United States. Growing up in colonist history and not being prepared, even being pitted with Asian individuals in their classrooms, Asian adoptees don't have any idea about their history because no one's telling them. I think about the rooftop Koreans and how horrible [it was with] Black bodies and violence that happened in the LA riots, and the idea of policing who gets to live or die. LA left everything to burn due to derelict leadership.

Holly Choon Hyang Bachman: So what do I know about transracial adoption? From my perspective?

So, my name is Holly Choon Hyang Bachman, and my experience is that I'm a transracial adoptee. I grew up in Minnesota, and I grew up in a predominantly white community. Minnesota is known actually for having the largest Korean adoptee population. I currently live in LA now. I found out that one in 10 Korean-Americans are adopted, so that's a lot of Korean adoptees. Particularly with the foundation called the Mixed Roots Foundation, I've gotten to know a lot of other transracial Korean adoptees. I actually did my research—I graduated from the University of Minnesota—and I researched if there's any difference between same race and different race adoptions. I think the whole experience of race and culture is not only a very powerful and personal one, but it's different for everybody.

One of the other aspects of knowing about international adoption is, from the immigration standpoint, one thing about international adoption is that there are over 35,000 international adoptees facing deportation because their adopted parents never did get citizenship for them.

Monica Kim: I definitely had to research Korean adoption, how the Korean War led to adoptions all over the world. I think just knowing how I was adopted in the '80s and how Korea has tried to do more to decrease the number of international adoptions is good. Koreans are all about the blood so it's hard to change that culture. There's just been more high-profile adoptees, like Kara Bos. Being more vocal is a super positive trend, and getting more transparency from agencies, and knowing how expensive it is. I like to know different stats on it.

SooJin Pate: The common foundation of adoption is taking non-white children as white Americans. I see it as a project of white supremacy. The adoptions across race are not being brought in to learn about their culture, but to assimilate. One of the largest enterprises of domestic adoption started with native children into boarding schools to assimilate, to make them white Christians. That was huge. That started in the early 1900s, so it's part of the cultural genocide. It's not only happened in the States but also Canada and Australia. They thought that if they can't kill natives, then they can turn them into white people. It goes back to Andrew Jackson. This phrase came from Robert Carlisle: "Kill the Indians, save the man"[22]. So that's the roots of domestic adoption.

The root of transracial/transational adoption is Korean adoption. That's the first kind of adoption that became an industry. That too was a project of white supremacy[23][24]. The white Americans [thought that they] needed to save the "heathen children" that, without them, will become communists. It was about assimilating non-white bodies into white Americans.

Tell me what you know about domestic and transracial adoptee history.

Young-wha: Domestic is in the foster care system. It's court-run. A lot of families get torn apart. They say it's neglect/abuse. It's very race-driven. It's more expensive obviously here. If families can't afford to adopt

---

[22] This was connected to the Carlisle Industrial Training School in Pennsylvania, founded by Charles Pratt (History of the Race Construct).

[23] This could explain partly why white male-Korean female pairings are the most common pairing for interracial relationships.

[24] I would also call it a project of identity theft, not in the traditional sense of the word, but as literal theft of one's identity.

domestically, they do international adoptions. Not as many hoops to jump through. It comes from TV commercials and Christianity. White people want to be saviors and think, "Of course I'm going to help the poor children in Asia, Africa, wherever." Most of our files, they stamped abandoned whether or not they knew we were abandoned. If we were abandoned, then the thinking is they won't return.

Rutledge (Black fiancé of Young-wha): I was kinda unaware of transracial adoptions in general until I found out one of my cousins was put up for adoption. Five years ago, he came back to the family. He was adopted to a Caucasian woman and Black guy. I didn't know much at the time. I was asked if I wanted a brother, but my father said, "No." My cousin's son is also adopted. It was a domestic adoption. On my dad's side there's a woman who was adopted too. I never saw transracial adoptions until I went to China, and I saw a lot of white people picking up Chinese girls. I thought there was some weird ring going on and that I should call someone. I had no idea what was going on. Even now, Young-wha's story is eye-opening. And I'm learning a lot here. So I'm learning how things have been working. I had blinders on.

Young-wha: There are a lot of domestic adoptees in my family. My dad is an adoptee in the '40s. His two sisters were adopted. My grandmother adopted three kids. On my mom's side, most of my aunts couldn't conceive. I have four male cousins who were all adopted. Even though we had that commonality, it was different for me because I'm transracial. I questioned "Who am I?" "What am I?" "Where did I come from?" I heard that "Your parents saved you." My parents never pointed out that I was adopted [to others] even though we talked about it. Some of my aunts and uncles introduced me as adopted to explain why I was different.

Jordan Davis: I'm definitely more familiar with domestic adoption history, mostly through African-American experiences with adoption, and I've been doing a lot of reading about Native American experiences with the Indian Child Welfare Act, why there's a reaction of non-Native peoples to that Act, etc. My understanding of transracial history is less except for the white saviorism and the colonial underpinnings of that. I'm still learning.

How do you feel that domestic Black adoptees are different from African adoptees?

JaeHee Melanie Chung-Sherman: [There's] so much in terms of identification in terms of how they've navigated their environments, knowing the positionality of Black identity of African-American adoptees or fosterees. [There's the] internal experience of "I'm white" saturated in this white-dominated culture that says, "I'm supposed to be this way", but then faced with Black culture that says, "I'm too much this or not enough that." How that intersects with TRAs [transracial adoptees], what that means in terms of finding "where I am" in time and space. Even as me being non-Black and East Asian, that comes up in terms of how that feels as they're processing through. "Am I African-American?" "Am I Black?" This is what I hear from my Black TRA clients. Then you add sexual identity, queer identity, gender identity in TRA spaces that aren't always amendable [amenable] for the vast majority of TRAs coupled with historical marginalization and oppression. It's the cognitive knowing and the body knowing. We're doing work on how the body feels like and how they claim their Blackness in terms of identity when they walk in the world and having that affirmed even when they don't always feel part of the Black community. I'm part of it, but can't always get to it. So much of my work is decolonizing, decolonizing the harm that's been done.

Tell me what you know about Korean adoptee history.

Yun-sook Kim Navare: It started in the early- to mid-'50s with Harry, Bertha, and Molly Holt with Amerasians [children born in

Asia to an Asian mother and U.S. military man], predominantly with strong Christian roots. They founded Ilsan. Even to this day it's a dog-and-pony show. God bless the adoptees with disabilities. At the time it was a necessity because of the Korean War. The Korean War was very controversial anyways because of the white and Black soldiers and the comfort women to service the white men and Black men, and poverty. There are a whole slew of reasons. We are the first country to have the oldest, longest history internationally, interracial [adoption], and overseas [adoption]. "Put up for adoption" came from this [time]; when the train would pass they would lift the baby up with both hands. It started with Holt International, and they started penetrating into Central and South America, the Eastern bloc countries, and African countries (Ethiopia and Tanzania). There were some independent agencies. Holt, Social Welfare Services, and Eastern Child Welfare [Eastern Social Welfare Society] were the three big ones. Yes, there was a true need, but I think the world now with the Hague, adult adoptees advocating for themselves, human rights, and women rights, 1) Is there still a need? 2) Maybe we could revamp, maybe we could reassess families differently in the home study. There's quite a bit of literature that started with the third wave about how and why foster parents and adoption agencies became a whole industry where there was a supply and demand. Because the foster care system is sometimes hard to adopt out of. That's the whole point of going overseas because [the kids are] not drug or alcohol exposed. Their history can only go so far. If you were to do a search and found someone… These guys are pretty strategic going overseas . They may not have made a lot of money otherwise. Going internationally was the better route for them. At first it was a need, and I think that eventually became a niche and then a market. Then when China opened up, "Yay, China girls!" Then Russia was even better because they're white. The food is very bread/dairy-based. It's not exotic like for a Korean or Ethiopian little girl.

Have you read any books about adoption? If yes, which books have you read? How did that book affect you?

SooJin Pate: I've been out of academia for five years so I'm not up-to-speed, but there's this graphic novel that just came out, and there are other Korean documentaries. *Palinpimpsest: Documents from a Korean Adoption* by [Lisa Wool-Rim Sjöblom]. She's famous for the "I am not a virus" campaign. It's powerful because her artistry is beautiful. American [Korean] adoptees have monopolized the conversation around Korean adoption, but now Swedish [Korean] and other [Korean] adoptees are adding to the conversation. The [Korean] adoptee diaspora is learning from each other and dialoguing with each other.

Yun-sook Kim Navare: I've read *Seeds from the East.* I've read anthologies, poetry. I've read *The Adoption Lifecycle*, a lot of different readings just from studying psychology, sociology, and social work. [I read] how it affects identity, how to provide resources to adoptees, research on why they're institutionalized at higher rates. An African-American friend was adopted by a white family in DC. She was interviewed by a Black adoptee interviewer for *In Our Own Voices* [by Rhonda Roorda]. I read some poetry. That was pure narrative of transracial adoptee voices. So either anthologies, poetry, or practical.

I asked you this before in 2007. Some poetry about adoption takes up the theme of waiting, journeying, or silence. Taking into context race relations, do you feel that you are waiting for something? Do you feel that you are on a journey? Do you think that silence is a large part of the adoption experience?

SooJin Pate: We're always on a journey. If you're not, then you should. We should all be on a journey to be more informed human beings. I feel like this moment is a journey.

It's very unpopular to be silent in this moment, which is an interesting thing. Police brutality is not new, and white silence isn't new, but now Black folx are not being silenced, so that gives me hope. We'll see if that will lead to action. Only time will tell. The fact that white folx are talking about this....

I never thought I'd see news pundits using the words "white supremacy." I was even in a role where I was a teacher, and my boss told me I couldn't use those words in front of mixed company, or I'd be chastised for saying it, and now we have journalist and talking heads talking about it like it's nothing. I think that's a positive direction because what protects them is coded language[25]. Now that it's no longer invisible because we're naming it, gives me hope. I remember my first year as a TA [teacher's assistant] in grad school talking in front of 300 students about the 81 shots that were fired at Amadou Diallo. [The police had] mistaken his wallet for a gun. That was in early 2000, so the point is that there's a long history of police violence against Black men and women. White folx didn't really care, but now I've never seen white people care more. I'm reminded of what Martin Luther King Jr. said, if you think about the Civil Rights Act in 1964 or 1965. He said that while it was great that all the protests led to this legislative act, he said we asked for too little. It wasn't good enough because white people didn't have to give up anything, and real change requires giving stuff up, giving up power, giving up their food, giving up their resources in order to make lasting sustainable change. I hope we don't make the mistake of asking for too little when we have the ears and hearts of white people for the first time ever in the history of the United States.

I see that you are currently living in LA. Tell me about Los Angeles.

Yun-sook Kim Navare: I'm a single parent in the Korean community. There's overt racism, and covert racism. Growing up in a blue-collar

[25] This is also called "The Southern Strategy".

Black and white community, it was like this: a) They've heard of Korean and b) They like kimchi. It was like, "We know you're Korean, we even like *sundubu* [tofu stew], but we resent that your kids are competing with ours." People would call me, "China girl". The microaggressions are there. There's nationalism. My daughter was raised bilingual/bicultural. She can be around Korean and Vietnamese kids. She has access to Korean makeup and kids with inside jokes. There are FOB [Fresh off the boat] Koreans, rebel emo Koreans, there's an Orange County piece of it. "Wow you speak English so well!" "Wow you're so educated!" It's like being Will Smith. It's a double-edged sword of "You're not really Korean." Not all of us were raised middle class. Our exposure of different things runs the gamut. I was blessed to be exposed to diversity. Coming to LA was a step down. In Detroit, Korean culture is huge. For Asian Pacific Heritage Month, it was "We're going to eat Korean food." Here it's "Oh we're going to talk about MLK Jr." My safety is a little bit different. Latinos are kinda kin because they're also POC [people of color]. There's a love-hate relationship with every group.

Tell me about the uprising that happed in 1992 in Los Angeles between Blacks and Korean people.

Renford Reese (Rodney King's mentor): African-Americans had gotten tired of what they found to be exploitative behavior. Koreans had a number of liquor stores and shops throughout South Central LA, and it was the lack of warmth [that bothered African-Americans]. Blacks would pay for something and the Koreans wouldn't want to touch their hands, so they would throw the money back at them. There was not a perceived reciprocal customer service. That was a culminating event. Everyone talks about 1992, but few people talk about Latasha Harlins, which I see you did. That was the foundational incident that led to April 29, 1992. Soon Ja Du shot this 14-year-old girl in the head. She got 500 hours of community service, and it didn't get national attention. People saw that as the height of injustice. How can someone shoot someone in the back of the head and they only get 500 hours of community service?[26]

Rodney King was the catalyst that sent it over the top. There was a disconnect. The Rodney King incident had nothing to do with Koreans. There was not a Korean officer who beat Rodney King. Koreans were scapegoated. You have to turn your anger toward something. Koreans had more stores in South Central than any other group. The exploitative treatment when it came to African-Americans, Rodney King had nothing to do with that. That's what people don't understand. There was nothing in the verdict or jury process. I know you said that perhaps they were more vulnerable. If they had been physically at their shops, there would have been more murders.

From the Korean side, Soon Ja Du were [sic] accustomed to young blacks coming in there stealing. That's what happened. I'm sure Soon Ja Du thought, "I'm tired of this. I can't take people taking product from my store." I'm sure that's what sent her over the top. If you look at the video, Latasha is clearly paying for the orange juice, but it was all the previous episodes that led up to it. Blacks had a legitimate concern. How can you be in a neighborhood and not invest it in schools, can't give a smile? I was at USC. That might be a cultural thing. That's where the cleavage is. Blacks are loud and animated, but you can't come do business with people you don't understand. In terms of the tension, it's organic and natural based on how different the people are.

So, we can say after the riots, "How can we make Black and Korean relationships better?" On one hand it's simple, but on another it's complicated. Simple because if you're going to do business you need to get over the fear of your customers or move. Deal with them like they're human beings. Get to know their names. Don't stalk them. That's the simple thing. The more complicated thing is how

[26] *This House Will Pay* by Steph Cha envisions a world where she gets her just rewards, but since it's a novel, it does not have to be based in accurate facts or reality.

do you change somebody's DNA? How do you change this approach to life? How do you train Blacks to be less animated, less loud, less aggressive? How do you train a whole race of people to not be who they are? That's the more complicated thing. In terms of Koreans doing business in the hood. If someone wants us to buy Girl Scout cookies or help with a school trip, let's do what we can to support them. If you're doing business in a community, you need to look at yourself as being a part of it. I'd make the same argument if Blacks have business in Koreatown. Learn some Korean. That's what we call good customer service. The essence of humanity is interpersonal communication skills.

Are you familiar with the uprising that happened in 1992 in Los Angeles between Blacks and Korean people?

Bree Davis: For me, it's a weird space to be in. I found the Black community before I found my Korean identity. So, I learned about that first. It's weird as a Korean adoptee. I know it's an uncomfortable conversation because there's a lot of anti-Blackness in the Korean community. I used to go to Koreatown fairly often when I lived in San Diego, from 2010-April 2019. I have a few KAD friends in LA and we'd hang out.

David Taylor: No. [I explain.] Oh then yes, I couldn't remember the year. It was a huge issue. A lot of rioting going on. I clearly remember watching video of it. It was a huge thing.

Enetty Taylor: No.

Holly Choon Hyang Bachman: I obviously was not living there when it happened. In the context of living there right now, I know individuals who experienced the 1992 racial riots, which resulted in racism and diversity work out of that. One of my longtime Chinese mentors, his mother was murdered by an African-American, and that's a whole dynamic that came out of that. But, as far as living here in LA, knowing the historical roots between the Korean and Black community during 1992, and also being Korean in LA (LA has the largest Korean population outside of Seoul), I feel very comfortable being here. From me coming from Minnesota, I did have a short living experience in the San Francisco Bay area, so that was different. It's interesting because living in Minnesota, with there being very few Asians there, being relatively white, being a Korean adoptee or Asian-American woman, when I moved to the San Francisco Bay area I said, "Wow! There are so many Asians in one place," but in LA I said, "Oh my gosh, there's a lot of Koreans in one place!" What's cool about LA is that it's similar to the work that I've done in both communities. LA's very similar from a community-driven standpoint as Minneapolis. I feel very involved with the community, civically. I'm involved in the LA Chamber of Commerce here, and some of the other Chambers, then doing the work in the community. But in the context of race and diversity, it's much more multicultural in LA. Whereas when you get outside of Minneapolis and St. Paul, it becomes much more white, European. I live in Pasadena, so it's still part of LA county, but it's more a suburb of LA city. I love it here. It's funny, my family always asks "Are you ever gonna come back to Minnesota?" and I say, "No, I'm gonna be staying here." Partly it's because of the diversity. It's interesting, and we'll probably get to this because of George Floyd and the whole civil unrest and racial protests that have been going on. From the historical fact of race and culture in LA to now it's kinda hard to believe that we're coming in full circle again with what's happened violently with the murder of George Floyd, but I've actually talked with people who lived the 1992 riots to now, and they're hoping this is different. And this is a cross-section of race and culture. I have people who are African-American and Korean and white that have shared their experience about why this moment in 2020 is different. Although it reminded them of the riots, they're hoping that this moment is different.

Hayley Hoffman: I'm a little familiar. I have a friend who's out there. She's Korean. She was abandoned by her parents. A Black family adopted her. She didn't know they adopted her until she got her transcripts later in life. [There was] escalation of oppression and resentment between the two communities and Koreatown. I think someone threw a rock inside a shop and that's how it started.

JaeHee Melanie Chung-Sherman: I am. So, I was in high school during the Rodney King events. I grew up in Texas. My adoptive family moved us. The lexicon I heard was very racist. I didn't understand the dynamics between the Blacks[27] and Korean. I didn't know exactly what happened and the growing tension historically the way I do now today. I was told as a child that the Black community had been the ones that had rioted and looted. I don't hold the same belief now. It's so much more complicated from what I understand today.

Jordan Davis: I have a very limited sense of knowledge of the riots. I saw the archival video. I know the importance of the media and how that's played in aspects of police brutality, as well as historically. More recently, I've seen recent articles from the Korean-American community regarding their connection to it that makes me want to learn more. I'm from the Midwest, and we don't have a large Korean-American community in relation to the West Coast. So the relationship between African-Americans and Korean-Americans hasn't been a big factor due to where I live now.

Matthew Goodman: The LA or Rodney King riots, I actually wrote a paper about it in college about how it's overhyped in the media. "Black mobs destroying Asian stores." But what you found was that *police were directing people into Asian areas and funneling them into minority areas, which created violence in those areas because the protestors were being channeled*. There was a great story about a

[27] Kept as part of the interview.

Korean who was disarmed by the police, so instead of protecting his store the police abandoned him. *It was about deflecting white shame so it could be a minority vs minority story.* [italics added for emphasis]

Monica Kim: It was a tense time with race relations. I won't claim I'm an expert. I was very young. I can understand it's been getting more attention in this political climate.

"But what you found was that police were directing people into Asian areas and funneling them into minority areas, which created violence in those areas because the protestors were being channeled. There was a great story about a Korean who was disarmed by the police, so instead of protecting his store the police abandoned him. It was about deflecting white shame so it could be a minority vs minority story."—Matthew Goodman[28]

SooJin Pate: I remember Lekisha or Letisha[29], the Black girl that was killed by a Korean grocer and had set off the riots. I don't mean the Rodney King riots. I mean between Blacks and Korean grocers, where you saw images of Koreans on the rooftops with rifles trying to protect the stores. All of that rose from the killing of this young Black girl. When I think about that moment and this moment, I think it was an opportunity for healing, but it created an even stronger wedge.

What I've been doing is holding workshops and webinars on how we can be better allies, which requires us to reckon with Black racism, which stemmed from the 1992 [LA] riots. The majority of

[28] This was only unknown to those not living in LA at the time. The Korean-Americans of LA were well aware and quite angry about it (Nguyen).

[29] Her name was Latasha Harlins.

the Korean population is on the West Coast, and the majority are business owners whose businesses are located in Black and brown communities. It's important to take this moment that we didn't use then. It's important that we reckon with our own bias in our own community so we can prevent things like this. If [only] we were to have this conversation in 1992. It was well-known that we were actively working to be allies. If we were to do that work in 1992, would Tou Thao[30] still have been complicit in aiding and abetting Derek Chauvin? But now we end up being complicit, so this is a ripe town for the Asian-American community. It's important to show up and fight shoulder-to-shoulder with our Black comrades.

Yun-sook Kim Navare: Yes, *Sa-i-gu* (4/29). That's one of my main motivations. Raising my daughter in Koreatown. I kinda figured there would be intergroup relations, also including faith, the queer community, class, POCs, community organizers, there are so many affinity groups. There are so many lessons that can be learned that we're still learning. Blacks have been pitted against Koreans, particularly merchant class/first-generation (1st gen) immigrants. You see it in almost every major city. One wonders why Koreans set up these shops and why those [Black] consumers and customers go to buy from them. Police brutality, LAPD is a whole other conversation and the gang culture and how LAPD is like a gang. Our financial and economic factors have been checked up, but you'll still be thrown underneath the bus conveniently. There are a lot of folks who use 1st gen stores as vehicles. It's lucrative to sell color contacts and weaves. I'm seen firsthand from working in these stores myself. The [different] groups read the same magazines, following the same pop stars. I can see both sides and have to act as a referee. At the end of the day, it's really petty. "Mister Kim only sells liquor." There are latent stereotypes on both sides. I think, "Do you guys ever try each other's

[30] Another hypothetical question was posed in Time magazine: "Did Tou Thao think he was proving his belonging by becoming a cop?" (Nguyen).

food?" They only see each other across the counter. There are so many who are integrated and have exposure. A lot of it is cultural beef. I think the media puts that wedge in to maintain the model minority-ness. I've seen changes, collaborations, talks, dialogues, ministers come together with ribbon-cutting , X amount of dollars into the community. It's also a symptom. If there wasn't all this violence, there wouldn't be a need to shift fingers [shift blame/point fingers]. The big elephant in the room was Rodney King. Oppressed, disenfranchised people. Why are we beefing with each other when there are larger systematic issues?

Young-wha: I remember watching it on TV. So, I was 19-20. I remember watching it on TV thinking how crazy it was. I also remember the Korean stores being looted and the tension between the Korean community and the Black community. I wouldn't say I was invested in it at that time. I did not see myself as Korean; I saw myself as a white girl.

Rutledge: In '92 I was living in the Midwest, and I was aware of the things happening. I was 16 years old, still in high school, and I really couldn't grasp the gravity of the situation. I wasn't aware of the Korean influence. I saw Rodney King (black guy) and the cops (white guys). I never considered the Asian aspect of it.

Would you say Minneapolis is similar to LA?

Renford Reese: There's no city in America like LA. It doesn't have the same dimensions in terms of geographic and historical perspective. If you look at the hot race issues, they're coming from LA, the low-ride Chicano culture comes from LA. LA is more diverse than Minneapolis. You have robust minority communities in terms of minority politicians that have become prominent in the past four decades, like Tom Bradley, the 1st African-American mayor in the United States. Sports icons like Kobe, LeBron [come from LA].

In terms of the similarities, it's with the police departments. They seem to have the same type of aggressive behavior toward marginalized communities. Machismo and bravado. The Minneapolis Police Department is not popularized like the LAPD, but there's a similar pattern throughout urban police departments in the United States.

I see that you used to live in Minneapolis. Tell me your thoughts on Minneapolis in the context of the George Floyd protests that happened in 2020.

Holly Choon Hyang Bachman: I just wrote a small piece for the University of Minnesota's alumni network. I actually co-chair the multicultural alumni network there. We launched it a couple of years ago. The foundation of Mixed Roots Foundation is in Minnesota, and it was birthed out of social justice. As I shared in my writing piece, it was literally the morning of May 25th we were honoring Memorial Day, also honoring the ones we've lost to COVID and war, and I posted about the 9-year foundation of the Mixed Roots Foundation. Then, in less than 12 hours later, I'm sitting in LA in my studio, and I'm watching the news and hearing about the murder of George Floyd, and then found out this was happening in my home state of Minnesota, Minneapolis. I'm still shocked. What was so powerful for me was that, not only did this happen in my home state, but I know exactly where it took place, but I also know personally friends in the leadership there. I know Keith Ellison[31], I know Klobuchar, and I know the Chief of Police there. My longest-time mentor (he's the leader of the Major Taylor Cycling Club of Minnesota, and he's known me since high school) is only four to five blocks from the murder scene. I was able to process with him within that day. We were just baffled. All the violence took place shortly after. I think for

---

[31] U.S. Representative for Minnesota's 5th congressional district from 2007 to 2019

me personally what really struck me with the George Floyd incident was that is was so blatant. I just talked with another mentor-advisor friend, a former CEO and president of the Minneapolis Foundation, and we both connected last night because he was checking on me and seeing how things were, and we both talked about George Floyd. With us both being in Minneapolis, and he's African-American, and I'm Korean/Asian, and we have the same sentiment of what happened to George Floyd—there's no explanation. It was right in your face. It triggered a humanity outrage, that anyone that would see that would be shocked, and, of course, triggering the global outcry and protest. I think for me personally, of what recently transpired, I'm personally connected.

I felt very proud of being an alum of the University of Minnesota where they're actually the first major education institution to cut ties with the Minneapolis police department, and that was a huge statement just across the country because obviously the University of Minnesota is a pillar. They're leading in research along with the Mayo [Clinic] now with COVID. So it was cool to see them step up, and then of course myself being personally tied to that effort through the multicultural alumni network. So, it's been a lot, but pain brings people together. Now even though George, Mr. Floyd's, not with us today, but he's literally created a movement that forced everyone to look at reality, the humanity, and actually, hopefully will really truly create change.

Tell me about Minneapolis from the perspective of a Korean adoptee.

SooJin Pate: I would say that it's similar to everywhere else in the US where there's this blatant racism undergirding how we think, how we operate. Minnesota is touted as one of the best places to live, for its high quality of life, low unemployment, great schools, but if you look at the data at the granular level, healthcare, etc.—it's only for white people. If you look at the data, we're the worst. We have the largest gap. One of the highest disproportionate rates of Black and brown folx in prison compared to the local population[32], as it relates to housing, on every measurement. It's only the best if you're white, but we are the worst for Black people. There's a huge gap in the treatment between whites and Blacks. White Minnesotans haven't been aware because they've turned a blind eye. Not thinking about that is part of white privilege. But we've known for a very long time that it's not paradise. We're on the heels of Mike Brown etc. All the things that happened here didn't lead to major systemic changes in how police treat Black and brown bodies. It's par for the course on how Black and brown people have been treated in our community here. It's been happening. The point I'm trying to make is that it's not new; it's been happening all around the country, but the fact that this teenager was able to record it.... This video footage, unlike video footage by the police, is different because of the length and the demeanor of Derek Chauvin, his smugness and callousness. It looks like he's just chilling, but while in a chill stature, he's committing murder. That's what's made it so powerful and compelled white folx to do something, say something. There's a Derek Chauvin in every white family. As for Thou, we all have people like that in our family that won't do anything. I'm so thankful to that teenage girl who took that video so we could all witness how brazen white supremacy is.

I also mention Baltimore at times, though not as often as LA and Minneapolis. Would you say Baltimore is similar to LA?

Monica Kim: I wouldn't know. I know there's K-town in LA, but I couldn't say.

Renford Reese: Again, LA is more diverse, more popularized and glamorized in popular culture. But Baltimore has a bigger Black population. People assume there are more Black people in LA because

[32] In 2017, Minnesota was ranked the 2nd worst place to live for the Black commuity.

of popular culture, but there aren't. They make up less than 10% of LA. [Checks World Population Review.] Or 8%. I guarantee you if you asked people in general in the United States and abroad what the African-American population is in LA, they'd think 40-50%. In Baltimore it's 63%. Compare 63% to 8%. That's the biggest difference. If you have 63% of any race in any city, it's going to be less diverse. It will be the predominant culture. Very few cities have an African-American majority like this. Baltimore has a larger Black population than Atlanta, which is really amazing[33].

On one level we can look at the cities, and the cities might be diverse and despite the diversity of the city, the police department's the same. The mindset is the same in urban America. In that we have hyperaggressive tactics, a type of bravado, a type of machismo that supersedes interpersonal skills and de-escalation techniques.

---

[33] This is where I have an epiphany of all the lost sympathy I could have given. I now know why my first (not longest) Black ex spent so many weekends in Baltimore.

Identity

In what ways have you explored your Korean side?

David Taylor: Sometimes we watch Korean movies. I don't remember Korean so much. I honestly don't know a whole lot about my culture.

Monica Kim: Obviously KADs have written books. Nicole Chung's [author of *All You Can Ever Know*] is the most popular. We're a minority within a minority. I was more involved a few years back in the KAD community, but I didn't feel like I had a lot in common with them. A lot of them seemed very white. It's taken me some time. I haven't always been interested in Korean culture. After college, I felt more comfortable with being Asian, going back to Korea and meeting family.

Milton Washington (Half-Black KAD): I know about my Korean side because I was 8-10 years old when I was adopted. After being adopted, that's when I learned English. That's when I started school with a new language, new family, new culture.

Yun-sook Kim Navare: In 1998 I was there for a summer, and I went to Holt International summer school. It also had European [KAD] adoptees. There was a whole curriculum where we studied the language, cooking, and martial arts. We stayed in Busan, the countryside, and the Holt office to look at our files. My peers adopted through other agencies found the other agencies to be more transparent and adoptee-centered. Holt was very much a factory. Even Molly said they were the "Cadillac of adoption agencies," which sounds very distasteful. One of the original eight [of the Holt empire] was a heroin addict. Other students would throw mud at them. [They got a taste of what it was like.] They have an office in Eugene, OR, and New Jersey. I said to myself, "As soon as I turn 18, I'm marching into the office, and getting my records." A couple graduate students brought their school-aged children. I was loving it because I was watching TV with them, going grocery store shopping, we'd give each other gifts. I met Ami [Nafzger] when I was a volunteer with GOA'L as an events coordinator. We celebrated for KADs overseas. When I was 16, I worked for a woodshop. She [the owner] had a daughter in college who would braid my hair. Next thing you know I'm learning phrases. One of my stepdad's best friends was in the Korean War, so he taught me some Korean. His best friend's girlfriend was Korean and furthered my cooking and language [skills]. Purple, my favorite summer, fashion, anything a young teen girl would like before Hello Kitty was big. I was often drawn to the aesthetic. [...] I had to seek it [Korean culture] out and keep it constant. I'm the only one in my family who went to college. To experiment on an intimate level was very enriching and was the missing link for what I was starving for. I liked going to K-mart with her, and people thought she was my mom. It made my adoptive mom so jealous and mad, but it was nice to not be stared at. These are small, trivial experiences. I remember going in their homes and just chilling, making kimchi. Then it was time to go home. "Wah wah." Back to Charlie Brown. My daughter has friends who look like her. You shouldn't have to be alienated. I come from a big family, and you don't buy or drive foreign cars. They were all autoworkers. My family was okay with Americans, and that included Black people, but they were more xenophobic. It was more about "they're taking jobs." When my Vietnamese friend came over, everyone was staring at him, but my Black friends were shooting pool with them. Where's the racial line here? If you're American like them, it didn't matter. They were union workers, they ate burgers and fries. It was very, very strange. They don't have issues with my partner being Black because he's American, but they're threatened by the Asian stuff. Maybe it's because they're afraid they might lose me. They know if I stay with an American I'll still be stateside, but if I'm with an Asian they might take me to another country. Nine times out of ten, the Asian will be educated. I was really, really confused by this. I thought they'd be happy [for me]. He just looked at him [my ex] like "What the hell is going on here?" because of their line of work.

My first husband was Vietnamese. My daughter is a double-foreigner. They [My family] have a nationalist and xenophobic piece. It's just too much otherness, and it's across party lines. They're okay with Jews too. Maybe it's their personal insecurity that I might abandon them. My daughter has a Korean first name and Vietnamese last name. It's difficult to raise my child culturally Korean as an adoptee. My family was all burgers and hot dogs. They didn't read. Whatever they saw in the media they took [as gospel]. I'm not the most environmental person. I have some middle America ways in me too. I can't see it ever changing. I'm Asian, Korean, and adopted, so clearly a minority, but I know where my loyalty lies. I want to make conscious choices and decisions. And I've always thought I'd be better off adopted by a Black family. I feel that there's a lot of positive Black parenting qualities I could have benefited from if I were adopted by a Black family. I would like to see more Black fostercare children going overseas because it's very one-sided and political here. We need to reevaluate what's perfect and preferred. Two women or two men could adopt or not adopt. There are so many ways of having a family. I challenge that Christian and white is right.

In what ways have you explored your Korean side? Have you traveled to your birth country?

Lisa A. Quaites (Half-Black KAD): I made a trip to Korea in the summer of 2019. I was fully immersed for the two weeks I was there. As a result of that, I returned home and got more into the cuisine in terms of cooking or dining at Korean restaurants. Prior to that trip, I hadn't eaten much Korean. The midwestern version was not the best. I was a little concerned that I was going to starve because there was nothing I thought I'd eat. I studied on the Internet before that trip to learn about Korean food so I could order it off a menu. I also researched for my memoir too. Some of it off of YouTube, reading things, watching K-dramas. I would never have thought to watch K-dramas before.

I have a good relationship with my adoptive family, but they didn't expose me to anything Korean, and I really wish they would have. I felt a little awkward going to Korea and not being able to speak the language at all. I use chopsticks in the states. In Korea they're metal, and I felt really awkward. I wish I had connections to my culture. [People would say things to me like,] "Oh, you're Korean and Black, and I've been to Korea this many times."

Rachel Kavanagh Baldwin (Half-Black KAD): I traveled to Korea in 2010. I visited Holt Korea via Holt International in Eugene, OR. My file from Holt Korea had some interesting information that was not included in my home files. I found out that I had a foster family. I was born/abandoned in Chuncheon, not Seoul (as indicated in my file). I visited my orphanage in Chuncheon, which is now a daycare center, and I discovered that a woman brought me there and I stayed there for 6 weeks (my file stated a few days). Chuncheon City Hall did not have any birth records, so still some unknowns. Also, my intake date at the orphanage was May 9, 1974. My legal documents indicate my DOB as June 18, 1974. As you can imagine, its taken me years to dissect this information and come to terms with it. To this day, I have no interest in pursuing a birth family search.

Jessica Farrell (Quarter-Black KAD): I was born in S. Korea. I made a point to be stationed there as a US soldier in 2004-2005. I fell in love with Korea. I love the culture but when I stayed I knew I would always be considered an outsider. It makes me appreciate my birth mom so much more. She spared me other racial prejudices; I know they would have happened.

Milton Washington (Half-Black KAD): Several times. The first time was in '98. It was cool. Lots of emotions obviously. It was cool to go back through those emotions and then be like, "I'm over it." I got what I needed. I got a good clean cut. I choose to keep aspects that are very Korean.

Have you traveled to your birth country together? Or do you have plans to?

Young-wha: We have plans to.

Rutledge: I've been to Korea in the '90s for the Navy. I was there for 24 hours. It was just "Let's see what kinda goods we can get" and then we got back to Japan.

Young-wha: When I was growing up, my parents always made sure we went back to Korea. I experienced Korea when I was growing up. Being a child and seeing it as an adult is two different things. I went to Korea on a birth search with a tour [as an adult]. It was eye-opening and life-changing, and I learned so much. When we first started dating, we were planning on going to The Gathering, but it's definitely in our plans. Maybe a honeymoon?

Rutledge: What?

Young-wha: I'm excited to show him old Korea and new Korea and teach him about my culture.

Rutledge: I need to show her Brooklyn.

A lot of people don't realize that if a Korean adoptee were to return to Korea, they'd be treated similarly to how Black people are treated in America.

Monica Kim: I felt shamed, but they judge me for not knowing Korean. I should learn, but I have a block around doing what people tell me to do. Even if I spent years studying, they'd still know. I know 10-15 words maybe.

Black Adoptees

The two questions that have historically plagued Black adoptees is, if they were to adopt a child, why would they not be able to adopt a white child? (However, now they can.) And why were they not adopted by a Black family? (However, now they can.)

In fact, there are Black adoptive parents now of Black adoptees, and what I've noticed about how they're different from white adoptive parents is that they tend to get their income from the military and they're more open to allowing their child to search.

Parents of Black transracial adoptees were more likely to support open records, 75% supported it compared to 51% of the parents of Korean adoptees. This resulted in 63% of Black transracial adoptees wanting to know more about their birthparents vs. 39% of Korean adoptees (Silverman).

In her Red Table Talk series, Jada Pinkett Smith interviewed Kristin Davis, a single white adoptive mother of two black children and asked, "Should white people adopt Black babies?" Most adoptees and people in general fail to realize that the support for colorblindness starts with the laws that forbid race to be a consideration in the adoption process. Many adoptive parents do not have the opportunity to choose the race of their child, and this is how white adoptive parents can be paired up with Black adoptees or how Black adoptive parents can even be paired up with redheaded white adoptees. (Black parents can also be the biological parents to a redheaded white child as well, though quite rare.) The closest parents can get to choosing the race of their child is specifying who they are not willing to raise as their own on paper forms.

White Canadians tend to adopt more Black children from the States than people living in the States. However, this does not mean racism is less prevalent. Register says of a Canadian adoptive mother, "As we talked, it became apparent that the mother knew nothing about the vitality of African American culture and had never questioned the superiority of her own culture" (Register 127).

There are some adoptees, mostly Black adoptees, who have noticed how their parents are prejudiced against the child's own race. For example, I watched Adoption Mosaic's Adoptee and Father's Day panel, featuring only male adoptees, and one of the panelists shared how his father worked in the Department of Corrections and told him that he would never call his son "Black" because to his father, Black was the color of convicts.

Ironically, that father did not realize that Black and white adoptees in general are also more likely to be incarcerated, with young people placed in group homes 2.5 times more likely to enter the criminal justice system, 90% of young people with more than five foster placements enter the criminal justice system, and a quarter of foster care alum enter the criminal justice system within two years of leaving care. Of course, Black children are twice as likely to be placed in foster care than white children, and are often called on police by their own foster parents or foster care staff (Juvenile Law Center). This is not just a problem in the United States of America.

What makes U.S. domestic adoption different from domestic adoption elsewhere is the legal ability to take a child from the incarcerated mothers who represent 10 percent of the prison population permanently. Out of the mothers in jail, 35 percent of the mothers' children are removed from their custody. Ellen Barry says, "Given the stringent legal requirements of the existing foster care laws and regulation, it is virtually impossible for incarcerated mothers to comply with the time requirements for reunification with their children. Even if mothers are on parole or probation, the obstacles for reunification are still enormous. Formerly incarcerated women have great difficulty getting jobs with adequate wages, obtaining housing, getting job training, arranging for daycare, and meeting the requirements of the juvenile court reunification agreement" (Oparah, Shin, and Trenka 65). Almost all of the women who give birth in prison are separated from their children legally. Even if a pregnant woman has nearby relatives, it's practically impossible for them to get to the prison by the very short time allotted to pick up the infant, so then the baby is made a dependent of the juvenile county court where the prison is located. Roberts said, "Because the majority of women's prisons are located in predominantly white, rural areas far from more racially diverse urban areas, these infants are most often placed with white foster families in relatively less diverse communities" (Oparah, Shin, and Trenka 66). Was this placement intentional? I wouldn't be surprised.

Many are not aware that the no fault clause was stricken for public housing, meaning that if a grandchild is found to be using pot that their grandparents can be evicted, or if a caretaker is found to be using pot that the elder they are caretaking can be evicted. This is why Black families are so reluctant and unwilling to house family members after they have returned from prison. In addition, the 24% of Black men that make up the prison population are not counted in poverty statistics (Chilton).

Statistically, we all know that most men in prison are Black and that most ex-convicts have a harder time finding a job. Statistically, we know that financial pressure is the #1 cause of divorce. However, whenever people hear the term "interracial marriage" they want to celebrate making love and not war. However, if it's Black men in these relationships, there is a statistically greater chance of financial pressure, and a greater chance that they're making war and not love. So not only does a Black man have to work twice has hard as a white man to get ahead, an interracial married couple where the man is Black, has to work twice as hard to stay afloat and to stay married.

Adoptees comprise the largest percentage of prisoners, felons, and patients of psychologists, therapists, or counselors. Mental health professionals are surprised at the alarmingly high number of their patients who are adopted. Studies show an average of 17 times the norm (Lifton). Fifty to seventy percent of the teens at The Haven (a resource center for street kids) in New Trier Township, Illinois, are adopted; that's 25 to 35 times the norm (Henderson). Sixty to eighty-five percent of the teens at Coldwater Canyon's Center for Personal Development (a private acute-care psychiatric hospital/

school in Southern California), are adopted; that's 30 to 40 times the norm (Ostroff).

High numbers of adoptees are sent to disciplinary or correctional schools or are locked out of their [adoptive] homes (Carlson). Adoptees are more likely to have difficulties with drug and alcohol abuse, as well as eating disorders, attention deficit disorder, infertility, suicide and untimely pregnancies (Mitchell, Ostroff, Lifton, and Schecter). Black adoptee Nicolle Tremitiere Yates says, "I've seen some adult transracial adoptees turn to drinking or drugs. Some have low self-esteem or even thoughts of suicide" (Roorda and Simon 151). Since addiction research has proven that addiction is only a symptom and that all addicts have some form of trauma and abandonment, which adoption causes without question, it's clear to me that the $1 trillion spent on the War on Drugs would be best spent on the War on Adoption. As for those adoptees who deny this (denial is always strong within addiction and adoption), they have only to experience key moments in what is considered a full life to understand what I am talking about. There are 44 anonymous or other recovery groups in existence and addiction can "begin" at any age and be realized at any other age.

In reaction to Black babies being adopted by white parents was "[o]pposition to the practice of transracial adoption galvanized in the early 1970s and led to implementation of same-race adoption policies at most adoption agencies by 1975" (Oparah, Shin, and Trenka 92). Due to the backlash at the idea of white parents adopting Black children, white parents who wanted to adopt had to go overseas. "[The] suggestion that American families find it easier to adopt children from other countries than to adopt transracially within this country is saddening," said former senator Howard M. Metzenbaum, author of The Multiethnic Placement Act (MEPA) of 1994, that was passed as part of the Improving America's Schools Act (Roorda and Simon Back Cover).

The 1995 movie *Losing Isaiah*, starring Halle Berry, may help answer why things are the way they are. The movie furthered the myth that Black parents did not want to adopt Black children and that "large numbers of white families would eagerly adopt Black children in foster care if these [race-matching] policies were eliminated" (Oparah, Shin, and Trenka 53). The movie was made one year after the 1994 Multiethnic Placement Act (MEPA) which made it illegal to use race to deny or delay adoption (Roorda and Simon, *In Their Own Voices: Transracial Adoptees Tell Their Stories*). *Losing Isaiah* propagated the stereotype of Black mothers on crack and welfare among the conservative whites. The fact that Halle Berry took this role, as a Black woman indicates either internalized racism or desperation for an acting role. In fact, I have found that it is common among all adoptive parents to be against the stereotypical welfare woman. When Reverend Bigelow was asked if he connected with his race he said "Definitely not. [...] Because African Americans are always depicted on TV as a group in need, a group that is always looking for a handout . . . and I wasn't raised that way" (Roorda and Simon 220).

Adoptees tend to get along with adoptees, in general. Ideally, there is an automatic affinity, connectedness, and special place in the heart, along with curiosity and fascination. (However, I had an opposite experience where a Korean adoptee bullied me because he thought I was just Korean-American.) A similarity I notice between the two types of adoptees is similar to what is called the "gaydar"[34]. Korean adoptees have a similar ability to detect other Korean adoptees out of a crowd. I call this "KAD-ar." Kari Smalkoski says, "I have adopted Korean radar, I'm sure of it. Perhaps all adopted Koreans have it built inside" (Bishoff and Rankin 73). Nicolle Tremitiere Yates says the same is true in the Black adoptee community: "I knew she was transracially adopted immediately. How can you tell the difference? The hair gives them away. Also, many transracial adoptees only feel comfortable around white people. That's my observation" (Roorda and Simon 148). In the summary of *In Their Own Voices*, the interviewers

---

[34] Interestingly, the only person I met who had a "bi-dar" was Björk's assistant, David.

noted, "Laurie, the most 'cosmopolitan' of the interviewees, who, before entering high school, had lived in Sierra Leone, the Ivory Coast, Panama, Bangladesh, and Thailand, also does not put her black identity at the top of the list" (Roorda and Simon 384).

Korean adoptees whether consciously or subconsciously do not tend to hang out with Korean-American immigrants if they are in an all-white community. Black adoptees experience the same thing with African-Americans. According to Arnold Silverman, 73% of Black transracial adoptees surveyed preferred white friends and 69% of the transracial adoptees dated white people exclusively. However, 70% of Black transracial adoptees took pride in their racial heritage, but only 57% of Korean transracial adoptees did. Part of this might be on the part of the openmindedness of the parents.

Adoptees as children are afraid of being bullied and fear that association could lead to being singled out. In some cases, this adoptee experience is even true for those who are not adopted but live in predominantly white neighborhoods (Sambou).

Perhaps Korean adoptees do not face as much blatant racism in the job market as, say, Black adoptees but "adoptees with a foreign appearance seem to have a disadvantage in the labour market [...] that cannot be explained by their educational background or qualifications" (qtd. in Hjern, Lindblad, and Vinnerljung 6). Due to such prevalence of racism when finding a job, it can take both an economic and mental toll on Black adoptees.

However, for those Black adoptees who struggle like this, I say that there are still positive things to focus on. Adoptees complain that they don't have any role models, but for the Black adoptee community, I can think of at least one: Black adoptee, Dan O'Brien, gold medalist in the decathlon. For Black adoptees, another great role model is Seth D. Himrod. Himrod is a stockbroker, fireman, and drill sergeant all rolled in one. From 1989-1992, Himrod served in the military during Desert Storm. He was a paratrooper and drill sergeant. Himrod began stockbroking at my age and received his license in 1995. He rose up in the ranks within ten months and became vice president.

Then he became interested in fighting fires. Himrod explains his reasoning, "a fireman can save people's property and their lives and really make a difference. As a drill sergeant, I can help teach young men to stay alive. That's the bottom line—to stay alive and do their jobs. [...] And as a stockbroker I affect not only their lives but their family's future" (Roorda and Simon 298).

I would be remiss in discussing domestic Black adoptees without saying anything about transcultural, transnational, and transracial adoptees (TRAs) from the 11.724 million square-mile land mass of Africa that is large enough to hold all of Europe, the United States of America, India, and Japan (Encylopædia Brittanica). Why does Africa look smaller on a world map than America? It's for the same reason why Galileo had such a difficult time explaining to the church that Earth revolved around the sun rather than the sun revolving around the earth. It's for the same reason why Korean is spelled with a "K" rather than a "C"[35]. (This controversial myth states that it's spelled with a "K" because Japan, with the tagline "House of the Rising Sun," wanted to be before Korea in the English alphabet.) I point out the size of Africa because by making Blacks believe they're small, in their minds they are small, but they're not. Poor Black children are as smart as rich, white kids. It would be helpful if we didn't measure all intelligences by how well they measured up to a standard white, or even Asian, intelligence. For example, I can tell you that I'm very booksmart, but can be embarrassingly ignorant about simple day-to-day matters.

This dynamic is not true of Black adoptees who were adopted within their own family. There are plenty of Black adoptive parents who adopt either within their own family or foster children, a much less racially charged way of creating a family. These adoptees get to deal with the different dynamic of "What happens when your older sister becomes your mother?" They must set up personal boundaries that no one can cross, even family.

---

[35] Kim and Yu 365

Photographers did more harm than good with their "poverty porn" as many places in Africa would be wonderful tourist destinations. For example, Ethiopia is mentioned in the Bible many times, was never colonized, and has a rich cultural heritage. However, despite being Black, African adoptees may feel somewhat like outsiders in the narrative between descendants of slaves and white people, whether or not they are descendants of plantation owners[36], since their ancestors did not go through slavery, euphemistically called the Triangle Trade Route in the South. They don't even relate as much to rap. The interesting thing to point out is that African immigrants are overachievers over other immigrant groups and US-born Americans, with more bachelor's degrees, with a third being in science, technology, engineering, and math (STEM) fields , and more master's degrees, medical degrees, law degrees, or doctorates. They are twice as likely to work in healthcare, like my Ethiopian adoptee friend, and we can thank them for saving our population from COVID-19 (Simmons). Isn't it interesting then that Asians are seen as the model minority when the truth is that the model minority is Africans? But that wouldn't fit neatly into the narrative, particularly since Blacks are lumped together much like Asians, where differences are diminished for a simplified political purpose.

Speaking of inaccurate stereotypes, I honestly believe that Koreans love *yongneom tongdak* (seasoned whole chicken), *dakgangjeong* (Korean double-fried "candy" chicken), and watermelon more than Blacks do. I could talk a little bit more about food. *The Hate U Give* has a scene where the main character's brother tests her boyfriend's "Blackness" with a food test. I have had similar conversations at work. Even though white people may be offended at the idea of white food, food can be considered racialized insofar as race is connected to cultures.

---

[36] By the way, most people don't realize that reparations are not always monetary and can even be cultivated as a daily practice.

Profiles of Black Adoptees

In what ways have you learned about your Ethiopian side?

Halsen Valdes (Ethiopian adoptee): I came here at the age of 18, so I had a pretty good understanding of my culture. So, it was more a struggle to keep it rather than learn it. I wanted to learn the culture here. So that was my main struggle. I didn't get the chance to be around people who looked like me. I would miss it. I knew it was there but couldn't access it.

In what ways have you learned about your Zimbabwean side?

Enetty Taylor: Considering that I was raised part of my life in Zimbabwe, I take my culture with me wherever I go. I teach my kids. Every day I'm with it.

In what ways have you learned or are learning about your Black side?

Helsen Valdes: At first, the first 3-4 years were a struggle. I know a lot of my friends have a different experience. I came here at a mature age[37], and who I was was already formulated [formed]. The battle was just trying to preserve it.

I went to a school that was pretty much white. When you are older coming to this culture, it's harder. I'm learning about African-American culture in America, but I don't fit in African-American culture nor the white culture.

I would like to add that the longer I lived/stayed in America, I realized and felt that Black doesn't have the same meaning that it used to. I realized moving forward I have to live defending it rather

[37] Arnold Silverman stated in his research that the effects of delayed placement are greater than transracial adoption in and of itself (Silverman).

than embracing it. For that very reason I used to say I'm not Black, I'm Ethiopian. For me, it felt easier to abandon my Blackness than to face the struggle.

Jessica Farrell: I have explored my Black side by joining big brothers and big sisters. With my big sister I'd attend Black churches until they made it clear I wasn't one of them. Later I found out my genetic make up is 1/2 Korean and 1/2 mixed with white and black. It makes my struggle more interesting yet frustrating. I know why the black community is angry. I totally get it but they aren't inclusive either; I think that's mainly because they've had it so rough. They've learned to rely on their own and shun what isn't theirs.

Jordan Davis: I went to school for history originally, and I have a broad interest in different histories. I started off with Medieval Studies, like the Crusades. Then when I did more reflection, I shifted my focus. I'll be starting my graduate studies at the University of South Carolina, focusing on archaeology and history, particularly African-American and the African diaspora heritage. So, in some ways, my academic life will be directly exploring it from a historical perspective. I'm still working on how I connect with present-day African-American communities. Part of that has been through reunion with my birth family. Most has been through my relationship with my birth family.

Lisa A. Quaites: I was raised in the Black culture, so I was fully immersed for 51 years now. So just living and interacting with family and friends and community members just with pop culture and music and movies and anything you can think of. When I view myself and think about how I live my life and what I've been exposed to, I'm Black. Just being fully immersed.

It's kinda funny because there's a game that's about Black cultural references. All the players of the game have to come up with the references. Like it would ask questions about *Fresh Prince* or *Living Single*. It was kinda funny because it was me and another friend, and we were in the lead. I found my biological father, and he's Black. And this was last year. And they were like how is she winning this game? It was quite humorous.

Rachel Kavanagh Baldwin: I haven't done this actively, but gained a greater understanding and experience during my undergraduate years at Notre Dame. While I learned a lot, it was also a polarizing experience, as it is when I started to learn about Colorism.

Milton Washington: I was a Black kid in a Black family that moved around because my father was in the military.

My husband's also an Army brat. It's a tough life.

Milton Washington: It's not necessarily tough. It just makes you less reliant on other people.

What is it like being Black, Korean, and adopted? How do you navigate?

Jessica Farrell (half-Korean/quarter-Black adoptee): You in are a world of your own. Nobody in my life understood how I wanted to fit in everywhere I went. Black families shunned me because I spoke proper English. I wasn't accepted with my white family in front of others who were close minded nor did Asian accept me either.

Lisa A. Quaites (Half-Black KAD): I will say when I was young, it was tough because I didn't know anybody who was adopted. I didn't know anybody who was Asian. There were a couple who went to my school, but not a lot. I wasn't Black. I wasn't white. Kids are mean. For Black kids to think I was not Black hurt when they would call me "China girl". I was born in 1967. It was right at the height of the Civil Rights movement, and there was a lot of focus on race when I was growing up. Maybe people are seeing more mixed races, or the mentality is changing toward race, but I think I became more accepted by my peers by who I was. When you're young, you want to be like everyone else because difference is uncomfortable, but when you get into your teens you want to be different. When I became a teenager, I started embracing my dual nationality. A lot of people would ask [me about it]. I would never think to ask people, but people ask me that all the time. I'd say I'm Black and Korean. Even though I didn't know anyone else who was Korean, I was accepting it and liking it. I grew to embrace it, and now I love it. It's so awesome! I would not want to change a thing. I love being multiracial, multinational. My oldest daughter is cool with it, but my youngest daughter embraces our Asian heritage a little more. It's definitely been a growth process. My thoughts and feelings of it have evolved with maturity.

Rachel Kavanagh Baldwin (Half-Black KAD): This is a loaded question. My 46 year old self has a different response and approach than my childhood or young adult self. Throughout my life, I've often found myself being held accountable or responsible for peoples' ignorance. They could never understand how I could be multiracial but then also be raised in a white family. People have always wanted me to chose, and they overwhelmingly assumed I was black, so thought I should "act" black...whatever that means. My life has been full of microaggressions. I've been ridiculed by the black community for being "too white," ridiculed by the white community for trying too hard to "fit in," and completely dismissed by the Korean and Asian community because of my brown skin and curly hair.

Milton Washington (half-Black/half-KAD): First of all, I consider myself Black first, then Korean, and then adopted. That experience has left me in a lot of ways as a loner. My life is more of a loner than any of those other things. I'm a strange loner because I'm social. But being disconnected from my [birth]mother makes it easier to stay away from people emotionally. It's an interesting way of being in this life. If you know what you're doing, it can be very powerful. So many people are emotionally vested in others. You know how deep pain feels like, so you learn quickly how to avoid it. You kinda stay away from folks. I can keep a good emotional distance from folks and navigate and be seen as a social butterfly, one of the drivers if you have to learn to have influence. I want to get some things out of life [by learning to have influence]. As a Black/Korean adoptee living this life at this time where isolation abounds, I'm used to isolation. This is an environment I know well, and I can thrive. Also, having emotional fortitude to deal not just with isolation but existential uncertainty. I had coronavirus and went through dark places, but I've gone through tough situations that require you to be calm and balanced before. If there is no tomorrow, then fuck it. I'm kinda old-school Black. I believe in Black values from the old school is doing for your own. Fuck what is going on. Fuck the government.

I feel like being a loner goes back to being an "Army brat."

Milton Washington: There you go. It helps you view situations in ways other people don't. White people been doing this for 400 years. Fuck that. They're gonna keep doing them. Part of our efforts requires a PR perspective, messaging perspective. Getting tight. The world changes for the better. Lot of us ain't ready. We gotta get ready. If you talking shit, that robs your credibility. We don't have the luxury of poor showing right now.

What is it like being Black and adopted? How do you navigate?

Helsen Valdes: At the stage I'm in, the struggle to fit in faded away. I realized I am valuable. I love me. The struggle more is concept-wise rather than accepting it.

Jordan Davis (domestic adoptee): Particularly because I was transracially adopted, I feel that I grew up in racial isolation, being the only person of color in my family. That has always been an unspoken tension with me and my adoptive parents. When they adopted me, it was the colorblind era of the late 80s when Michael Jordan and Oprah were going big and they thought racism was over. It's been a long process unpacking that, particularly recently with Black Lives Matter. There are racial disparities. There are things marginalized communities experience in this "post-racial" society. I grew up in Milwaukee, Wisconsin. It's ranked in the top 3 most segregated cities in the US. I grew outside of the African-American community. That's really shaped my experience. I don't have a real sense of connection to African-American heritage. I'm spending a lot of my 20s trying to reclaim and explore that.

How do you feel that domestic Black adoptees are different from African adoptees or international Black adoptees?

Enetty Taylor: I have no idea how to answer that. I have a few African adoptee friends. The experience is not the same. Everyone's experience is different. I can't generalize. I can't conclude because everyone has different experiences. Everyone's individual experience depends on the family, where they grew up, and so forth.

Helsen Valdes: Massively different because domestic adoptees don't have to deal with culture shock.

When you bring the cultural difference, it's realistically hard. You have to be willing to try to meet halfway. When you can do that, all of that is good. When you can't do that, family gets separated. Domestic, they're already here. They know how a kid should function in a family dynamic. The parent knows better how to help that kid. They know how to maneuver it. Definitely international adoptions are more challenging.

Jessica Farrell: In a long round about sense domestic black adoptees are international. It [If] one was to forget the whole slave trade— (which will never happen in my eyes). It wouldn't be seen that way by most. But being a product of international adoption I think "immigrant" means directly moving from country of origin to another country and that doesn't apply. Nor do I think mainstream black adoptees will agree. But I guess that [is my] argument.

Jordan Davis: There's common themes of when you come to the United States, there's a level of racialization that occurs. If you don't have an accent or culture markers, you get lumped in as a Black person. From talking with my African friends and from Congo refugees who came to the Midwest, they experience racism in a lot of similar ways to African-Americans. One of the major differences is the history of slavery and having that long-term contact with white Americans, whereas Africans may have met one to two white missionaries or development workers doing "good things." African-Americans have a much broader range of interactions. That's making a broad generalization.

Lisa A. Quaites: I don't know if I can answer that question. For an African child to be adopted to a different country, I don't know what they would think or how they would feel about missing out on their African customs. I think how an adoptee adjusts to a new environment has a lot to do with their family and how supportive or abusive they are. I don't know if I can compare and contrast that.

Milton Washington: Yeah, they [domestic adoptees] got adopted, but they still pound for pound turn regular Black, like "woe is me, and I'm owed some shit." Someone who comes from a different nation and understands scarcity, you know you ain't owed shit in this world. Yeah, you can fight, and you should fight for reparations, but also receive as the collective. If it do come in our lifetimes, we need to get tight anyway.

Rachel Kavanagh Baldwin: Not sure, as I do not know any.

Do you think that African adoptees are expected to marry other Blacks?

Enetty Taylor: Possibly. I know most Africans prefer to marry within the African culture. Most people want to marry within their cultures. In these progressive times, I'm seeing a lot of difference. We don't have a lot of arranged marriages anymore. I'm seeing a lot of marriages based on love. I'm starting to see that right now, but I'm pretty sure that if you go deep down into the villages where they believe in the "natural order of things" they believe in marrying within your culture.

Connection to the Black Community

You have or had a Black spouse, Black fiancé, or Black boyfriend. This is rare in the Korean adoptee community where many people marry white people or other Asians. Why do you think there are not more of these types of interracial marriages among KADs?

David Taylor: My wife had two kids, and I had two kids from a previous marriage. She's from Africa, her first husband was Black, and the second child's biological dad is white. That's a good question. I met her in a running group I created specifically for Asians who like Black females. There are a lot of Asians guys that prefer Black women. One of the common questions I get asked is "Why do you prefer a Black woman over a white woman?" That's just what I prefer. I grew up in Boston. Predominantly, my neighborhood was white. When I got into middle school, there were some Black kids. I don't know if that's when I got into preferring Black females. That's who I was comfortable with. I could relate to the Black kids because they also get teased a lot. I don't know if it's their appearance or culture. I've been asked that so many times. I live in North Carolina now. When I was growing up in Boston, most Asian females were with white people. Most of the feedback I've gotten here has been pretty positive. Sometimes people glare at us, but it's a friendly stare. They comment on how great the kids look. But with the rioting, I've gotten flack from Asians, Blacks, and Whites. My wife was adopted too. She's from Zimbabwe and was adopted by a white family.

SooJin Pate: Korean adoptees are taught to be white people. We are inculcated with white norms. So much that we grow up thinking that we're white. To use the twinkie metaphor, we look Asian but the way we see the world is through a white lens due to how we're raised. That's why, that's why it's rare. It's way more common for Koreans to be with white folx. Even marrying other Asians, that percentage is smaller than the percentage of those who partner with white folx.

I know less than a handful of Korean adoptees who are partnered with Black folx. The common denominator is that they've done the work of decolonizing their minds to become racially conscious folx. Once you come to that awareness and consciousness, you end up partnering with someone who's not white.

We're actually divorced now, but we're co-parenting our daughter. Even though we're not together romantically, we love each other as family and friends. I spent almost my entire adult life learning about Black culture, Black literature, Black history. That's what my Master's and PhD degrees are in. For both Alex and I, we never saw us being part of an interracial couple. Things I might experience as an Asian-American woman, I didn't have to explain because he's already educated himself on that, and he's very active in the Asian-American community. Because of that, we were on the same page and could just be there for each other. This moment isn't any different. We talk, breathe, mourn. Memorial Day is when this happened. A week after George's murder, Alex called me up and said, "I just need someone to cry with." We have that type of relationship. Because of our longevity and how we've been immersed in each other's cultures. There's just so much synergy. Alex and I from the get-go were very communicative around these issues.

Young-wha: Because we grew up with white people. We're more comfortable with what we grew up with. There's always that underlying racism we get from our parents that marrying white is better. I think that's the reasoning behind it. I remember at one time, I know it was influenced by society in general that "Black men are kinda scary."

Rutledge: [Laughs]

Young-wha: "You have to be careful with them because they're all players, and white men are better to women." Our family and society plays a role in that.

Yun-sook Kim Navare: I have a lot of issues with KADs. I think they go with what they know due to trauma, loss, and separation. Our intimate bonds have been severed. [They've dealt with] the adoptive family environment, whether there was abuse and neglect. I came in the mid- to early-'70s and the focus was on integration. I'm glad to see more KADs are having more relationships with Asians. Many of them typically go for white partners, whether gay or straight, because it will protect them and it's socially acceptable. Then there's fetishism, eroticism, exoticism, geisha, and prostitution stuff, so we're more palatable to white people. We're placed in places where there's not a lot of diversity. Some of us never leave their hometown, and they like predicatbility and what's safe for survival. I'm the total opposite. I have to follow my gut and soul. I have to keep searching for my family because that's my truth. I never bought into the American dream. Some KADs don't want to, not because they're racist; it's just because. They don't want to disrupt the adoptive parent fantasy of the KAD world, but I think that's changing. Things are more open and more acceptable. The older generation fell into assimilation, but the younger [generation is different]. There are other KADs in relations with brown and Black folx, but they're few. It takes a lot to challenge those notions. "Oh, I can't search because my parents would be so offended" etc.

Bree Davis: I think it's because we're raised by white folx. There's that adjacency to the white community and because there's anti-Blackness in the Korean community. My parents even had issues with me dating Asian. When I moved to California, I cut off contact from them. I was married to a white man, but I realized I couldn't do it because of racial issues and white men fetishize Asians a lot more, so I chose not to date white at all. An ex I dated was half-Mexican half-Black so my child is Mexican, Black, Asian, and white. His mom's side is Black and his Dad's side is Mexican and white.

Monica Kim: I could talk all day about why I think this is. A lot of adoptees grew up in predominantly white communities, and they just feel more comfortable with white people. The advantages that can come from being white can be appealing to some, plus [there's] negative stereotypes about Black men. The biggest [reason] would just be trying to have white privilege and the comfort. That was my experience and a lot of adoptees'. I don't know; there are so many answers. I'm interested in what people's reasoning is. My dating preference is Korean or Black. I'm mystified about what the appeal is to only dating white. Sometimes I'm genuinely confused. For many years, I like dating non-white because there's more common ground, being able to related on a deeper level.

Holly Choon Hyang Bachman: It's kinda interesting, the cross-section of race, adoption, and culture. I've always shared with my experience that I'm white, but my heritage is Korean. It's interesting because even with my longtime mentor who's African-American, he has kinda adopted me as an adopted daughter. Having that kind of feeling of being discriminated, prejudice, and racism, I couldn't go to my family because they don't understand that experience. I kinda felt that I was drawn to—and I'm gonna go deep a little bit if you don't mind—with my experience of being white but being Asian on the outside, with my relationship with other African-Americans or Black women or Black men, there's somewhat of a camaraderie, the social justice piece where we can kind of share. And the same with other people of color, but I get into relationship, say with my most recent relationship was African-American, and I've had past relationships. What I think is interesting, and I've been trying to figure this out, that even though my most recent and past relationships are Black, I married a white guy. I had dated African-American men prior to my actual husband and then I dated them after. It's really interesting because I married a white guy but had dated African-American men, and there was maybe interest in other races. I think it's the identity piece. It's the commonality and the context of culture and experience. Even with my most recent relationship, we were both from the Midwest. He had been living in LA for many years, but there's that kind of commonality. "You're not from LA; you're from the Midwest" so we had that connection. There's a whole different culture and work ethic. He was saying he'd never go out with anybody from LA. So it's interesting how that worked out because we had that connection. But what's interesting is my ex-fiancé—for me, I've never felt like I fit in anywhere—so even when I was dating my ex-fiancé, I kinda made a commitment that I would go to his mom's all African-American church, but I said, "When we get married I want to go to a multicultural church." I don't want to belong to one race. That's really been my mantra and my mission all my life. I said to my white [ex-]husband, "I'll go to a Catholic church once a month, and that's it." But I want to go to a church that's diverse. Partly that's because I grew up being a minority, even perceived as a minority, even though my culture's white. I innately have felt always this social justice in me of fighting for the underdog and always helping the less fortunate. It has been a mission in my life. So all those different factors play a role in my relationships.

I see that you say you're a Diversity, Equity[38] & Inclusion Professional. In what ways do you practice anti-racism as part of your job?

SooJin Pate: I'm confused by this question. It's not something I shut off and turn back on again. I live it and breathe it in every aspect of my life. I don't think I have to be anti-racist now but not some other time. That's not how I think at all. It's a value that I hold 24/7.

In what ways did you practice anti-racism as part of the work you did with Division I college football?

Monica Kim: It wasn't blatantly called anti-racist then, but you have to understand how individuals are treated in the classroom. I worked in academic counseling. The coach would tell Black kids that they should sit in the front, but I can't say that race didn't play into that. Stats show that Black kids are more likely to be suspended, and their troublemaking is seen as aggressive. If students told me about negative interactions with professors, I'd act as a mediator. There was a Male Athletes Against Violence program. It showed football players in a positive light, and, by extension, Black men who were somewhat large and intimidating. It was very unofficial and informal in conversations about how they felt isolated. I think being able to relate with them on that and having that culture. I never did diversity training with them. I was the only Asian on the staff. It was a huge challenge: underrepresentation of people of color in staff.

---

[38] Note that the preferred word is "equity," not equality. Equity has been compared to more plumbing in the poorer neighborhoods or even giving a slingshot to King David, who defeated Goliath.

I also wanted to mention an experience that I had in college. I worked at Barnes & Noble, right outside Baltimore. One day, I was going into work when I was stopped by a large Black man. He immediately invaded my personal space and said, "You all are so racist. You just like us when we buy stuff." Part of me thought, well, I work in retail. It's my job to be nice to people so they will buy stuff. I'm nice to anybody who might be a customer, regardless of race. But, in the moment, I was scared because he was a big guy who was comfortable enough to aggressively approach me in broad daylight. He also was clearly angry already, so I worried I would be physically injured[39]. In spite of my fear, something inside me snapped. I was really offended. So, I swallowed my fear and did my best to explain how I actively tried to be as anti-racist as possible. I stood my ground, despite the fact that he remained up in my face the entire time. He took it well and I was able to successfully diffuse the situation. I think he walked away with a bit more understanding. I have thought about that incident a few times in my life. It made me think of how I hope even a little exposure with someone Asian could help the future perceptions of the kids I worked with. It also made me realize that he had lumped me in with my other coworkers (who were almost all white). This hurt because I had experienced racism just as I'm sure he had. I also think about the continued segregation in Baltimore, how there is not a lot of opportunity to have these types of conversations. There are not enough people challenging negative perceptions, facilitating dialogue between individuals from the Asian and Black communities.

Helsen had a lot of good things to say about you in your practice as a psychotherapist. In what ways do you practice anti-racism as a psychotherapist for intersectional Black and Indigenous People of Color (BIPOCs)[40] and transracial adoptees?

---

[39] A similar thing happened to me.

[40] The legalistic/data gathering European version of BIPOC is BAME, which stands for Black, Asian, and Minority Ethnic.

JaeHee Melanie Chung-Sherman: That's a good question. It is baked into the way I experience the world, how I see the world, and how I've integrated and reapplied psychodynamics into the work I've done. It took a lot of years and unlearning, particularly [from] clients of color who've shared that with me when I've micro-aggressed. For the clients I do see, it's so nuanced and then we add all the other intersections among gender identity, religious and non-religious beliefs, and racial identity, etc. that constantly keeps me curious, as well as energized. I seek the best and most affirming ways to understand who that person is. Adoption, particularly, predominantly for most TRAs and TRIs [transracial immigrants] has hetero-centric family systems, predominantly evangelical Christian. [It takes] a lot of the work if and when the individual is really dismantling a lot of internalized factors they experienced on an external and continuous basis.

In what ways do you practice anti-racism as part of your job?

Matthew Goodman: The entire idea is based on research, two major pieces of research on how to keep 3rd-6th grade attainment. I did a lot of work in criminal justice. When they calculate prison rates, they look at 3rd grade attainment rates. If they think of it that way, we need to think of it that way. Harvard looked at public investment. Only a few have a positive rate of return, $1 for every dollar invested: childhood health and childhood education. I didn't know about health, but I knew something about education, the 3rd-6th grade attainment in largely African-American and Latinx communities. We take pictures and collect stories of our students. Our students aren't lazy. They're remediating several levels in a year. Educators see the kids self-managing. The kids learn to manage themselves. They're not acting out, not getting in fights. People come and see our students. We have two-year-olds that do our work! We have two-year-olds doing homework! It's fundamentally anti-racist. Black bodies doing this work, mostly math. They [these people] get to see them do it. No amount of rhetoric is more powerful than being in that space. The kids are awesome. They're so cute and excited. It's uplifting.

In what ways do you practice anti-racism?

Renford Reese: I never think about it or frame how I live my life on being anti-racist. What I try to do is embrace a certain type of humanity. That's respecting other people, trying to challenge yourself with your own stereotypes as a conscious, active process. Asking yourself, "Where did that come from?" and "Why did I think it that way?" Treat people with respect, kindness, warmth, and giving [sic] them the benefit of a doubt. I just look at it as being a good human being, a good neighbor, a good professor. It takes a certain level of sophistication to deconstruct [race]. It's easy to be lazy.

I'll give you an example. When I was living in Seattle, I was at a garage sale, in this nice upper-class area. It was a white-person-owned house. I was looking at snow skis. I bought a beanbag and put it up front. It was $3. I put it up front [to get more]. When I went to leave, the owner asked me. He said, "You didn't pay for this beanbag." I said, "Yes, I did." I turned to the guy I bought the beanbag from and asked him to tell the owner that I bought the beanbag. [Afterwards,] I found myself in the car shaking.

I went through the difficult process [of deconstructing]. First of all, he didn't see me buy the beanbag. I don't think he was wrong in that. Then I asked what would he have done if I were white. It's $3. Who cares? You're trying to get rid of this stuff. I came to the conclusion that he was being biased or racist. I had to go back and ask the question and didn't just think he was racist out of the gate without asking.

A buddy was at a restaurant as a couple. He was African-American and his wife was African-American, and the white couple got their food first. The kneejerk response is that they're racist. But there's more variables to that. First of all, you don't know what they ordered.

They could have ordered hot dogs and you ordered filet mignon with lobsters. In this environment, people have a kneejerk response to think things are racist when it might not be.

I have a friend and when he asked maintenance for help, maintenance asks if he's a professor because he looks like a student. Is that him being Black or him being young? How you gonna get traumatized by a maintenance guy? We let too many small things traumatize us. We're stronger than that. We came as slaves. That's why they use us in the field because of how mentally and physically strong we are. So that's the problem that I have with parts of the movement. Of course, I think we should fight institutional racism, systemic violence. Show me who's on your board. That's quantifiable. How should we start to recruit people who look like the community?

Holly Choon Hyang Bachman: How I practice anti-racism is not making assumptions, not playing off stereotypes. If you're looking at being really active and intentional, really thinking before you speak and creating inclusiveness and diversity. There was an awesome comment or post on LinkedIn from an African-American woman about corporations stepping up with anti-racism. There was a really cool statement, "That's great all corporations, stepping up for diversity and anti-racism, but can I see your Board of Directors? Can I see your executive leadership?" Drop the mic! You can have diverse players, managers, but in the NFL there are only one or two owners of color, and everybody else is white. Looking at boardrooms of corporations can tell you if they're really truly creating an inclusive, leadership and society. And also naming it, that's the other thing too. Part of being anti-racist is calling out the behavior and also to work on systemic change where you do go to the council, you do go to the school boards.

That's what we do with Mixed Roots. As a high school culture diversity group, we petitioned the principal and the [school] board to say we want Dr. Martin Luther King Jr. Day off. This was back in the mid-90s, and we got the day off. But prior to that with no student movement or voice, if that hadn't happened as a student group, then we would have had to have Dr. Martin Luther King Jr. Day at school. I feel like that's exactly what's going on right now. This conversation I had with my friend last night, we talked about a lot of stuff! You should have just been recording that and that would have been your interview. He had mentioned, and I agree with him, that right now, the whole fabric of society has been upended, uprooted, and now the question is "Are people actually going to do something about it and stay consistent and really truly make change and not just be on the bandwagon?" Because right now, I was telling him, my Black friend last night, that every single email I get is Black, all Black, Black, Black, Black. That's cool, but let's really see if these corporations and businesses and leadership do anything, and it's not just jumping on the bandwagon.

Rutledge: I'm keeping it PG. I'll let her go.

Young-wha: I think it's more having those conversations. I'm on the Diversity Committee at work, and we talk about what we can do. Through the George Floyd incident, it broke my heart. What can I do? Especially with COVID. I'm a mom. Did I want to go to protests? Heck yeah! But I had to consider if I'd be bringing COVID home or to my clients. I did a lot of Facebook posts and let my voice be heard within my Facebook community and spoke up about it when people commented on the George Floyd incident or even the protest. As they talked badly, I'd try to have that educational conversation with them. Being a mom and my son being biracial—he's white and Black—we have that conversation all the time. And trying to educate him on what racism is from very young. We had multicultural friends [over] all the time. He'd gravitate towards Black people. Even our dog's name is Tyrone. My son was 10 when he named him. I always try to educate him. And he went and protested. I was very proud of him.

Rutledge: I was against it because of the protests turning into riots.

Young-wha: If I had not talked about racism, he may not have done that. He takes it on as his own issue. It's very close to his heart.

Rutledge: He does Facebook posts. For me, I don't care to let hate win.

Young-wha: Me neither.

Rutledge: One of my friends is Native American. I have friends that are white. They're family and friends, and I love them all. You can't just say to stay with just your kind and hear the rhetoric that's put out. You have to talk to people. I was in the military. Instead of going off what's taught to you, I'd talk to people in my unit. One guy in the Navy was from Missouri. He told me "If a black person is standing near an orange tree, then he'll die." And then I said, "Wouldn't there be no Black people in Florida?" When people take the time to know others, it opens up lines of communications. It's not about the color of your skin. It's about who the person you are is. You can't go by what a politician tells you because they try to pander. Go and talk to people about what's going on in the world.

Young-wha: For me, I love movies that talk about racism that gets into deep conversations. Rutledge doesn't at all. He told me a couple months ago, when I was talking to him about it, and he said, "But I'm not interested in those kind of movies." I said, "1) I don't expect you to because you live it every day, and 2) if I'm going to marry you, I need to know everything I can about your community to know more about you. That's part of why I get really into it.

David Taylor: I've never heard of that [word]. My wife and I, we try to… with all the crazy racial stuff that's been going on, we teach our kids that everybody's equal. That's where we're at with that. We just try to teach our kids right from wrong. We try to value everyone's opinions and respect everyone's boundaries. We believe some people can change regardless of how they feel about other races[41].

Yun-sook Kim Navare: I made a commitment to stay in social work and want to continue to always advocate for communities that are oppressed. I continue to work in homeless services, low-income welfare, high-rent communities that are disproportionately African-American, most of the clients. That's what I'm doing, trying to get people into a hotel. Maybe [I'm] an Asian Karen or something but I have to be like "Why is this family able to do this, but this family is not able to do the same thing?" They say, "Thank you." It's always important to stand up for people in public who are being harassed. If there are two prostitutes, guess who's being handcuffed. It's important to always extend yourself in all of your peer groups whether it's in the YMCA, in the employee groups at my job, Black Lives Matter in LA, women of color groups, to always make my voice heard because I know other Asians aren't stepping up so I feel I have to speak up for us and say things like "She should be able to wear dreadlocks to college." "Why did the mom get jailed?" All this inequity. We are POC too, and we get it too. It's important that we articulate our stuff. Especially Black women are like, "No, really?" We can be denied medical care. [People ask,] "Why did you fill it out?" A lot of times people aren't given education on how to make the transition smoother. I see it all the damn time: Checkpoint on Saturdays to do DUIs. I think it's important for other people of color to know we get passed up for promotions, we often don't qualify for social services for some crazy loophole reason. I'm tired of seeing organizations cherrypick. Why does staff and leadership look the same when the clients look different? I will defend Maria

[41] For example, Derek Black, son of the man who developed Stormfront, disavowed white nationalism (Saslow). It was ironic that his last name was Black. In addition, there is a Black man whose mission it is to get white nationalists to disavow their former beliefs (Wanshel).

[and others]. Since I have some amount of privilege, I feel it's my obligation. That's what makes me so mad with Asian people (though I have love for them too). How many Asian doctors could step up during this COVID pandemic? I feel that the Black community values are very, very different from Asians. [With Asians,] if you're not in the inner circle, you can forget about it. I like the [Black] philosophy. The people who fall through the cracks are the darkest and poorest. We were orphans ourselves[42]. [I ask adoptees,] "You do remember that, right?" I don't understand that at all. They've crazy Protestant values about "Pull yourselves up by the bootstraps." I feel that I offend a lot of people because they don't get it. More and more adoptees are changing their names, are searching. The #MeToo Movement. Everyone's talking about their rights. Empathy is changing. It used to be more politically conservative. There's now space in the room. There's a budget for it, a program, a legislation for it. We have a terrible, horrible legacy. I've been blessed to be around amazing, amazing individuals. Sometimes I get dragged down by inappropriate, unjust discrimination that throws me off. The Black community teaches always take the high road, give what you have, good fundamental values and morals, just a basic way of life. I know I have biases. My family was abusive and neglectful and never should been approved. They actually lost their foster parent license[43] so they went under the table. I'm spread very thin because there's so much work to do. I've seen people go from rags to riches. I've seen pivotal moments and conversations that opens

[42] In industrialized countries, people define an orphan as a child under 18 who has lost both parents to death, but Unicef defines an orphan as a child under 18 who has lost one or both parents to death, which does not always apply to adoptees. Unfortunately, the difference can lead to people assuming children need to be adopted rather than supporting the families that need help (Unicef).

[43] Harry Holt, who started Holt International, was also rejected by an adoption agency.

up hearts and friendships, all these beautiful things to make more. I feel compelled to speak up, like if a bus driver is being rude. I say, "They're counting their change." Sometimes I have to be even aggressive for people to take me seriously. Gen Z and millenials will continue to be vocal and have different expectations, and hopefully those norms will change. Everyone deserves basic respect and courtesy.

Hayley Hoffman: I went to the protest here in my community. I'm very vocal about it on Facebook. Most of all, it's I'm a good human. I treat people fairly. I continue to educate myself on how to stand up for marginalized communities. There's a group called Hollaback! that works with the Asian Justice Coalition. It's training on how to be a bystander and how to intervene when you witness racial discrimination in its many forms. And also, it probably isn't race, but I volunteer with the LGBT community, and I have a friend who has a mentorship program for parolees. I said, "Hey I wanna be involved with that." It's mostly African-American.

Talking about bystanders makes me feel like the bullies from high school have moved out into the world.

Hayley Hoffman: I was listening to *The Tipping Point* by Malcolm Gladwell on audiobook. The whole book is about the anatomy of epidemics. And I think that could also be very telling and timely of what it is now. Looking at the influencers, the connector, etc. There are different points in our society where you have communities connecting with influencers creating this rhetoric or movements. At times it reaches a tipping point. You don't always know it's coming. I feel that's what's happening. We've reached our tipping point of marginalized communities. Now we have voice and influence to make some change. That's why this movement is different. The Internet came out when we were in high school. We have all this information at our fingertips. If you have a conscience, intelligence, critical thinking, and reasoning skills, you're forced to do something with this influence. There are enough who are educated and informed enough to say they have an obligation to do something or be indifferent and pretend "It doesn't affect me."

I was reading *White Fragility,* and she tells the reader to contemplate how many teachers they had that were the same race as them, and I realized I didn't have any in my official schooling.

Monica Kim: I had one Korean professor, but she didn't talk about diversity at all. Since she was in developmental psychology, she could have talked about it a lot. I also took Japanese in high school and had a Japanese professor.

I'm in the generation that thought Japanese animation was trendy.

Monica Kim: When I was younger, I pretended I was Japanese because it was trendy, but now I'm like "Internment camps[44], comfort women, oh dear." I also liked that Japanese is so phonetic.

I feel that Asian-Americans are kind of in a spot like the white female pioneers of anti-racism; we're people of color but also closest to white Americans and can have their ear.

Monica Kim: I definitely try to impart that in my classes I teach. I do a whole session on microaggressions. I try to make as strong a case as possible. There are things that happen every day that can wear you down. People agree that microaggressions can be more powerful than blatant racism. It's not something people think about every day. I've trained to be an implicit bias trainer so people on hiring committees can be less biased. It's really ingrained though. When

---

[44] She is referring to Japanese-run internment camps in Japan, not Japanese internment camps in the United States of America.

I was in college, I never talked about diversity issues, and now it's my mission. Especially now, more than ever, it's critical to show that white people are providing mental health services. If you're any type of minority, the field needs you. It's been an awakening because I had mostly white professors.

In what ways have you learned about your spouse's Black side?

David Taylor: We've been married for three years. We still have a lot to learn about each other. She tends to cook African dishes for the family. We share both Korean and African food. We try to teach African languages. My wife does what she can to share stuff about where she's from. Our kids [that we've had together] are still pretty young. We have a 2-year old and 1-year old, and they don't have a lot of interest in cultures.

In what ways have you learned about your spouse's Korean side?

Enetty Taylor: I've always been fascinated with different cultures. I was already into Korean culture before I met him [my husband]. I watched Korean dramas. A couple years after I got into Korean culture, I met my husband. Now I know how to cook a lot of Korean dishes. I know how to speak some Korean. Writing is not easy, but I'm learning a lot of things.

Tell me about your relationship with your husband.

Enetty Taylor: When my husband and I met, we were both going through rough breakups and had two children from our previous relationships. We were more than friends and were making sure each other was okay. Eventually we moved in together. Blending our families has been the hardest thing ever. As much as we love each other, it's difficult to blend two cultures together, but [it] can be done. I speak 6 different languages and am open to other cultures, which helped. He has almost all his life been in interracial relationships with Black people. It was easier to start different traditions based on our cultures. He was adopted at age 6. He doesn't speak the Korean language. My oldest daughter speaks more Korean than he does.

He's starting to get in touch with the Korean side. Before he didn't at all. His mom also adopted a girl who is Korean. It was not easy for him to get in touch with his culture. He said, "you sound more Korean than I do." We're going to Korea one day because I want him to know. He doesn't know his family or where they are. That does not mean he cannot get in touch with his culture. We've celebrated our 3rd year of marriage.

In what ways have you learned about each other's side as pertains to race?

Rutledge: I don't have a lot of experience with the KAD community. So, to go to some of the events and to see how close the family they've made is really cool. You don't get a chance to choose your family. With the KAD community, you don't get to choose, but there's so much love amongst each other.

Young-wha: You do get to choose in a sense, but the caveat is that any KAD, if they could switch with another family that knew our history, they'd give it up [being a Korean adoptee] in a heartbeat because there's a sense of loss. It's a loss because we have no connection to our bloodline at all. Most of us long for that connection. Most of us in a heartbeat would switch, we'd give up the membership of being in the KAD community.

I grew up thinking I was white, thinking I'm white, thinking I have white privilege, thinking there was no racism anymore. I went to a liberal university and that's where I got connected with my community and what racism is all about. Prior to that, I knew more about the Black community than the KAD community. I remember dating this one Black guy back in my 20s, and I remember he said something outrageous, and I called him "boy," and he stopped laughing and said, "Don't ever call a Black man boy." From that day forward, I understood that I should never call a Black man "boy." It's demoralizing and dehumanizing and making them objects.

Rutledge: Same as "oriental."

Young-wha: Within college, I learned what racism really was. That's when my passion really opened up. That's when I wanted to learn everything I could. I remember watching a movie called *Animal* and remember learning about the letters of Willie Lynch and how to be a good slave. It was so heart-wrenching to me that there was so much hatred from the white community. From then I took a strong stance and was aggressively anti-racist, then I matured and stopped shoving it in their face, coming at them more with a softer communication and with a learning process.

Rutledge: My dad is Black. I'm multiracial—"biracial" is the new word. My mom's a Caucasian woman. I lived with my mother for years but would visit my dad's side of the family. I remember a cop pulling over asking where I'm running to. I thought "Who the fuck are you to ask me where I'm going?" I never had a conversation with my dad where he told me I can't do certain things because of how I look, like jaywalk. It wasn't until later on. You're always in the wrong, that's just the nature of it.

Young-wha: Very sad nature.

Rutledge: I can be considered intimidating because of my size and because I'm Black. I have nothing but love for my family on my mom's and dad's side. Racism is not something we gave up 50 years ago when we integrated drinking fountains. When my parents got married there were still some states where it was illegal.

In what ways have you learned about your boyfriend's Black side?

Monica Kim: We definitely discuss race and racism quite a bit. Dating anyone, you learn about their culture. I didn't date because he was Black, I just gravitate toward people of color. I think it's just been a hard time, but a good time. We've had more discussions since George Floyd. It's been positive because we've had so much to talk about. We watched more documentaries. Culture is something you see, but I guess as a kid I went to a predominantly white school.

My sister volunteered for a camp for city kids, and I was the only non-Black. I attended one summer, and it was interesting. A lot of adoptees are minorities surrounded by white people.

I grew up close to Baltimore. I would go to Baltimore in high school and worked with mostly Black kids [as an adult]. Since I grew up in a white neighborhood, I've been interested in going outside the bubble. Growing up, I didn't seek out a lot of Asian kids. Baltimore is an extremely Black city. I worked in Division I college football in Maine, which is one of the whitest states. There are mostly Black kids recruited living in a very white state.

My partner is pretty light. Some people think he's white, but they aren't sure what he might be. Black people see him with me, so they think he's white. He has to tell people he's Black. He's the lightest one in his family. We also relate on that level because people think I'm Asian, but I was raised white, and people think he's white, but he was raised Black. It's also interesting too. Have you heard the Cut videos? They had one "Guess if I'm white" video and only two were white, and he got every single one of them right.

When I saw his [dating] profile, I thought he was white and was like, "No, I don't wanna date you." But then he sent me his DNA test. There are things that are easier to talk about. I've dated white, Asian, Latinx. When I first met him, he had his hair really short, and I told him to grow his hair out. The only times people didn't think he was Black was when he was with me. People are used to seeing white men with Asian women. Someone posted something about the alt-right's Asian fetish. My jaw dropped. I can't believe it, but I can. It's super interesting.

Before I met him, I assumed that when someone's lighter, there's one Black parent and one white parent, but both of his parents are mixed. Mixed people are like Korean adoptees. People decide for them whether they are Black or white[45]. I consider him Black because he didn't have any white influence growing up. I wish more people would talk about it. When he was in 6th grade, someone called him the N word. It could be worse if he were darker. We were at a party and a white girl asked him what he was, but it's inappropriate, like the "Where are you from?" question. Especially at family gatherings, it's a spectrum from light to dark. You shouldn't have to prove your Blackness. People feel compelled to talk to us because they can't wrap their head around it. I personally feel offended when people assume he's white. He also has lighter colored eyes, which are not common in the Black community, and is not something I've normally been attracted to.

In what ways have you learned about your boyfriend's or child's Black side?

Bree Davis: My boyfriend is from Cleveland, and we met in San Diego. He's a jazz musician. He started diving me into the history of Black music. He's constantly having me watch Black movies, Black history. He's constantly teaching me stuff. If he had a gig in LA, I'd go with him. Leimert Park is very Black with lots of Black-owned businesses, bookstores, music stores, drum circles. He's played in the concert hall called the World Stage. That's part of why we moved to Ohio, because he hated how white the jazz community was, and he wanted to be around Black musicians.

In what ways have you learned about your child's Latino or Latinx side?

Bree Davis: Not a lot. I didn't know my ex's family very well. She's seven going on eight, and he was abusive. He didn't tell his family about her until she was four. There was a lot of stuff that was left out.

---

[45] However, high performers don't let others define who they should be, according to Brendan Burchard.

She has very mixed hair, and I asked people to help with her hair. His family was more into the Black culture. His Mexican side of the family are estranged because his father married a Black woman. But in San Diego, there's a lot of Chicano culture, and I would take her with me to school sometimes.

In what ways have you learned about your ex-fiancé's Black side? Black history, culture.

Holly Choon Hyang Bachman: I truly thought this guy was the one. It was really perfect, but it was a humbling experience because you can't really judge a book by its cover, and that's regardless of race. One thing I did learn about which was really interesting is that he has mixed roots. This is kind of an identity issue with my ex-fiancé. He identifies as African-American and was very pro-Black, but you look at his ancestry, and his mom is very light-skinned and his great-grandmother was Indian[46]. It was interesting talking about race with him because culturally he identifies as African-American. When we get into discussions about Blacks and people of color, and how I saw him interact with and his comments about the Black community vs the multicultural community, I could sense he still has a racial identity issue. And then again, talk about the whole slave history. His whole family's roots are from Texas, being more from the South, and you can hear it in his mom's voice. His mom has a Southern drawl even though she didn't grow up there, but her mother grew up in the South. So it's interesting how that translated over to his mom because he grew up and was raised in Peoria, Illinois. It's interesting how some of those cultural traits are there. And I could tell he has Asian-y eyes because he has some Native in him, and I think that's what's caused interesting conversations with him because he hadn't had anyone call him out on that, his mixed identity. We actually did a DNA test. But it's interesting learning about the Black culture from his perspective. One of his brothers would really

[46] Indigenous

only date white women, so I thought that was interesting too, but they have this pro-Black mentality. It was interesting how he saw race and culture. My educational degree is in sociology and social psychology.

I have a three-step process of becoming your full self. I've been kind of reflecting on it even for myself through this journey of race and culture. There's an identity stage, a diversity stage, and a unity stage. I feel like even with my ex-fiancé, I feel like he's still in his identity stage where he's still trying to find out or know his roots. I had the opportunity to process all that by going back to Korea, learning about my roots. The diversity stage is where you can go beyond your own race or cultural group or yourself, and you have the desire to learn about other people. And then the unity stage brings it all together, and you come together. It's been an interesting process, even interacting and having a history with my ex-fiancé.

Identity is "Who are you?" Diversity is "What are you?" And then what we say in Mixed Roots Foundation is unity is "Where are you in your life and giving back?" If you can find out who you are and what you are, then you can step out and be able to give back. You can't give what you don't have. If you don't know your roots, if you don't know who you are, it's gonna be a struggle, and it's gonna be hard. This is in every race and culture group. I feel like there are certain groups still in the identity stage where it's always about them. This could even be for women; it could be for any group stuck in their one box. Until you can get out of that one box... You can apply it to religion too. You could be Christian or Jewish. Adoptees have that identity stage of who you and how you come out and present yourself.

In what ways have you learned about your cousin's Ethiopian side?

Hayley Hoffman: She came to America almost as an adult. She's Ethiopian as far as culture and upbringing. She was able to cook for us and share some of her experience. She had this beautiful food and coffee and way of doing things. The way her mind works is more Ethiopian, and her worldview. It's been about 15 years that she's been here. I was in my 20s when she came over. She's definitely changed through the years. She was so vibrant, but over the years I can definitely tell that she's a little more removed. I think it's hard. We've had discussions of how it's hard. How hard it is to be Black. Her family is very unique because she has brothers and sisters from all ethnic backgrounds.

In what ways have you learned about your business partners' Black culture and history?

Matthew Goodman: I'm not religious. I was adopted and raised in a non-religious Jewish household, but here the church is the beating heart of the community. I work with the church and community center in St. Louis. I had to learn this whole new vernacular for this African-American church. [I deal with] the actual problems versus the problems people believe the community faces. White people teach coding. To do coding you need access to the computer, Internet, and good math skills, which less than 5% have. These kids have no aspirations to go to Ivy League schools. We focused on reading, writing because those are the actual skills the communities face. Or how to get meals to elderly people during COVID[47] because there's no public transportation, in a way that's safe and a no-contact way for communities that have no money, as an Asian person in these spaces to make sure I'm serving them in a way that lifts them up. [I've learned] how to keep my mouth shut until I have something useful to offer them. I don't tell them what to do. I say, "This is what I hear, and I will work to find a solution within a week." You don't often see these partnerships. It's awakened me as a person of color and my firm belief that the liberation of people of color depends on us liberating ourselves together. If we remain divided, we're playing into the hands of people who want to keep us down.

---

[47] Short for COVID-19

In what ways have you learned about your client's Black and Indigenous histories?

JaeHee Melanie Chung-Sherman: Significantly, I've learned by diving deep by both reading and learning directly from social advocates through interpersonal relationship. I've also learned from their own experiences.

How do you feel about Korean adoptees?

Enetty Taylor: I have a lot of friends who are Korean adoptees. I love connecting with other adoptees. It doesn't matter what culture. Most are adopted by white American families. Almost everyone I know were adopted by white parents. Back in the day, there was a lot of adoption going on. That's just something I've noticed. I think I've also noticed that most of the Korean adoptees are struggling with who they are. They don't know their families. Most African adoptees know their families. A lot of my Korean adoptee friends spend a long time trying to find their families. It has cost a lot of emotional time. They just want to know. It's eating them emotionally, which is not something that should ever happen to anyone.

Rachel Kavanagh Baldwin: Not sure how to answer this. For those who've been raised in loving homes, we should feel grateful and privileged. On the other hand, it makes me sad to think that my country of origin did not have the infrastructure or care to keep so many of us, especially those of us who do not appear to be traditional Korean.

Tell me your relationship with Korean adoptees.

Helsen Valdes: My cousin Hayley Hoffman is adopted from Korea. I feel comfortable to talk to her about our shared experience.

At some point I did Tapestry[48] for this company. I was at the Tapestry conference to talk about my experience as an adoptee in America. There I met another Korean adoptee [JaeHee Melanie Chung Sherman]. I was at the Tapestry Conference to talk about your experience as an adoptee in America. She was in the panel, and I remember I looked at her and thought, "I wish she were my therapist." What an awesome thing it would be for someone to have actually gone through life that is similar to you! Not only did she have the experience, but also the understanding of the emotion of life as an adoptee in America. She's so good at bringing awareness at this issue, not only just an adoption experience, but also African-American and Asian culture, the race issue even within that in the Asian-American community and African. And her experience overall. It's very amazing. She works in so many areas where she gets to be connected with so many different adoptees. She's obviously a top, top counselor or advisor or something like that. She's very submerged in the understanding of that concept. Everything that she says consists of honesty, truth, and I look up to her in a sense because sometimes you want to say things, but first, I have a language barrier; second, I don't know how to put it in words. I feel it inside but don't necessarily know how to put it in words. And I would go to her page, and she'd just have a beautiful way of putting it. She speaks what I feel inside even though we're totally a different culture. I don't know why I forgot about that.

Lisa A. Quaites: The Korean society is the most homogenous, purest society. I learned that it was mandated that all half-Koreans had to be adopted out to countries that would accept half-Korean

[48] "Tapestry is a church-based, educating parent about adoption and for those who want to adopt and have adopted and how to maneuver through it, so they had a lot of adoptees come in and share their experience with it." For more information, go to https://www.tapestryconference.org.

children[49]. The founders of Holt understood the challenges half-Koreans would face. Me and the translator walked around the village [where I was born]. It only took 15 minutes to walk around it. We talked to people who were older. And they were very uncomfortable. The translator, bless his heart, wouldn't tell me everything he was saying. He told me later there were lots of racial slurs and hateful, hurtful comments coming from that village. He said, "Your mother's probably dead. You should stop looking." And my translator was a young 20-year-old, and he had never faced racism on that level. But that's the older generation. I kinda expected it.

It was my fellow KADs who rallied around me and picked me up when I was at my low. When the Korean natives were looking at me, they told me "You're beautiful." I received a lot of support from the KAD community. We're all in the same boat, and we're on this journey where we need reassurance and encouragement from someone else on that journey. I can talk with them about things my husband wouldn't understand [like about] some of the things my biological father said. My husband doesn't understand why those things would affect me so much.

Renford Reese: African-Americans are not thinking about Korean adoptees. If you told the average African-American that you're a Korean adoptee, there's no context. I bet over 95% of Blacks in LA don't have an Asian friend. If you're talking about something so specific like that, they don't know the concept. It's hard to talk about something invisible to this population. As you state in your book, there should be some sort of dialogue. There's a commonality there.

Do you think KADs share many similar experiences, issues, and concerns as with Black adoptees?

[49] The South Korean government viewed the birth of 1,000 mixed race orphans, or "honhyol koa," as a PR crisis as they were obvious reminders of Korea's dependency on the U.S. (E. Kim).

David Taylor: Honestly, I don't know a whole lot of Black adoptees. She's really the first one. I didn't know a lot of Korean adoptees either. Mainly they were Indian. We have talked about that she had a whole lot of other siblings. I don't get a lot into [talking about] her siblings. She had a pretty good experience growing up. Our moms are in their eighties. I don't know if she dealt with any major racism growing up. I don't know if there are a whole lot of similarities. It never really came up. I struggled with it for many years. Mostly we've been focused on our kids because they've been keeping us busy. We never sat down and talked about the adoptee experience. She supports me because I'm in some adoptee groups, and she says we should get together. I didn't really know she was adopted until a couple months after we got together. We talked about going back to Korea, and she thought it would be good to have some closure. I've had some reservations about it, but she's always been very supportive, whatever adoptee issues I've had.

Enetty Taylor: To an extent, yes. I believe they do. The most crucial thing, when you don't know about the circumstances, the main question is why were they given up? Africans know why we were adopted. Most Koreans don't. We're all adoptees, but the difference is the knowledge. We have more closure than most Korean adoptees. All of my friends who are African adoptees know their birth family, they know where they are and communicate with them. Other than that, our experience is the same. We try to get used to our new family. We try to find our identities.

Hayley Hoffman: They do. I think so. I was talking with my daughter's friends an hour ago and her father just died. He died having his fourth wife. She kept referring to his daughter as "She's his daughter, but she's adopted." She just found out she's half-Nigerian. She grew up not knowing she was half-African. She grew up in Manhattan Beach in a very white community. She and I were talking about what it's like growing up in a transracial family. And you're not understanding that you're experiencing racial discrimination or someone's being racist against you. Yeah, I think as a child I don't think it matters what race you are if you're part of a transracial family, you assume an identity of your surroundings, so it's a shock when someone tells you differently, but you're a child and don't know how to identity. I've had this conversation with my parents. Parents see us as their kids. It's as equal of a shock for them as it is for me. "What do you mean?" "How dare they put a label on you?" It's hard for them to see that and to accept that, for both adoptees and parents. For adoptive parents it can be a rough go-around.

Helsen Valdes: Yes, definitely. There's a lot of similarity. If a kid is adopted from Korea or Ethiopia at the age of 10, they would both struggle to understand the new culture. They would also both struggle to fit into a new family dynamic. When you come at an older age, the kid knows their culture, and it becomes more challenging for them to adopt to a new way of life. Also, when it comes to a new family at an older age, trust has to be built in order for the kids to start loving their new home, their new family. They share a similarity in which they both need trust, and love comes afterward.

When it comes to race aspects of it. That's different. Koreans have a lighter skin tone that's closer to Caucasian. For that reason, I feel that Koreans would feel more comfortable than I would as a Black person.

Jessica Farrell: Yes. The whole am I [way I am] accepted for who I am in an adopted family will always be in any adopted child's mindset. The addition of it being international adds an extra layer.

Jordan Davis: I think definitely in terms of adoption, in terms of the themes of family separation, searching for family members, limited access to documents. If they're transracially adopted, separation from their birth culture. One of the major differences is that African-Americans don't have a state-to-state or national-to national relationship with the United States. South Korean adoptees have a contact with South Korea, whereas the African-American adoptees are a minority within the United States, so there's no advocacy. South Korean adoptees have a lot more in common with Native American tribes because they have a nation-to-nation relationship that African-Americans don't have because we're a minority. The citizenship question isn't a major factor for African-American domestic adoptees. African adoptees would also have a nation-to-nation relationship. Some African countries put a ban on transracial adoption, but that's not possible in America. NABSW [National Association of Black Social Workers] don't have legal standing to enforce because we're not a separate nation. Native Americans were able to pass the Indian Child Welfare Act, so the tribal nations within the United States get a say as to if they enter the foster system, who they're adopted to, etc. Native American adoptees would have more similarities therefore.

Lisa A. Quaites: I think adoptees, no matter what race they are, share a lot of similarities. The sense of belonging, the desire for a biological connection or bond, fitting in. Another thing that helps me too with the adoptive community is being a part of social media groups. I didn't even know they were there until last year. I see common themes that come across. No matter what your race, even if it's a domestic adoption, I think that biological bond is something that some think about more than others. For a long time, I didn't think I missed it, but once I had kids and they were the only biological connection on Earth that I knew, I had a desire to meet my mom. I think there are similarities. it's gonna be the environment that you're raised in. Korean adoptees are seen as a minority and Black adoptees are also a minority. Both of us are non-white. I don't really feel that white people who are racist hate one group more than another. I think they don't like anybody who's non-white. I can't say I've seen or experienced— I dunno. I guess the news reports more on white vs. Black racism and not the whites vs. Koreans. I know Asians are discriminated against for sure, and if you're not connected to the Asian community you might not know the extent of it.

Monica Kim: I think so, just the identity struggle. I think particularly too if you are distanced from your culture. Just something as basic as haircare or makeup. I think hair is a bigger issue than makeup. There are commonalities for sure. There are plenty of stereotypes of Asians and Blacks.

Rachel Kavanagh Baldwin: In terms of marginalization and discrimination...yes.

SooJin Pate: I would say, yes and no. It depends on the level of consciousness around race. There are a lot of Korean adoptees I know who are really blind to race who have adopted their parents' colorblindness. It's only an issue if you bring it up. For those Korean adoptees, I think there's very little in common.

Even for those, what they do have in common is not fitting in, that their bodies betray them because they can't pass as white, no matter what.

I have domestic adoptee friends who have been adopted by the same race, and they also talk about how they don't quite fit in, so I think it's a universal adoptee feeling. There's always that anxiety. I think that's true for all adoptees regardless of race. We have to constantly overperform, show our appreciation because there's this fear that if we do something wrong that will somehow lead to the manifestation of that anxiety[50]. That the fear of not belonging will truly come to pass.

For racially conscious Korean adoptees, they have a lot, a lot in common. Black adoptees also have to go through the process of decolonizing their minds. It's rare to hear Black adoptees say they

[50] This could explain at least one-tenth of why the model minority came to be.

grew up thinking they were white. That's a major difference. I've heard them say, "only with other Black people do I feel like I'm not Black." That's also true for Korean adoptees. You think finally I won't be the only person who looks like me. Finally, I'm among my people. But for some, myself included, that was the expectation and hope, but we felt more like a stranger than ever because of our inability to communicate. Here our body gives us away, but in Korea our voice gives us away[51]. There are certainly some similarities and differences. The more conscious they are, the more they have in common. Black adoptees' abilities to assimilate is a lot more difficult because they're darker and how Blackness has been racialized in our society.

Yun-sook Kim Navare: Yes, I do. I think there's the racial dynamic. There's a plus and minus of it. Because of what Black means in this world, there's a bigger burden on the Black adoptee. However, there's the international/intercultural piece; we have that burden too. "So you're born here, all your ancestors are here, you're American as apple pie, baseball, blah blah blah." So there's that tension. We're forever a naturalized citizen, we're a perpetual foreigner, we're an immigrant. Both of us have different huge elephants in the room, and everything is relative. It's easier for the Black adoptee to embrace their identity because there's a large Black culture, like in the South. But for us, it's a little more limiting. You have the *hapas* and the language barriers. At the end of the day, Korea is still your motherland[52]. But Black adoptees don't know what country they came from before their ancestors were in America. They're disconnected from their roots in a different way. [It depends] on the adoptee, the temperaments, the community, the school, the family dynamics, the family socioeconomic status, how to navigate race outside of the family. Clearly people knew something was going on [with my family]. I remember removing myself from

---

[51] ...as well as the way we walk.

[52] "Moguk" in Korean. Ideally, one has a deep love and special spiritual place in the heart for the motherland.

that dynamic. I was this random Korean kid. I would go back to my family unit and it would be like "Who's this?" "We don't know her name. She was abandoned." The racial dynamics in terms of relativity to whiteness. I can see plusses and minuses to both sides.

Matthew Goodman: Yes and no, I think that from my personal experience. My brother and I were adopted together. I call it [living between worlds] "living on the hyphen." The kind of racism I experienced was very different from what I see Black adoptees face, but there's the same connection. You're exterior to it sometimes because "The space wasn't made for you. You're not supposed to be here." I wanted to be white because it would make my life easier, but I've found as I've gotten older that being an adoptee is my superpower, that I can find a level of commonality with anyone. In the adoptee world, we call that being a chameleon.

I was at the grocery store. We specifically chose to live in an African-American neighborhood. There's this white mother with her Asian daughter. I could tell they were mother and daughter. The little girl was mimicking her mom. She [the mother] looked at me and was like "How did you know she was my daughter?" She said how lovely it was to be recognized as a mother of her daughter. It gave me access to people living in these spaces. My mom's family was here [in St. Louis]. I have a lot of connections.

I spend most of my time in the Black communities. I live in a neutral area, so police don't know what to do with me. I've done civil rights litigation here as well. It lets me communicate different sides with each other. Anyone who works in St. Louis who works in antiracism, your goal here is to raise up and lift up Black voices. As an adoptee, it let me see that more clearly and build trust with multiple groups. I don't think Black adoptees have the same access to that.

Young-wha: That's a good question.

Rutledge: Asians are considered more demure. That's why they're sexualized. When you're Black, you want to fit in. That's true for either side. If you're Black and want to do things white kids would do, other Black kids are like "What's up with this dude?" I don't know the difference between Black adoption and Asian adoption, but if a white family adopts a kid from a culture that has Black people—who's the cousin in *Fresh Prince of Bel Air*? Carlton—they'll raise them to be Carltons. They might laugh at them because they're a joke.

Young-wha: I would beg to differ because you say they were made fun of. We all went through that, and we still go through those identity issues. Black adoptees also go through that as adults as well. I think they're very parallel because we want to fit in as well. I remember being called Bruce Lee or "ching chong" or "karate." I remember thinking, "But I'm one of you" and didn't understand why they would pull their eyes back. I thought, "Why would you do that?" I convinced people I was white. My mantra was that I was yellow on the outside but 100% white on the inside. It's very parallel. Even though the struggles look different, they're similar because they're based on identity.

Milton Washington: Yes and no. Yes on levels of feeling alone and being disconnected from your mother, but there's a stark in-person experience as a Black person in America. There's a hierarchy. Black folks are the darkest folks who will always be on the bottom. There is a difference by being Black. I happen to love Black. I know Black in a way a lot of people don't. I wouldn't want it any other way. I'm sitting in a brownstone in Harlem living like an artist, living like an entrepreneur, with big plans to be an entrepreneur. That ain't all that bad. And [censored][53].

I don't wanna put that in here.

[53] Not censored due to curse words.

Milton Washington: You'd get more readers. Just the hint of naughty or illicit can work wonders.

How do you feel that trauma is different for adoptees versus the traumas unique to the Black experience?[54]

Hayley Hoffman: I think for adoptees we don't have that connection to our heritage the way the African-American community does. Theirs is an inherited trauma. We're the first to go through this because we are the first generation[55]. As the African-American community had 150-200 years[56] to inherit the horrific inhumane— It's horrible the things that came along with being an African-American in our country. I don't know which one's worse, not that there has to be a worst. Our legacy wasn't to be owned and to be stolen from our homeland to serve somebody else. That wasn't how we got here in one regard. In one regard, our parents and the landscape that was there, it was last resort as opposed to people coming here in cages. I really feel for the Black community that that was their origin story in the US. When I think of my origin—and I don't know if all KADs or adoptees feel this way—I think my origin was from a place of love and desperation with hope that there would be a better life for me. I'm a mom of two kids. I think of how desperate they must have been to not be able to care for a child they cared for nine months.

---

[54] JS Lee says that at worst adoption can resemble indentured servitude but is in no way comparable to slavery as abusing a child can result in severe repercussions (J. S. Lee).

[55] There are technically multiple waves of Korean adoptees by now. The first wave was mostly half-black, half-Korean adoptees or half-white, half-Korean adoptees. They're over 50 years old by now. However, we are first generation immigrants.

[56] More like 400 years.

Holly Choon Hyang Bachman: It's very interesting. I got into a deep conversation with my mentor-advisor friend last night, and we related it to COVID and racism. Racism is a fact. I think—depending on how you want to segment it out—it's funny because I also talk about the LGBT community. No one knows you're adopted unless you actually come out, and you say you're adopted. It's kinda interesting with identity. One thing I've learned about the adoptee citizenship and adoptee rights with the original birth certificates, that it's a civil right to have that medical information. It's a race and culture issue. I've had Black friends having dialogue about this. Just last night, my Black African-American advisor friend of mine—we talked about how the president of the United States, Trump, calls the COVID the "Kung flu." And I'm Asian-American, and I shared with my friend last night how crazy that is and offensive, and my African-American friend said he agreed. We're on the same page of feeling that discrimination or that racism.

I do mentoring too, and one of my African-American mentors talked about how being a transracial adoptee during these times is actually very difficult. We can't really go to our family and talk about our race and being discriminated against in public, because in the family we're just their daughter, just their son. I went to a particular hotel in Vegas, and I get assumed that I'm a prostitute when I was with my white husband. I've boycotted the hotel. I won't name it. Those are kinda those different things where when I share with other people, regardless of race or who I'm sharing this with, people are appalled but it is a fact that when I go out in the world, and I share this with my family, they're shocked to hear that I get discriminated against with stereotypes like that. So with that those are some commonalities I can exchange and share with other Blacks or African-Americans because they get discriminated against as well on how they look or how they grew up or how people perceive them. It's interesting, the cross-section of identity and race and culture, and also just of how people perceive you and then how I perceive myself and how you bring those two together. Some people could say I'm pretty much white because I listen to pop and country. What's really cool is watching the news this morning, and they showed that top country singer is an African-American[57] country singer and a female!

What's so cool is that the paradigm shift I'm seeing now is sharing the stories that are out there, getting all voices out there. Even in the last two days, with the whole situation with Bubba [Wallace] from Nascar, I'm so glad they brought his dad on because for me personally trying to figure out the identity with mixed people is that they're forced to choose. If someone didn't know he had a dad, everyone would assume he's just Black, but, hello! His other half is white. And so is Colin Kaepernick, and so is Barack Obama, and even senator Kamala Harris. They all have an African-American mix, but a lot of people forget. And this is an interesting study on identity, how we're all forced to be in a box. If they identified with their whiteness or their Asianness other than Black, especially in a racialized society that we live in, then it's automatically assumed that they're not fighting for Black rights. It's really interesting. It's only at convenience when society will allow them to be their full self because, otherwise, they're just Black. But they're also Asian, Indian (which is Kamala). Even senator Nikki Haley, her family is Indian, and a lot of people forget even though her politics are different. If you look at a race and culture perspective, she got put into a white box. Not only with her politics, but because she looks more white than Indian. It's deep. Going back to your questions about identity development, depending on your race and culture too as an adoptee and the race and experience of an African-American, it's interesting.

Monica Kim: It's apples and oranges. Especially in America. There's been discrimination, prejudice, and racism for hundreds of years, and adoptees are protected from a lot of it except for the coronavirus. Our issues tend to be not violent. We're subject to microaggressions, but we're not having to fear for our safety, the fear of being pulled over by police.

[57] Rissi Palmer, who will start a podcast for women of color

Adoptees also have more challenges because it's not open, not mainstream, not highlighted. White people are never gonna get revved up the same way about Asian issues. It's not a competition, but there are not enough Asian-American voices that white people are going to listen to. I can understand because we're not subject to violence. My friends are all about Black Lives Matter, but when I post Asian issues there's just silence[58]. For example, with *Ghost in the Shell* and the whitewashing. And now there's uproar over animé [Japanese animation] characters. [But] there's never enough uproar.

JaeHee Melanie Chung-Sherman: I think, first, the universal qualities of trauma are from a white lens, so I question that. Oppression is oppression that is deeply embedded into history for black adoptees. The racialized and identity-based trauma are constantly nuanced. Our largest organ is our skin and to be embodied in something that is traumatized and can bring trauma and to not be acknowledged is trauma itself in a way that non-Black and non-adopted people will never experience. The impact that happens is so many transracial adoptees and non-black POCs will get into a "trauma-lympics" even in our own community, which can be so invalidating, especially for Asian adoptees and lighter-skinned adoptees. Even being asked; they won't ask my Black sibling to do that in the TRA community. Even for transnational adoptees (East Asian), to know our own privilege when it comes to publications, speaking engagements, and pay raise [is important]. It's another place of co-opting experience and privileging ourselves on the backs of Blacks who experience more oppression. I look also at Latinx adoptees, the disproportionate services provided in social services to save and rescue them. It's sick. There are so many layers

[58] I've noticed this as well. I can experience someone whitesplaining on Black Lives Matter, but be completely ignorant to Korean and Korean adoptee matters.

to it, when it comes to trauma. Ultimately, it's up to the client to decipher what has been traumatizing for them.

Jordan Davis: I think that the trauma related to poverty and police violence are more widely understood and accepted as reality than the trauma transracial adoptees get from being called an "oreo" or traumas related to having to not deal with white people as an external thing, but having family members who make racial slurs and comments rather than someone outside of your family. Those kind of traumas are not as accepted by the larger society.

Rutledge: I can't really speak on the traumas between adoptees. I know how I feel trauma. I'm half. I can't even speak to how white people or Black people would experience trauma. I can only speak to my own experiences.

Young-wha: We all have trauma, and our trauma is being taken out of our home country and being assimilated to a whole new country with different smells, people who don't look like us.

Would I ever say that it's as traumatic as what Black people go through? Absolutely not. They were forced into slavery, forced into being treated like animals, forced into the prison system. I think our trauma is our own trauma as KADs, but the Black trauma is within the Black community; it's not individualized. They fully understand what the Black trauma is. We take it personally in different ways. I'm not saying they [Black people] don't take it personally. I would definitely say the Black community's trauma is worse. Asians are looked at as the "model minority." We tend to assimilate better. We don't want to rock the boat. With the Black community, they don't want to rock the boat, but they don't get a chance to not rock the boat or to rock the boat.

Rutledge: When it comes to the traumas of coming to this country, I was born here, my grandfather was born here. Five generations of my family have been here. It hurts when people say to go back to where I came from. "Takoma? Why would I go there?"

There were two kids in the back of a pickup truck when I was 4 years old, and they said, "N****** can't play with us." I couldn't play with them because of my skincolor and my hair (I had an afro). Every now and then that memory comes back to me. Systemic racism was ingrained in them. There's nothing we can do to hide our skin. We don't want to ingratiate ourselves to a culture that doesn't want us.

Have you been more traumatized being adopted or Black?

Helsen Valdes: For me, both. Being adopted at an older age brought its own struggle. And also being Black living in America has its own struggle as well.

Being adopted at an older age, my struggle was learning a new life, land, and family. Learning to function in a family dynamic was a big challenge for me. I was older and living to some degree independently when I was in Ethiopia. So to come into a new family and having to be a kid again was very challenging.

Being Black and living in America had its own impact as well. I didn't quite fit into the African-American culture. I didn't understand the history of African-American. I struggled to make and keep friends, with African-Americans. I also struggled to accept me as a Black person in America for the obvious reason that Black didn't have a positive meaning anymore.

Jessica Farrell: Black. Sadly— Adopted I know I'm loved. But having my own children I face racism directly from my in-laws who made my Black side stand out like a sore thumb. I felt different as I never had before. It made me feel less than, like only my side was tainted. Our kids are Asian, Black, and white but my spouses family is white. My adoptive family has always stood up for me.

Jordan Davis: It's very difficult to disentangle those, but I would say that a lot of African-American adoptees now talk about that we have a level of white privilege when we're around our white families, but that goes away when we move out of those spaces. If I'm with my parents going to the store, I'm less likely to be followed inside the store or racially profiled, but if I'm by myself, I'm more likely to experience all the stereotypes. In a lot of ways, Black transracial adoptees have an awareness of white privilege. A lot of our early years we're shielded with white privilege due to our proximity to our adoptive parents. It's a cloud of protection.

I remember in elementary and middle school that once parent-teacher conferences came up, the way they interacted with me was very different from how they interacted with other Black students. If I was succeeding in school, they'd say, "This is great because your parents must be so proud of you," but talking with the very few Black acquaintances I had, they were told, "You're raising yourself up and doing better than your parents and community." They wouldn't attribute their success to their families.

Lisa A. Quaites: Honestly, I would probably say I'm more traumatized being Black. And the reason why is because when someone looks at me, they don't see adopted, but they do see a person of color. So that's more of a threat to me than not knowing who my biological parents are.

Rachel Kavanagh Baldwin: They're not mutually exclusive and they both bear their own weight in shaping and affecting my growth and development. However, I do feel a sense of relief that I am not currently living in the US given the racial landscape.

Milton Washington: I have to say adopted because my kind of relationship with Blackness understands a less burdensome path of life. So, I know how me being Black has resulted in me in certain situations, but I don't get so emotionally caught up in people's feelings in trying to keep me down. I treat it like the rain. It is what it is. I pound for pound get more that I want than the average Black person because I don't spend too much time sweating the problem.

When I was in Korea and all the Korean kids were rejecting me, I was crying every day. "Mom, where's my Dad?" "Let's get to America" fixes every problem I got. This Black couple got out of a Ford LTD. The woman had caramel skin and a big afro. And the dude who came out was the manifestation of who I thought my dad would be. I grabbed his leg and jumped in his car and locked all the doors.

It sounds like you had a good experience.

Milton Washington: There's a lot of context to that we don't have time to get into. I have a fascinating, fucking life, and I know this and love it.

How do you feel that trauma is different for adoptees versus the traumas unique to the Black and Latino or Latinx experience?

Bree Davis: It's very different. That's hard. It's different but there are similarities. I think with Korean adoptees there are certain parts that can be a little more difficult because they [adoptive parents] try so hard to suppress us. There's a lot of police brutality and racial profiling for the Black and Latino communities. I was in the woman studies department and learned about it there. I found the Black community before I found the Korean community, so I was learning about police brutality and racial profiling first. People in the Black activist community are very supportive of my adoptee issues. I have these conversations with my boyfriend since Floyd's death. Even the stuff with the coronavirus, with Asians being targeted. And he said, "Now you know how we feel." We live in a very white city too. His and my experiences with racism are different.

I thought you moved to Ohio to be around Black musicians?

Bree Davis: Where I work is very white. I work as a stylist in a kid's hair salon but I'm the only Asian and there are one or two Black hair stylists, but everyone else is white. The coronavirus has made it difficult to meet people. He grew up in Cleveland, not Columbus. There's a big adopter community here, because I see a lot of adoptive parents come in, and that's a little weird. Myka Stauffer, who's getting all the heat and who has 7,000 subscribers on YouTube, she's in this city. There's an investigation going on. I want to show up at her door and give her a piece of my mind, but that's not okay.

How do you navigate through today's polarized society?

JaeHee Melanie Chung-Sherman: For myself, I gotta get a lot of self-care. I've got a great community of support, particularly those who identity as women people of color who are also doing similar work where we can vent, sympathize, and grieve, particularly for people of color. I see all are people of color in my practice. Racialized trauma is happening every five minutes it feels like. The polarizing's always been here; it's just being elevated to an international platform. This is how they've survived. For transracial adoptees, we've been silenced or not exposed to it. I hear it so often from other TRAs. I hear that quite often from Black adoptees who are really coming to terms: "I had no idea this was happening to my people." "How could no one have told me?" For most TRAs it's been there and is much more energized.

Monica Kim: I think I just do the best that I can. I've grown up used to it. I can't say I haven't been preparing for this my whole life. I was the only Asian kid in K-8. I transferred schools because I was bullied. People may not like me because I'm different. I want to say I'm surprised, but I've always seen it. But it surprised me that it's white people's "first" experience. I've always seen it, felt that, particularly working in education. You'd think they wouldn't be so ignorant because they're educated, but degrees don't mean that. I make do the best that I can. I'm more fearful than I was previously due to verbal and physical attacks on Asians, but I can't say I'm shocked by it.

I hope all people of color can be unified, but unfortunately there's a lot of division, particularly between the API and Black community. Like in Baltimore between Korean-owned and Black-owned stores[59]. There's a lack of understanding and opportunity to interact. My [Black] ex grew up in DC. He said I was the only Asian he'd ever dated. He said he didn't know many Asian people even though he grew up in DC. Lack of exposure breeds misunderstanding. Just with me volunteering in the schools as well, people would say I'm "Wendy Woo" [singer/songwriter]. That was shocking, the lack of exposure[60]. Baltimore is highly segregated.

Renford Reese: I grew up in the segregated South. I went to the Westside School for Coloreds. My town was segregated by the railroad track, parts of it. The part of town I lived in was Blacksville, GA. We had to burn our trash in the back of the yard. The white politician would come to the church and would talk about what he'd do for the Black community and don't fulfill their promises. Black people are the most forgiving people in the United States. We might put on this veneer that we're hard and tough, but at the end of the day we'll accept. Especially when it comes to other races.

I'm not talking from theory; I'm talking about how I grew up. I grew up knowing we had to have a certain discipline. And it's about

[59] Baltimore's uprising was in April 12, 2015 after the Freddie Gray incident, and after Baltimore paid over "$5.7 million since 2011" to respond to police brutality lawsuits (Starr). It's interesting how when major newsworthy cop brutality is the issue, Korean-American neighborhoods take the hit. It's interesting how Korean-Americans (KADs) included think it's not their issue, when it obviously is.

[60] Exposure doesn't always eradicate racism and can backfire. Oversaturation of negative exposure is what was most likely behind Derek Chauvin's hatred of Black people.

thinking outside of the box. That's really abstract because the box is your job, your university, wherever you work, society. You have to understand the rules and regulations of the spaces you traverse. I understood that you had to have a certain type of focus. You had to understand people and their motives. I understood that you have to have jealousy, envy, arrogance. So you have to navigate. As one of a handful of senior-level African-American professors, I had to be first dedicated to my craft, which is political science on a university campus. My approach was I wrote my first book after I had tenure, *The American Paradox of Young Black Men*. By the time I was a full-time professor, I wrote *American Bravado* and the ugliness of the American brand, the hyper-aggressiveness. I wouldn't have written that book without tenure. Gradually, I became more radicalized in my writings. As an African-American professional, you have to be strategic and think your way around your career and make certain chess moves. (Someone who's white can go through the process without being strategic, and it's based on the sheer force of your personality.) And be careful not to get in trouble.

We have book buyers. As a professor, we get books from book publishing companies to adopt books to teach books. A book buyer came by in my second semester and said, "I want to buy the books you're not using." He said I could give you $25 for this, $20 for this. He said he'll pay me in cash. I just knew somehow that's illegal. I've never read rules against this and knew my colleagues did it. I understood there's no margin of error for me as a Black man. I'm under scrutiny so there's no margin of error.

My dad was the first sportswriter. He walked in the tradition of John Lewis. They were there together. He was a pioneer journalist. My parents were part of the Civil Rights Movement. You have to be strategic. He was the first black guy to work in the sports section. It didn't take but a couple weeks for them to warm up to him. They loved that man. If you look at his retirement, people loved "E." That was his nickname, for Ernest. The way he broke down barriers was one-on-one. He knew the son's name, the daughter's name, he knew they [were] having a big competition coming up. That's what we need, when people know they're interested in their family. That's how you become anti-racist, by connecting to their backstory. That's what I did when I came to CalPoly [California Polytechnic University - Pomona][61]. I got to know people's kids. If they had a choir or recital, I would go. I remember going to their dinner and playing saxophone. Now how you gonna hate me? The cleavage between races is so deep that we can't do some of those things. We're prohibiting and inhibiting ourselves from doing those things. I'd go to three to four colleagues houses on Thanksgiving Day.

Of course, we can't travel now, but traveling and seeing other cultures [helps]. I've been to 104 countries. I've been to every major city in the world just seeing how people live. I've been to Africa 14 times. They have nothing and everything because they have each other. Over here we have everything but nothing because we don't have that human connection. How does a fish discover water? The fish is born in water. In order to discover it, the fish has to come out of it. In order to discover ourselves, we have to get out of our enclaves. You can't discover yourself if you're just around people who talk like you, walk like you, think like you. I became a "fish out of water" when I travel.

[61] He has spent 25 years teaching about social justice outreach, restorative justice, and criminal justice reform and will continue to teach classes as part of a mandatory three-unit social justice course in 2023-2024 (Jones).

What was it like to have Black adoptive parents? How do you think they handle race differently from white adoptive parents?

Lisa A. Quaites: Here's what I think the difference is between Black and white culture: Black culture stems back from slavery days. If you have an ounce of Black blood, you're Black even if you don't look it. When slaves had children, those children weren't considered white at all even if they could pass as white and were treated with discrimination. The Black community has been very accepting of me being mixed race. If I were half-white/half-Korean then the white community might see me as Asian. The Black community see[s] me as Black, some of them, not all of them. I felt very comfortable being raised in a Black culture because they didn't treat me as different. I grew up thinking I was Black and not focusing on my Asian half.

What was it like to have Black adoptive parents?[62]

Jessica Farrell: I had white adoptive parents. I think the culture of having white parents isn't as bad as it seems. I didn't have anything else. My upbringing stressed fairness, truth, integrity, family, and love.

Rachel Kavanagh Baldwin: I don't know. I was raised in a white, Irish-American, Catholic family.

Milton Washington: What is it like having *my* Black adoptive parents, not just Black adoptive parents, but a military Black family. There's an asterisk at the end of that, having that perspective. It's the kind of mixture or environment out of the four kids that they had [besides me]. Don went to Northwestern, Donna went to Northwestern, Duyen went to Northwestern, Darren went to Florida A&M and Stanford

[62] I kept this question here to show that I too make assumptions.

MBA, soaring in the top of whatever exam they took. With regular Black families you're not going to find those numbers. You'll find that in military families because they know the value of discipline and if you'll succeed in life. My parents were very good at parenting, keeping books around, keeping us athletic, having rigor around schedules and timing for all sorts of things, giving us this great balance of freedom and rules. Never argued in front of us ever. We never saw it, and we never heard them arguing in their rooms. We've seen a couple things, but we always knew they were a unit. How important is something like that to be filled with that culture as a child who was adopted! They would be filled to a degree with just the models my parents were. Even the closer influence—my brothers and sisters—they were really smart kids. One of the values of our family was articulation, being able to talk and get what you want. I feel like it's almost this perfect complement to my life. As a kid who didn't start school until I was nine and hates to read, it was perfect to be adopted by a family of smarts that permeates everything we do. Great skill to have when it comes to my deficiency in education. There are a dozen instances. In this adoption story, my adoption experience is heavily skewed to the fortunate. If you have to get adopted, this is the kind of outcome that is the best-case scenario.

It sounds like Law of Attraction[63], how you attracted your adoptive parents.

Milton Washington: There's a case that could be made for it. My [birth]momma was a prostitute. One of the ways I saw my [birth]

[63] Even though Showing Up for Racial Justice (SURJ) says that part of white supremacy is being logical and looking for solutions, according to Law of Attraction, negative emotions prevent expansion and looking for solutions is preferable in terms of manifesting what you want. Even ranting to a friend can create more of what you don't want.

mother was as a boss. I learned how to know what I want and get what I want. I was very fortunate.

Did you have white parents?

Enetty Taylor: I was adopted by an Austrian family when I was a little older. I knew exactly what was going on. I was in the orphanage for a very long time. I was almost 11 when I got adopted. It was a very nice family. I don't know what I would have done without them.

How were your parents when dealing with race?

Enetty Taylor: They did not just adopt me. I have brothers and sisters. They did not want us to ever question what our race is. They encouraged us to be one with our cultures. We celebrated holidays from different countries. It was nice. I liked it.

That's quite unusual.

Enetty Taylor: We were very lucky to have been adopted into this family. We call ourselves the little United Nations.

Do you think that white adoptive parents don't know how to deal with race?

Bree Davis: Mine didn't. It's my experience that a lot of adoptive parents do not, but I have come across some who do, but they are few and far between.

David Taylor: My mom raised me to respect everybody. Have good morals and manners. My mom wasn't racist, and she taught me not to be. My family is predominantly white. From what my mom told me, my grandfather didn't like his own race, let alone others. He didn't understand why they had to adopt a child overseas instead of here. Mom taught me to be a good person, to be respectful. It's never really come up. At some point she might have wanted me to marry a white person. At some point she might have wanted me to marry a nice Korean girl because she had a Korean fetish. She'd decorate the house in Korean decorations. For her, it was a preference. It's something I'm still trying to figure out.

Helsen Valdes: No, I say that because. A family can be very kind but very closed up. It's easy to understand Korean if you grew up in a Korean culture. It's easy to understand African-American culture, if you grew up in an African-American culture. But when another culture gets in the mix, you have to adjust to that person's culture. You have to try to learn their language.

When I came to America, I made an effort to learn the language, to learn the culture, and tried my best to be a part of it. I believe if most people are openminded about learning and experiencing other cultures, we can create a better understanding. And with understanding, comes acceptance.

JaeHee Melanie Chung-Sherman: No, I don't believe white adoptive and white prospective parents know how to discuss race, racial identity, and racial integration.

Matthew Goodman: They struggle. I love my parents, but they struggle. My father was Jewish, but very Aryan. He was very used to passing. He didn't realize race was such a force in the world until a few years after he adopted me ,and it became excruciatingly obvious. They never told us we were wrong or making things up. They started seeing how other people treat us [me and my brother]. "That's your parent?" It hurt them, so it obviously hurt us. My dad was blown away by how racism affected dating. My dad passed in 2012. Him and my mom massively shifted to the left in a way his other friends didn't. I think it was a transformative experience for them and made them better people. I was proud they were able to embrace without any hostility. He was more resistant to it than my mom. Maybe being a woman, she was more sensitive to those things. He started realizing we were experiencing racism from the Korean adoptee perspective. Once he understood, he really got it.

Milton Washington: Yes, most white parents don't know because they have the privilege of not having to deal with it.

Monica Kim: Yes, the majority are not equipped to deal with race. My parents were not, and that's part of why I have trouble maintaining a current relationship with them. My adoptive mom gets very defensive. They mean well, but just because you love your children, doesn't mean your kids won't have racial challenges. I've learned not to talk about those things with her because it doesn't go over well. It's hard without her denying. That obviously upsets me. I would say adoptive parents were told to assimilate their children, and that's changed over time to educating kids on where they come from. But there's still lack of understanding. I watched a really good documentary called *Black, White, and Us*, about adoptive parents of Black children. These parents didn't really understand racism until they had a child of another race. I found it inspiring, but also sad that my parents didn't do that [what those parents did]. It shows progress being made even if it seems like not enough.

Advice

What advice would you give to adoptive parents thinking about adopting?

Matthew Goodman: That your kid is right about these issues. You need to listen, you need to watch, you need to observe and not [think about it] the way you would see it. The best thing he [my father] learned was how other parents interacted with me on the playground when I was by myself. When your kid tells you something, you need to believe them. It's the only way you're gonna learn. I did tell my parents they were racist, and I was lucky that it was a moment of self-reflection.

Helsen Valdes: Recognize that you are different. Different doesn't have to be a bad thing. When you realize there's a difference, it's beautiful by itself. It's also important for the kid to preserve their culture. Your body can walk around anywhere, but you're empty if what's put in you cannot manifest itself. With a different culture, how do you preserve it, keep it? That's going to be different for every family. The way you preserve the culture of that kid is up to you. It's a beautiful country and culture. That's who you are. A lot of times, my friend and I, we battle with wanting to be grateful, but at the same time, we wish for our parents to be more proactive with who we are. If I, as an adoptee, don't have the same perspective, that's okay, but don't push me to believe. Just because I'm your kid doesn't mean I need to believe the same thing. I have a battle of "If I say this, would I offend my family? Would they feel I'm less of a grateful child?" Being openminded to listening to their kids, recognizing and preserving that difference [is important].

What advice would you give to other transracial adoptees during this time in history?

Enetty Taylor: Love who you are. Your situation does not have to define you. Sometimes you have to understand you won't always find that closure but you learn what you can about your culture. Maybe it'll bring you closer to understanding your identity.

Hayley Hoffman: I would really say that it's important to listen because there's a lot out there. To listen to yourself. To take the information and sit with it and see how it affects you and be very deliberate in how you move through that. For myself, I've done a lot of work from a mental and emotional health standpoint. For myself, I wanna know how the feeling sits inside of me and be able to unpack it. One of the things is I really had suffered from racism and didn't realize it and that's why I reached out to the KAD community. I'm a huge Brené Brown fan. She's always talking about owning your story. If you don't own it, it owns you. But if you own it, you get to write the ending. That's what I've been looking at. What does this mean for me? What is my responsibility as a person and a human? How do I want to show up in this world? Do I want to show up with solutions? What am I going to do with that pain? It's okay to feel the pain, hurt, and frustration, but if we're taking it all in and putting it back out, that doesn't help anyone. What I've learned is that everybody's different. But what I hope for is that no matter what our circumstances are that we can find the humanity and beauty and know that's what defines us, and we all have a right to love ourselves. When we can start loving ourselves and all of our imperfections, that will be the only way to promote change and live a happy life. Whole individuals are what changes the world and bring change to this world.

Helsen Valdes: I would advise them to be openminded, willing to learn and embrace new cultures. If there's understanding on both sides, there's always acceptance. My advice is to learn a new way of life willingly without anyone having to impose it. When you understand something, you're willing to embrace it. Be willing to understand how to live a new life.

I have other friends who were adopted. Some of them resisted learning a new culture. Because of the resistance, they struggled to stay with their new family. If both the parents and adoptees meet each other halfway in learning a new culture, they can build beautiful, healthy relationships.

Matthew Goodman: I think the biggest thing is to consciously identify as a person of color and use your voice and intensely listen to what's being said in the Black community right now. Our role is not to lead. Our role is to amplify and elevate.

People ask, "How does it feel leaving your company?" I'm in no way the leader. I develop plans and lend the expertise and whatever privilege I might have. Our role is supplemental. Not to fall prey to the idea that the white community will offer goodies to us to defect. They're already offering a carrot in the educational space. It might happen in the short-term. It might help the East Asian community. The Hmong community won't get a huge amount of benefits. This is the core of what I say to everybody. Center yourself and ask what's best for your broader community. We either do it all together, or we don't do it at all.

Your body is on the line. We're half as likely to get killed as a proportion of the population. The police are far less interested in beating me. They don't see me as a physical threat. If I put my body in between, I can defuse the situation.

It's interesting how you use the negative Asian male stereotype to your advantage.

Matthew Goodman: Yes, if I do get the crap beating out of me, if there's a non-threatening Asian getting beaten, they're less likely to believe it was justified.

What advice would you give to other transracial adoptees?

Holly Choon Hyang Bachman: I would say to gather and connect with one another. I think it's a tough time right now, particularly for

Black transracial adoptees and transracial adoptees of color. There's an interesting story even with this Bubba [Wallace], and how his white dad shared he feels bad for his son because, and even George Floyd, he has to carry this whole racist incident on his shoulders because he's Black.

So, with my mentoring group, we mentor adopted and foster care kids. One of the interesting things is that one of my fellow mentors is a white adoptive parent who adopted an African-American boy. He shared a story that just a couple weeks ago, his 15-year old son was at a park and somehow fit the description of a criminal. He had 12 cop policemen on him, questioning him, and he was put into handcuffs. This kid is only 15-years-old and plus he was adopted by white parents. I encouraged my fellow adoptive parent white mentor, and he was LGBT too, to stand-up and be an advocate for his son. He said, "I tried calling the police." I said go to the council, go to the mayor, get the government officials because right now everyone's on edge, but the most important thing is you gotta call your elected officials, and that's really where you can make change. I thought it was completely wrong. My heart totally went out to my mentor's son. He said, "Dad, I didn't know what to say, and they kept yelling at me, and I was stuttering and almost crying because I'm scared. I've never been in a situation like this." That's unfortunately the sad story that that was his first ever encounter with the police. His white parent hasn't equipped him. But what's twisted on the flip side is that because he's a white parent, he might actually have more power, if and when he gets the attention of the authorities, to let these officers know they're wrong, and they may listen to him because he is white (the parent, not the kid). It's such a twisted situation with race and culture.

We're going through the "China virus" and how Asians are looked upon. There's been a huge rampant wave of incidents against Asian-Americans. Someone could come up to me and bop me on the head, and I could be like "I'm actually white." In your mind you're thinking I can go about my day. When people see me, they won't know I'm adopted or have a white family. It's an interesting dichotomy, identity. It's almost kinda like how we have to live double lives unfortunately. That's the plight of people of color. We as adoptees personally have to carry that. Family—that's a core need that any human has, and to struggle with that from an identity perspective, it's very powerful. It could either weigh you down or help you rise you up (if you have a good family). For me, I always kinda have to check in with myself and think, "Is this worth the war? Is it worth the battle to bring up or should I just let it alone?" Not just with my family, but any friends. Do I really want to bring this up about racism or discrimination?

Milton Washington: I'd have to say, looking around and to see all the pain and duress so many people are under is proof positive that there's plenty of pain to go around. It's not just you. There are a lot of people in pain. Confirmation that you're in a big boat instead of a tiny one by yourself is kinda comforting. We're now living Black Lives Matter with corona[virus]. If you want to fight with the cause, if it's gonna put purpose in your life. (I'm not out there because I'm trying to stay healthy and have my own way to positively impact the world.) Really, really get to know yourself to ultimately find yourself because peace is one of those things that's a prerequisite to survive because there's a high probability—the highest ever in our history—that shit's gonna go down. You better be ready, and you got to give yourself a rest now. You won't be so subject to duress as your counterparts because you found peace within you.

So you're Rodney King's mentor.

Renford Reese: Yes, I was the only mentor he only had from 1997-2000. The reason why I knew he didn't have a positive male role model in his life: I saw him in the parking lot and he couldn't tie a necktie. [There was no one] in his first 32 years of life who could teach him how to tie a tie. I gave him books to read. He had a rap group at the time. I gave him advice, helped him set up his website, played golf and tennis with him.

Would you recommend that people need more mentors?

Renford Reese: I think so. To have mentors is a good thing. I think it's important to have mentorship.

You have a lot of mentors. Would you recommend that people need more mentors?

Holly Choon Hyang Bachman: I wouldn't be here without all the mentors I've had in my life. It might be because of those orphan roots we have. It's not like you're trying to be taken care of, but...

I think for me, I also mentor a lot myself to give back. That's where I tapped into a lot of mentors who are African-American because they were the only ones who could understand my issues of race. They had the most lived experience. And also because when you're in that context of diversity and racism, the African-American community are leaders of that. I'm compelled and naturally driven to people in that space. Many of them are African-American. Mentoring is [for] the next generation. We have a mentoring program or initiative for the Foundation. How do you provide role models for adoptees and foster kids? It's all about connections, resources, just someone to listen to or share things with that are not of your parents or family. I truly believe I wouldn't be here today without them. People say, "Don't say my kid is adopted." Well, but they are. That's a fact. "Don't call them adoptees." From the perspective of identity, it's a fact that we are adopted. Steve Jobs, Larry Ellison[64], all these famous people, but even us regularl people, were adoptees. I have embraced my Asian and Korean roots. But interestingly I've had very rare older Asian

[64] The founder of Apple and co-founder of Oracle, respectively

women mentors who were adopted. That would be an interesting area to research. Maybe we're not old enough yet. We know a few Korean adoptees, but women is different. With the mentoring piece, I'm a huge advocate of mentoring. That's one thing I would give advice to Korean adoptees: have a mentor and be a mentor.

Additional Topics

Are there unique perspectives that you think we're missing in the discussion of race relations?

Jordan Davis: Broadly? Yes, I think it's normally presented as a binary as a Black or white perspective, but that erases others, particularly with Black transracial adoptees; we're in an intersectional space in the same way mixed race and multiracial children would have. And I think in race discussions, there's an overlooking of African-American or Asian relationships or African-American and Native American relationships. Those kinds of relationships don't get talked about because the focus is on the Black vs. white dynamic.

Rachel Kavanagh Baldwin: If so, yes. Race was never discussed in my family, which meant that I experienced discrimination, racism, colorism and microaggressions on my own. I didn't learn or measure the impact until I was in my mid to late 20s.

Renford Reese: Yes, I think so. The complexity of the issue. It's so complex that it can be overwhelming. The fact that there's no one solution. We're used to everything being finite. There's no finite answer to the issue of race because people are living it every day. If you're driving and a person cuts you off and that person is being insensitive, you want to curse the person out irrespective of if that person is Black. Are you being racist if the person is Black? You can't say no Black person is insensitive.

For instance, when I was fishing last week. It was peaceful and bucolic. People were walking, hiking, fishing. All of a sudden, I hear this noise "From the windows to the walls…" Because we're in this Black Lives Matter period, no one wants to criticize her. It exists. They saw that with their own eyes. It's a speaker loud enough to hear 500 yards away. Was there anyone else that had their music up that loud? Will that mean no one else who's Asian or Latino will do that? No.

We're living in the real world, not a sociology textbook. They have to deal with impersonal, insensitive, mean [people] irrespective of their race. But if that person is insensitive, and they're Black and you call them out on it, are you a racist?

Rutledge: I don't go out of my way to be like "You're like me. Let's hang out." I just say "Let's grab a drink or do whatever." Race isn't a prevalent thing in my head. I don't go out of my way to seek out the Black or Korean community. I'm just myself, and think "If you want to come along for the ride, we'll see what happens."

JaeHee Melanie Chung-Sherman: Gosh, in terms of adoption community or universally?

In terms of the adoption community or Black community or the intersection of those.

JaeHee Melanie Chung-Sherman: For so long it's been dominated by white cis parents, evangelical identified individuals. It's left out significant portions or intersections, Black, queer, trans, non-Christian, non-black POCs, not allowing dialogue at the table or building a new table. Race is always a bookend. I'm hoping there's a positive shift that's happening. I'm hopeful but also a realist in terms of justice and equity. Time and time again it's in terms of numbers, wealth, ability status, and voice. It's not dominated by marginalized voices. [There's] the stereotype of the angry adoptee coupled with race coupled with angry Black adoptee with the angry Asian trying to silence the voices trying to get to the table talking of racial justice and identity from the white colonialist lens. I'm hoping people will divest some power.

We're having the same conversations, and it's 2020. We're having the same training on how to talk about race, and I'd like to move beyond that and culture camps. Korean adoptees are the largest collective international voices. The integrated culture camps and culture awareness—I was part of that. We were complicit in that movement for Asian adoptees. The Black community, Black multiracial intersectional community were still being talked over. They were talking about racial identity for decades. None of this is new information.

Is there anything else you would like to add?

Bree Davis: I'm interested in this project. There's not a lot of conversation about this.

Enetty Taylor: No, not really much, just that I hope that one day most of us adoptees who are struggling mentally [don't have as much] mental exhaustion [anymore]. Most people suffer [from] depression. As a social worker, [I see this]. Where you don't have closure, where you're constantly struggling to fit in, the depression will sink in so bad. I hope one day that something can be done, and that people can find the closure they need to live their lives. And, suddenly, I wish that all families that adopt have great intentions like my parents did. But most don't and it doesn't sit well with the kids that there was an agenda or that they weren't loved. It's a mess on their mind[s]. There's a lot of depression going around with Korean adoptees. (Don't get me wrong; I'm sure that happens with African adoptees too.) But I haven't seen it to that extent because they don't have the closure or support, they need.

I'm glad that there are adoptee groups on Facebook. That's great. My husband suffers from severe mental depression. Being able to join, I noticed a difference because he doesn't feel as alone in the struggle. It's an outlet for him to get his frustrations out. It helps our relationship, and it helps others to know they're not alone. I think that group is doing a lot of help. I hope there are more groups like that. The excitement in his voice, I'd never heard that before. He was so happy because it's been an uphill battle. It really helps.

Jessica Farrell: Being adopted isn't easy for anyone. Being a KAD and being black presents a whole extra layer of fitting in. Finding yourself and ones [sic] own truth while being accepting to others regardless of skin color, birth/adoptive parentage is who I strive to be. I want to identify with my genetics but not loose [sic] myself in one race or another. I find keeping an open heart and open mind helps erase hurt and helped me heal. Throughout my life I felt broken, but not anymore. I see black ppl struggle, I see adoptive kids struggle. I turned out okay and I'm here to say to other KADs with either white or black parents you can to [sic]. Finding true self is coming to terms with realizing hurt but also striving to go past it a [and] heal others.

Matthew Goodman: We're at a really important moment. We've seen more shifts toward Black Lives Matter in the last several months. People are finally waking up to how much violence the police inflict on the population, on women's bodies, on the poor. This is a moment for adoptees because we can float between groups. It's the time to build bridges. Things previously seen as radical are no longer being seen as radical. That's what I hope for all of us. We can't physically be with each other, but we can be together. If racial justice is seen as a spiritual calling, we can build communion. We can come out of this with more lives than coming in.

Monica Kim: I think for me, I've also become more aware of if you're with 1-2 Black people, how that's perceived when you go out. I know now I was totally being racially profiled because of who I was with. A lot of times racism is subtle. I think it's harder to call out, and I also try to get better at calling things out, but I'm a slow processor. I'm getting education about how to best handle that. I try to get involved with any diversity initiative. Also having that challenge of representing AAPI but not feeling like a "representative representative" because I grew up in white culture. I'm the Asian voice on my diversity committee in my school. I also always worry about being the model minority because I don't want to play into stereotypes. People assume I'm smart, and I work in education, so that doesn't really help.

We do a lot of education and programming about diversity and inclusion without really highlighting AAPI issues. It's always about Black and brown children and not Asian children. I understand why the focus is on Black and brown but the wealth disparity in New York is high, and there's very many AAPI liquor stores, nail salons, low-income, low-education levels. People think of *Crazy Rich Asians*. People aren't seeing poor AAPI in the media. As much as I like working in diversity inclusion, I feel very isolated. There's not much said about those challenges. Like in the case of foreign exchange students, [there are] language barriers, cultural differences. Diversity conferences only talk about Black and brown. I find it disheartening because my school is predominantly white. If I'm not the voice, who else would be? Our upbringing was not so conventional.

Personally, I have always felt more welcomed by the Black community than the white one. I can also relate to how common Black single moms (my partner's mom being just one of many) are[65] and how my bio mom was a single mom who struggled.

Hayley Hoffman: I'm really sad. This has been a really, really hard time. I cry a lot. The individual pain I experience, but also.... It's so sad. People want to be loved. People want to be seen. People want to be heard. I think it's on all sides. White people want to be seen and heard. Korean adoptees want to be seen and heard. Black people want to be seen and heard. We're all guilty of bias toward one another in wanting to be right. I don't think the point of life is being right. It's about having a shared human experience. It makes people really sad. [She cries]

[65] My first longterm Black boyfriend's mom raised him as a single mother, but my second longterm Black boyfriend's mom divorced when he was in college, so though she's technically single last time I checked, I wouldn't say it was a similar experience.

I just want people to get along. So many people are walking around wounded and hurt and then it creates all these problems. We can assign and blame it on politics and race but our basic needs as humans is to be seen, heard, and belong. If you're trying to be right, some or all of those things have to go. As adoptees we have a unique perspective. I would always say and still believe, I don't know what it's like to belong to a particular group. I don't know what it's like to be Asian or white. I don't know how to be internally and externally aligned[66]. I don't even know how important it is. I didn't know it was wrong to be colorblind. I just know how to be Hayley. I don't know how to be Asian. I don't know how to be white. If people knew what I experienced, maybe that would be better. I get the aspect of it that colorblindness might prevent people from empathizing. I look at humanity more than I look at race or gender or sexual orientation. The LGBT community—I have a real sensitive place with them because I know what it's like to not fit in and not be able to do anything about it. No matter how hard I try to be white, I'll always be Asian. I understand trying to be a woman, when you feel like a man. The conversation will come back to the marginalized communities, Latino, Asian, LGBT. Until we are all able to come together collectively, that's what has the potential to change. Our voices have to come together and not continue to be siloed and not think our issue is more important than another's. There's a large portion of the white community that wants that too. Creating allies, having that conversation. What can we do better for all of us? We all have to take ownership and do our part.

In terms of being a mom and having biracial children. My oldest is Korean and Mexican (last name Chavez) and my youngest is Korean and Caucasian (last name Perry). We have more biracial children than ever. I try to teach my kids to be good people. I'm not sure that I talk to them so much about race. I don't know if that's right or wrong. My husband and I have five kids all together, three boys from his first

---

[66] That is something I very much relate to.

marriage, one girl from my first marriage, and one girl together. The kids' ages are 23, 20, 17, 11, and 3. We all look crazy and have different last names. It's a beautiful family where nothing is standardized. As long as you're having a good time and not hurting anybody. That's what life is all about. This is one of the places where I recognize I have privilege. I have the luxury of not educating them on how to be safe when they go out in public. Just be careful how you dress. My daughter loves everybody too. I feel like I'm doing something right. I have relationships with people that are transgender. I try to give her exposure to diversity through the natural course of relationships. All walks of life are welcome. It's harder for my husband. His family's Italian and Irish. Even he's really progressive for his age and what was acceptable. We all have different levels of tolerance. He makes fun of me for being so progressive. I grew up in West Texas, George Bush country.

Renford Reese: Regarding Black baby adoptions, is it better for them to know their race or to be loved? The fact that white's can't adopt is not right.

How can you not have a savior complex if you're trying to good and you're white?

I run the largest prison [volunteer] project in the country [Colorful Flags]. Ninety-five percent of all volunteers are non-Black[67]. Am I gonna call my white volunteers and tell them they have a white savior complex? They're helping inmates transform their lives. Irrespective of if they have a savior complex, it doesn't matter. They're changing lives.

Someone asked me, "Can you comment on how to be anti-racist?" They wanted me to be on a panel. I said someone else can talk about this. I'm talking about people who spent 20, 30 years in a prison, someone who's been flushed down the toilet by their mom. We never hear from the ones who really have entanglements with the criminal justice system [even though we often talk about them].

---

[67] Half of the facilitators were formerly incarcerated (Jones).

How do you envision what it will take to make people see that we should join forces?

David Taylor: I don't know. I think back to being a kid. A lot of Asians and Blacks have both experienced racial discrimination and racial stereotyping. That's a really good question. It's one of those things. I've had some Koreans ask why I'm siding with Blacks. I've had Black people saying the same thing. They weren't crazy about my wife being with me. I think it's petty. I really don't see what the big deal is. I love her. She's been supportive. We have a lot of similar issues. We've connected on a lot of personal levels. We don't really focus on skincolor like most people do. After a while it gets tiring. People ask me "Why don't you be with an Asian person?" We fell in love, and we have a great family, and we're happy. I don't know if I have the right answer. My wife feels the same way. I know in the past we've both talked about past relationships. I've had a lot of exes who were white and Asian, and she had exes who were Black, but we don't focus on "Did you leave them because they were Black or white?" Historically, Blacks and Asians have suffered a lot. A lot of Asians were slaves too. Right now Asians are targeted for the virus. It's just one of those things where I just feel like I don't have a right answer to that one, and it frustrates me because I wish I could. It's been a while since I've been asked these kind of questions, but it's not the first time. Most people I've been attracted to have been Blacks because that's who I was surrounded by. I grew up in a predominantly white neighborhood. By the time I was attracted to them, I didn't know a lot of them, and they were friends of mine that just happened to be Black. I don't think she dated any Asians before she met me. We talk about little things here and there about it, but nothing heavy duty. We didn't care what other people thought about it. With all this stuff, it saddens us, "Why can't everyone get along?"[68] I had some Asian friends who didn't like it, and I lost some family members due to

[68] This is similar to Rodney King's "Can we all get along?"

political or racial reasons from both sides. We experience hatred for our beliefs, politically, racially. We get targeted because people don't like Asians being with Blacks. We try to stay off social media to get away from all the harassment.

Enetty Taylor: I think by sharing our experiences, by reaching out to other people who are adoptees. If we can all give each other support, that would make a difference in somebody else's life, particularly someone who's struggling to find their identity.

JaeHee Melanie Chung-Sherman: Oh gosh, particularly after George Floyd activating Asians for Black lives, Asians have been trying to find a place. Model minority identity—that great lie and pathology we as Asians need to dismantle and deconstruct. Our liberation is bound in with Black liberation. I didn't realize this until—It's embarrassing to say—I was working with TRAs and Black adoptees and confront[ed] my own whiteness and my own shit that I put up with . I would not harm and do harm in our therapeutic space. That's my paradigm: to be in such a vulnerable place, especially with kids, and to see the pain in terms of their own trauma, what I know my Black siblings have experienced—decades and generations of murders and violence. We as Asians have still benefited is a hard pill to swallow. As oppression continues, our own oppression continues. It's real. The lies and policies and legislation are all on racist ideals. We all fight to not be at the bottom, which is ridiculous but human. We need to use our own privilege and white adjacency not in the place of saviorism but to stay in our lane. Not submissive Asian, not co-opting Blackness, not co-opting movements, but aligning with them and joining with equity. So now when I'm asked to speak on race, especially in the TRA community, all of us are marginalized. We know the seats at the table are extremely limited. If I'm asked to speak, I always research the organization to see if it's anti-trans, anti-Muslim. If it's anti-Black, I won't speak or if there were no other TRAs before me or if they pay them.

It wasn't just proximity—we were in it as a family system, particularly Korean adoptees. *And the Korean culture is anti-Black as hell*[69]. So we're getting a lot of mixed messages. It's really complicated. Not doing things out of sympathy or patronizing and having open conversations with colleagues [is important]. I wouldn't want anyone to patronize me. God! Keep me accountable. I'm really glad I have colleagues who will call me out.

Jordan Davis: I think that brutal honesty on the part of minority communities between African-Americans and Asian-Americans is needed.

There needs to be a recognition on the African-American side that, as Americans, we are complicit in some ways with American foreign policy. We served Black veterans from the war in Korea or the war in Vietnam as part of the American empire. African-Americans were complicit with the violence done to Asians, not in the ways white Americans are.

Asian-Americans—I'd like them to recognize how the differential treatment we've received (I don't like the term "model minority"). There are distinct ways the groups are treated. By only looking at themselves, they cannot see the full picture.

We need to get away from this oppression hierarchy. "Who's more marginalized?" "Who's more oppressed?" It's not a conversation I like having because it doesn't go anywhere. I think the two communities, Korean and Black, need to have those difficult conversations before they can do meaningful coalition or solidarity building.

Hayley Hoffman: I think we have to ask ourselves "What's the purpose? What is our vision?" If we have a purpose for equality or if it's for ego, to be right. You could say you're fighting for the same thing, but if you're serving the purpose of equality that's different

---

[69] Emphasis added

from serving ego for self-validation. All humans deserve dignity and respect. We all have hearts and brains and bodies and fingers and toes, so until we stop trying to dissect and segment who we are, nothing's ever going to change.

Matthew Goodman: I think for the Asian community, I beat the drum of understanding how white supremacy operates and how they cleave communities apart. Like the affirmative action on Harvard. The same guy [behind that] is a white supremacist. He doesn't want more Asians in college. We're being used as the tip of the spear. Instead of getting the losing scraps of white, that's a losing battle. Our fates are inextricably linked. Liberation means liberation of the Asian community. They're the last. The more [liberation the Black community gets], the more Latinx and Asian-Americans and everyone else will get. I try to do that through my work showing how these partnerships are mutually beneficial.

The white community is harder because some white people will lose honored privilege. I'm working an article about this now. If you want to get rid of racism, try to train [people]. You gotta replace them. You got to boot them out. That's the solution. Will that mean a loss for them? Yeah. I've actually turned to white women as the allies. They're often more aware of the downsides of white patriarchy and the historical subjugation of white women. There are nine dudes on the Supreme Court. We should have our shot. Honestly, I don't try so hard with white dudes and they get super defensive when you point it out.

SooJin Pate: It's going to take a recognition that we are all humans and share a common humanity. George is not some "thing," no, he's my brother. He's my uncle. He's my cousin. We need to recognize the humanity in ourselves and others. What white supremacy does, in order for it to operate, it requires us to dehumanize ourselves in order to dehumanize others. Derek Chauvin is so dehumanized so he could do this act. He must not see himself as a human being. To do something as inhumane, you have to be inhumane yourself[70]. It's going to take recognizing our humanity. Humane people commit humane acts. Inhumane people commit inhumane acts. There are more inhumane people out there than humane people out there. He's an extreme, but those in the war rooms keeping Black and brown people away from the decision table, that's also an inhumane act[71]. There's a wide range we need to tackle.

Yun-sook Kim Navare: I think, refreshingly so, we've seen a lot of exposure and validation due to the virus and the critical mass that responded to George Floyd. There were some riots, but largely they were peaceful protests. The solidarity is already there. Even back in 2015 and before, I've been noticing that there's a more tightly laced threading of what POC means. I think people are starting to see that we're all oppressed and divided by white supremacy. Those seeds of KAD and Black alliances have already begun. Then all of a sudden, we [Korean adoptees] were all Chinese and vandalized and kicked and stabbed, not looking at accountability of the government and funding. Today an economic plunge, then more excessive police brutality cases, nurses, essential workers, white people, Filipinos, Koreans. I feel like there has been federal events and intiatives to push for ethnic studies. I think most KADs are on board and seeing themselves as Koreans more and more. I think that Black people have always known, "Look, you're not white, you're one of us." Their anger was never directed toward us. I think that the Black community is a little more inclusive and collective. I think there is an Afrocentric core and justifiably so; there's a space for that.

---

[70] On another hand, my husband believes that it takes ugliness to root out ugliness.

[71] Trauma can sometimes result in detachment, which can also lead to lack of empathy and dehumanization of others. Both the person with trauma and the person without trauma must be ever mindful of what trauma can entail.

Then there is a space where they do want allies. They can be more flexible in non-Black people supporting them. As we're aging, Korea has arrived to the rest of the world formally. The views of Korea have changed. It could be a very smooth shift and alliance. When I was going to college, the medical assistant (MA) was Latino. That's who I felt affinity with. She'd have her dorm open. I wanted to go to a big university. We had an Asian student fashion show. We had a Latino fashion show. Black women have always been beautiful. I'm glad you noticed. Fake tans, botox, butt...I never understood all this appropriation. There are middle-of-the-road adoptees that can be moved. There will always be conservative, static adoptees. It's always class-based. They might not have a problem with the Jewish community, but with the Black community, it's more class-based. There will always be KAD Trumpers, but there are a lot of KADs that are flexible and open.

Renford Reese: Obama.

Obama didn't work.

Renford Reese: He's a coalition builder. You need a person, or a generation. You need a generation of people to give people platforms to work on projects together. To do things together. You say Obama didn't work. It didn't work because people didn't want it to work.

I played in front of 96,000 fans in the SEC [Southeastern Conference]. There are 12[72] SEC states. He only won the state of Florida in 2012. There are people worshipping the Black athlete, but then you can't vote for a president. In the *American Myth* documentary, a man says, "Son I want you to pull your pants up. I want you to be humble, educated, and to go to school." The young Black man says, "Oh you want me to be Obama." "Don't burn your buildings down. There's a better way to protest." The Black guy says "Do you want me to be

[72] I believe there are only 11 SEC states now.

Colin Kaepernick and take the knee?" There's little oxygen or space for Black men outside of entertainers or athletes. Let's look at the contradictions. Now you have 100,000 fans in Texas A&M obsessed with the Black athlete, but you don't want to give them any benefits. Let them know they're bigger than the sport they're playing. Give them mentorship. Let them know how you got your yachts. You want to exploit us on the one hand, but don't want to invest in us on the other hand.

When people talk about reparations, that's real. Everybody wants to be Black, but nobody wants to be Black. They want to appropriate, be cool, listen to Black music, but they don't want deal with the pain. They want to use slang and all of that. I think Blacks should have reparations. How do you get educated if one-third of the teachers in your school don't have credentials? The teachers are not incentivized to come to the inner city to teach.

It's hard to quantify the stuff of coming together. [People need] elucidation, enlightenment. Let's give people chances. Support study abroad. If I took a group of 16-year-olds on a study abroad to Korea, don't you think their perspective would change?[73]

Black people need reparations. I was hesitant about this 10 years ago, but [have changed my opinion]. Collateral dysfunction is because of poverty and lack of a strong family structure.

Koreans have a strong family structure, two parents in a household, emphasis on education. And that's how South Korea became the miracle that it became, through hard work. They sacrifice for your generation, through education. They make sure their kid gets the best education. I think another reason you have resentment between Blacks and Asians is because Asians don't get the same virulent treatment, but Asians think that Blacks have been here so long that they think they could have their own businesses. What does it mean if Asians have the same perceptions of Blacks as Africans have, if the Africans have the same perception?

---

[73] Sounds great in theory, but I would not recommend it.

Post-Interview Thoughts: Beauty

On Facebook, you spoke about how you had an emotional breakdown as a cosmetologist because you couldn't make your sister-in-law look like a Korean bride in Korea and that something you were passionate about turned into an object of shame because you only knew American beauty standards. Do you feel that the same thing happens for African adoptees regarding the differences in American and African beauty standards?

Hayley Hoffman: I didn't know there was a difference in Korean and American makeup. That had never entered into my mind. That was a new experience and shock for me. That was my experience as a professional, [not just as an adoptee]. For the African-American community, I'm sure if they went to Africa there might be different [standards]. Their ideas of beauty would be different than in the US. I think every culture has a different expression and acceptance of beauty, and every geographic location.

One thing that I found interesting about doing these interviews is that I interviewed both a cosmetologist and a hairstylist. Even though they have a specialty in beauty, it is only a certain kind of beauty, namely white American and/or Korean-American beauty. However, both have had to confront the area of beauty in their lives with which they were unfamiliar, with one dealing with Korean beauty in Korea and the other dealing with mixed hair that was a cross between African, Latino, Korean, and white. Beauty wasn't even on my radar when I decided to work on this project, but I feel that I definitely need to say something about it.

To me, I was obsessed with beauty when I thought I was ugly for being non-Aryan. Then I despised beauty when I was fetishized, because it caused so much pain and annoyance. Now I do not care about beauty, valuing health instead. However, I didn't learn how to apply eye makeup correctly until I was 33 and stopped when I was 36 because of uneven eyelids.

I am good friends with Erykah Soleil, a white cosmetologist. I remember when she invited me to a costume makeup class in college but had to retract her offer because the teacher told her that she was only teaching costume makeup on white people. Though we've had a pretty smooth interaction with each other, one of the more challenging times was when she was being enthusiastic about the fact that I should wear makeup, but I was reluctant because of my one monolid and one double-lid, which is relatively common in Asian communities, but almost unheard of in white communities. It reminded me of all the slumber parties I'd been to as a child, and how everyone ended up looking prettier after their friends did their makeup except for me. By the way, solid blocks of color à la runway model style is not going to work at work. I've even had an ex break up with me for the sole reason that I didn't wear makeup.

When I was in kindergarten, I remember someone touched my hair and announced to me how my hair felt like straw. My hair is even different from my Korean counterparts because it is coarse, thick, and 2A wavy, so I've even had to learn the LOC acronym (leave-in conditioner, oil, and cream) and "squish to condish." Later in life, I used to model when I had symmetrical monolids, but even that was racially challenging because photographers would try their best to get me to tan, which was the beauty standard of the day, but it just wasn't happening.

I can understand how challenging beauty is in the "face" of American beauty standards. Though it was relatively easy for me to trim my ex's soft African-American hair, wearing unnaturally red faux locs for a few months made it difficult to sleep and style. On one hand, I learned to take better care of my scalp, but on the other, I had to cut off the hair that matted. My adopted Ethiopian friend even went to touch my faux locs and later realized what she was doing and was embarrassed.

I got a glimpse into how much more expensive and time-consuming it was to style African-American hair when my ex invited me to a wedding. I was with her when she was getting her hair done into a weave, only to find out that the weave was going to make her three hours late to her own wedding.

One area where we definitely need to actually diversify is the beauty industry. Putting pictures of diverse models into magazines is not going to cut it; we need actual understanding of beauty differences throughout the beauty industry. Sheertex is a model, pardon the pun, in the beauty industry by hiring plus-size models and models with vitiligo. The Toca Life app includes vitiligo in its game for kids. And BTS has two singers with uneven eyelids like me.

Post-Interview Thoughts: Biracial and Mixed Race

Do you feel that people forget about biracial people in conversations about race?

Lisa A. Quaites: I don't know if they forget. I think we are just lumped into the people of color category because I guess in my mind there's white and there's everything else. I'm a minority on a whole lot of different levels. I don't think that Koreans are treated worse than hapa Koreans. You're gonna get whatever treatment you get. I think now, and it wasn't so when I was growing up, that there are so many mixed-race people. I wasn't exposed to that but now, in my mind, they're everywhere.

Rachel Kavanagh Baldwin: I think we finally live in a time where being bi or multiracial is somewhat normalized; however, I do not think that we've fully escaped the ignorance of attitudes that comes with understanding people with more than one racial background.

Jessica Farrell: Ppl forget others all the time. I walked through a white world always seen as "black sheep". I was seen in the black world as not black because I was biracial and never seen in the Asian world because I was biracial and black. But not being seen, probably until high school, when rap when [went] more mainstream let me fly u see [under] the radar.

Young-wha: Biracial children are excluded from that conversation a lot of times because society is fixated on people being one race. A perfect example is checking off the boxes for "What's your race?" Only recently did they say, "Mark all that apply."

Rutledge: I used to mix it up. I've been everything.

Young-wha: I would agree what people have said about biracial. It's not talked about. If it is brought up, people don't know how to address it or how to have that conversation.

Most adoptees who are half-Korean and half-Black, or a similar variation, tend to be treated as and identify themselves as solely Black. Whereas while most Korean adoptees from the 1st-3rd wave are raised as white with no to little discussion of race, half-Black adoptees are raised as Black with no to little discussion of the rest of their identity, such as Jewish or Chinese.

There are Black adoptive parents now of Black adoptees, and what I've noticed about how they're different from white adoptive parents is that they focus on the mixed race part that's Black to the detriment of other racial identities.

In general, Asian (and Latino) adoptees are expected to act white, but Black adoptees are expected to act Black. In general, Asian (and Latino) adoptees are expected not to date Black people, but Black adoptees are expected to date other Blacks, with a few exceptions (Marr).

Biracial and mixed people are the answer to peace, but as long as biracial and mixed people claim to be only Black, society will not change, for such a person kowtows to the one-drop philosophy established by whites and breeds nationwide if not worldwide hatred for his non-Black parent whether or not that parent was the more responsible one.

KOREANS AND KADS WITH THE LATINO/A AND LATINX COMMUNITY

Koreans with the Latino/a and Latinx Community

Though the majority of this book is focused on the relationship between Blacks and KADs, I also thought it would be important to add a chapter on the relationship between the Latino/a and Latinx community and the KAD community.

Perhaps Koreans and Mexicans became close when Koreans and Japanese people would not associate with each other. Their history, among their own race, is far more complicated than comparing it to Trinidadians who have rivalries with Jamaica or African immigrants that warn each other about dating Black Americans because, to Koreans, the Japanese represented the colonizers, the oppressors. In the 1920s, Asians hardly spoke to each other, and if you knew anything about Asian history, you'd understand why. Young Kim says, "Asians were not like today; they were in isolated, hostile camps. [...] You had to depend on Caucasians, Mexicans, Jews, and other people" . In the 1920s, Young Kim continues, "Asians weren't even able to buy homes [...]. All my playmates were minorities—Japanese, Chinese, Italians and Mexicans, until the Italians found out they [themselves] were white and moved out of the ghetto[74] [...] Mexicans and Chinese accepted us" (Kim and Yu 297).

Even though the Japanese and Mexicans unify before the Koreans and Latinx folx[75] do via the 1903 Japanese and Mexican farm worker strike, Koreans and Latinx folx have a lot in common. Both tend to be immigrants. Neither fit into the Black vs. white discourse. They both tend to watch TV dramas. Mexicans are one of the few Westerners

[74] This word was kept because it is part of a quote.

[75] A version of "folk" that is specifically inclusive of underpriviled minorities, particularly the LGBTQ community.

who caught onto the Korean craze, called the *hallyu* wave, that was happening simultaneously in China, Japan, and Korea that began with Korean dramas. "Even in Mexico—land of the telenovela—a flock of local women stood outside South Korean President Roh Moo Hyun's hotel during a recent visit, holding placards with Korean stars' names" (Faiola). K.W. Lee noticed that Asians and Latinos intermingle a lot (Kim and Yu 22). Korea responded to their Mexican fans with K-reggaeton.

In Los Angeles, Korean neighborhoods tend to be next to Latino/a and Latinx neighborhoods. This dynamic is also true for Virginia's Little Korea. In Denver, this dynamic plays out slightly differently, with Latino/a and Latinx neighborhoods being next to, or combined with, Vietnamese neighborhoods. Both groups also tend have higher rates of integrating into white neighborhoods. After Asians, Latinos/as and Latinx folx are the most likely to be in interracial marriages with white people and are the second most likely to be adopted by white parents (Marr).

For Kyu Min Lee, a Korean who grew up in Columbia, the first people to befriend him when he arrived in the United States were Spanish-speaking Mexican kids. Understandably, this made Korean kids angry. He often had to translate between the two groups (Kim and Yu 118). He was such a trustworthy friend of the Mexicans that he belonged to the Malditos (Spanish for "evil" or "damned"), the highest clique in the 18 Street gang (Kim and Yu 121).

Hyun Yi Kang said in her essay "No Spokesperson" that she helped her parents with their garment factory. Her parents had hired many Latinos/as and Latinx folx. She believes that they needed to declare an alliance and work together to address issues of racial exploitation and economic disparities (Kim and Yu 191). In 1993, some Korean-American youth protested layoffs of Latino/a and Latinx workers in LA by the South Korean owners of a large LA hotel. In 1995, they protested against South Korean factory owners in Guatemala for preventing workers from organizing (Kim and Yu 374).

As for the Latino/a and Latinx community, I remember a student in one of my classes at George Mason University who was Asian but intensely fascinated with Mexican culture, similar to the Japanese fascination with cholo culture today.

Some Koreans are attracted to Latinos/as and Latinx folx. Kyu Min Lee could not imagine dating a Korean. He has dated his Latina girlfriend for a long time, but his mother thought that she would be lazy, spending his money (Kim and Yu 127). Lesbian Sandy Lee shared that she took for granted that her ex could go with her anywhere because she was Chinese, but that her current Latina lover would not have felt comfortable being the only Latina among Asians (Kim and Yu 242).

Not only are they just attracted to each other, but occasionally Koreans and Latinos/as and Latinx folx are attracted enough to make a marriage out of it. Non-adoptee Sandy Lee's mother married a man from Peru (Kim and Yu 236). One Korean man likes how he is respected in her culture. Latino cultures are paternalistic, and they value men's opinions highly. Young Shin married a "fair-skinned Mexican American—he could pass as Chicano, Mexican, Arab—but not as European white. To him, being Chicano is a kind of political statement." She explained that when naming children they had "decided on one Korean name and one African or Hindi one. [...] Aisha [African or Hindi name] calls herself Korean and Mira [Korean name] calls herself Chicana" (Kim and Yu 331). And a few Koreans already happen to be mixed between Korean and Mexican. In Dallas, Texas, a half-Korean, half-Mexican DJ for a famous rap group won the annual world championship more than once (Kim and Yu 128). Kyung-Ja Lee (yet another Lee) directed *Koreatown Blues*, a movie about the love between a Korean immigrant and a Mexican mechanic (Kim and Yu 171)[76]. Youn Jae Kim's parents operated a Mexican restaurant in California (Kim and Yu 174).

---

[76] No longer available

One Korean used to be racist towards Mexicans until he discovered that they have the common thread of immigration. Maeun Koch'u, a self-avowed former racist said he changed when he saw *El Norte*, an emotional movie about Mexican immigration, and he realized that they were immigrants like his family. Of course, just because a few have crossed over to the Latino/a and Latinx side, not all have gotten with the program. Some Koreans are still quite racist toward them.

KADs with the Latino/a and Latinx Community

There are at least two KADs I read about or have seen whose adoptive parents were Latino/a. Sunny Diaz and Zara Espinoza are the only KADs I have come across who were adopted into a Mexican family. Diaz "grew up speaking English and Spanish, eating tamales and menudo during the holidays in her Mexican-American family" (Fox and Wilkinson 85).

White oppression has often sought to separate biological families, whether Black, Asian, Latino, or Indigenous using various means. Most adoptive parents never think about the commonalities many POCs share—that white oppression often involved the separation of families, either forcibly or not—or that they (adoptive parents) continue to participate in such a system. What many adoptees have found, which is useful in this conversation, is that even if you do not know where your parents or ancestors come from or even what they're named, you can still build a created family of your choice by choosing those who uplift and challenge us to be better people.

As for the American side of the equation, adoption and immigration law was so set up as to prevent chain migration, keeping them forever separate from their birth family (E. Kim). I believe that I'm the only KAD interested in my parent's genealogy. Law treats KADs as if they are genealogically related, but Daughters of the American Revolution treats KADs as if they're not. No matter where KADs go, there is no place where they will fully belong.

Also, we all tend to be lumped together, with all Latinos/as and Latinx folx called "Mexican" and all East Asians called "Chinese." In *Mambo Mouth* (1991), Colombian-born John Leguizamo impersonates Asian Americans in stand-up comedy.

I used to date an undocumented Canadian who was raised in the United States of America, and even though he was not the typical undocumented immigrant from Mexico or the Northern Triangle of Latin America, I could see the damaging effects that being undocumented had on him. I'm also well aware of the damaging effects it had on KADs living in Korea before the F4 visa for KADs, as Korea's social security counterpart is based on blood relations, which KADs are legally not a part of because we had been disowned. Of course, Koreans continue to disown us by not processing our legal ability to get the F4 visa, turning us away, which has caused a lot of annoyance and anguish among the KAD diaspora.

If one realizes that 1) half-Korean babies were mandated to be adopted out because they were a reminder of Korea's dependence on the U.S., that 2) Korean adoptions increased to better foreign relations, and that 3) KADs welcomed back to Korea are both economically and euphemistically called "cultural ambassadors" or "valuable assets" as opposed to just overseas adoptees, "haeoe ibyang," one will realize that what truly fuels the Korean adoption industry is nationalism and money. The Korean word for adoptee, "ibyang," is one letter away from the Korean word for stranger, "ibang." Many Korean adoptees do not realize that, despite their genetics, if they return to a homogenous and nationalist Korean society that 1) they will be labeled a foreigner, or "oeguk saram"; 2) they won't be allowed to have the equivalent of a social security number, or "hojuk," literally family registry; 3) they will only be able to belong to a community of other KADs, 4) they will be told to speak Korean, 5) they will not allowed to date Korean natives' sons and daughters, and 6) they will be treated by the average person with just as much xenophobia as the Latino/a and Latinx community experiences in the United States. Politically, Korean adoptees are just ploys of a nationalist country.

Minneapolis, is a major city in Minnesota, originally named Mni Sota Makoce by its original inhabitants. It is the most tribally diverse state in the country and hosts the Dakota, Ojibwe, and Ho-Chunk tribes (Pate, *How Asian Adoptees Can Support Black Lives Matter*).

Some Korean adoptees who grow up in predominantly white neighborhoods in the Midwest find Indigenous Americans to be the closest in appearance to themselves. Sometimes indigenous adoptees, before adopting from indigenous tribes was banned, would say that they were sometimes mistaken for Korean. Even for myself, after I realized I would never look like Disney's Aurora in *Sleeping Beauty* decided I was most like Tigerlily from Disney's *Peter Pan*. (In my childhood there were no such Disney princesses as *Mulan*, who represents both East Asian and transmasculine communities, as the animated *Mulan* came out when I was already in high school. I refuse to watch the live action *Mulan* for ethical reasons).

I remember hearing on a podcast that the speaker's grandmother passed as Black because it was perceived that Black Americans actually had more privileges than Indigenous Americans. What I mean for that is that Black people were rarely skinned. Dr. Leo Killsback said that 39 Indigenous American men who were hanged in Mankato, MN in 1862 "were skinned and preserved by the Mayo Clinic for further 'scientific' study" (Harjo). As for other injustices, currently, Indigenous women are murdered and sexually assaulted 10 times the average in the United States (Smith-Morris). Even though Asian statistics don't come to that, Asian women were four times more likely than Asian men to have sexually transmitted diseases (STDs) in 2010 (Lin).

Indigenous Americans have had the most difficulty with the trope that white women had to be saved from indigenous hands. Even though the news propaganda wanted the country to believe in 2003 that private Jessica Lynch was saved from Iraqis (who were actually treating her in a hospital), Jessica named her own daughter

Dakota, which is Sioux for "friend" or "ally" because it was an indigenous woman who brought her to the hospital (Zara). This case also illustrated the comparison between the Indigenous and Muslim communities as treated by the white media, in referring to Osama bin Laden as "Geronimo," as referring to Iraq as "Indian country," and as evoking "Wanted Dead or Alive" posters from the time of "cowboys and indians."

ADOPTIVE PARENTS

One of the differences between Black and Korean adoptees is in the adoption process. Dr. Wilkinson concluded that adoptive parents of Korean adoptees (this advice is different in the case of Black adoptees) should not bring other Koreans into their life until the child is ready. Even though many adoptive parents of Korean adoptees have already done so, Wilkinson says that in her research findings "encountering a Korean adult may disrupt rather than assist their adjustment to the family" (Wilkinson 70). The adoption process is different still for Russian adoptees as Russian adoptees are matched to birthparents by their facial features, such as their eye color and face shape.

COLORBLINDNESS

One cannot talk about adoptive parents without addressing colorblindness, euphemistically called "non-racism," but realistically called "aversive racism."

Adoptive parents see their children as White, whether the child is Korean or Black or another race. Colorblind, color-ignorant, or color-denying? To deny that an adoptive family is now an interracial family can be as detrimental as explicitly making prejudiced remarks about people of the adoptee's race. An extreme example of colorblindness is in Germany, where they do not talk about race or racism despite the fact that many people throughout the world know about Germany's racist history. It is a different matter though when non-family members are colorblind too. Adoptive parents need to know the healthiest spot between denial of race and obsession with race.

A lot of POCs assume that white people are willingly complacent or ignorant, but such is not the case. Just as POCs use their experiences to understand race, so do white people. The difference is that they have far fewer reasons to experience racism unless vicariously through POCs.

My father has told me that he's more Korean than I am because I didn't grow up with Korean culture. This is not an intentional microaggression on the part of my father; this is how he was raised, how many white people were raised. In *White Fragility*, Chapter 2, the author talks about how a white woman would shush her child if that child pointed out in the grocery store that someone was Black, instead of something healthier like saying, "Yes, that person is the color of mocha, or cinnamon. Would you like to speak with him/her?" What the child picks up is that it is not polite to point out race. What that child learns is not just "non-racism," but censorship and the preference for using euphemisms, as was popular in Germany during World War II.

The phrase, "I don't think of you as _; I think of you as white" exemplifies colorblindness. Colorblindness does not mean being treated as if you have no color; it means being treated as white because white is "the new normal" (or rather the old normal). This phrase is a phrase you will hear mostly from adoptive parents, who are overwhelmingly white.

I have noticed this from a friend who shushes me whenever I refer to someone as Black when I'm telling a story where that's an important point for understanding the story. It irritates me, but I let it slide because I suspect he has autism and has a hard enough time socializing. This was the same guy who sincerely thought I was white and wasn't just saying it because he was "colorblind." I have noticed this too from my mom. One time I complimented the cashier's [tattoo] sleeve in the grocery store. She admonished me because "it's like complimenting someone on a birthmark," which made no sense to me because that person obviously spent good money for the artwork to be noticed. This is something a lot of people do not understand about white people. It might also be a thing in South Korea, where tattoos are looked upon with disdain.

Ijeoma Oluo makes it clear that the ways race is not talked about is both damaging and actually making race an issue, to include when an employer ignores hairstyles in the dress code, when Parent and Teacher Association (PTA) meetings are during school hours (meaning Black and Latino/a/x parents could risk losing their jobs if they attended), or when movies are made with only white people (Oluo). I would also add when people assume that all people drive cars.

Those raised by white parents, whether adoptive parents or not, suffer from internalized racism, including me. One of the darkest examples I can think of regarding the underbelly of adoption is that the siblings of J. Alexander Keung, one of the officers complicit in George Floyd's death, were black adoptees adopted by his white biological mom. Even though her biological son and adopted children were Nigerian or Black, and even though Alex dated a Hmong woman, his mother did not talk about race. Somehow that environment of not discussing race fostered an environment where Alex ended up participating in a black man's death (Barker).

Depending on where adoptive parents raise their Korean adoptee child, racial epithets thrown at them or their child will vary from none at all to just as bad as what adoptive parents who raised Black children encountered. Ignoring bullies does not always mean they will go away; I know this from personal experience. Interestingly, when faced with Korean adoptee questionnaires, I swore then that I was never subjected to racism, but it was peculiar that having ten bullies was not common. However, in hindsight, I believe the model minority stereotype contributed to my massive amount of bullies. I also remember someone hating me for being "perfect" because, she said, she could imagine me playing piano. I was also subjected to positive racism and positive verbal abuse, which is often overlooked but just as damaging because it still involves seeking approval and is still as much of an imposter as triumph (reference to "If" by Rudyard Kipling). See *You Are Special* by Max Lucado.

Not all things about adoptive parents are colorblind, white nationalist, or negative. Sometimes they say some sweet things even if in interesting ways. For example, my parents often told me they were prejudiced "for" (or biased for) me rather than the way the word is normally used, as prejudiced "against" (or biased against). All parents are naturally, or at least socially, prejudiced for their children, meaning that they have a preconceived notion that their children are the best. For example, a mother could compare her child to historically great modern artists, whereas everyone else might see a lack of talent as well as a lack of understanding of art history.

One way to get adoptive parents to understand the damage of colorblindness is to go with them on vacation to a non-white country and ask them how they would feel if no one acknowledged their feelings about not fitting in. For an adoptive parent to be in Korea would be like being a Black person in Switzerland (that is a James Baldwin reference). If an adoptee chooses to return to his or her origin country and decides to bring family along, the family will finally get a glimpse of what the adoptee has felt like for the adoptee's entire life. Most adoptive parents have never been the only white person in a room, but my mother was the only white person in a room one time. My surrogate birthmother's family invited us to a traditional Korean celebration that was in Korean. My mother clung to me, for the first time in her life experiencing what I experienced most of the time.

WHITE SAVIOR COMPLEX

Many adoptive parents fall prey to the "white savior complex," whether consciously or not (Shorts). White savior complex could also be known as a race-specific codependency, though codependency exists across all racial spectrums. Why else do you think the United States of America is in everyone's business? Because it has a codependent culture, starting with the idea of America being a "shining city upon a hill." It's so bad that even a Black *Republican*, Jason L. Riley, wrote a book called *Please Stop Helping Us*. I will not get too into codependency here because that is not the focus of this book, but I can recommend the introductory books, *Codependent No More* by Melody Beattie and *Boundaries* by Henry Cloud and John Townsend. I will share a well-known anti-racist quote here. As aboriginal Lilla Watson said, "If you have come here to help me, you're wasting your time. If you have come because your liberation is bound up with mine, then let us work together."

As with Black adoptees adopted during this time, I imagine many of the Korean adoptees adopted in the '60s (many at that time, half-Black), were adopted by parents who were believers in the Civil Rights Movement. Other ways adoptive parents can prosthyletize can be through Christianity, politics, or even through anti-Communist sentiment. And some unsavory adoptive parents will even adopt for work, and keep their own adopted children in slavery, mistreating them from a place of power.

The idea that the world requires white parents to save the little orphans of the world is just a nicer way of saying manifest destiny. Since whites accuse Blacks of having a sense of entitlement, one could also say the same for whites who believe they deserve to have children, no matter what the cost because, of course, everyone knows that children are the answers to all life's problems. (I hope you understand I'm being sarcastic.)

HOW TO CALL IN ADOPTIVE AND/OR BIOLOGICAL PARENTS (QUICK START GUIDE)

1. Understand that you are called to this purpose.
2. Understand the role of the amygdala and be mindful of each other's amygdala.
3. Understand their mindset, or at least make an attempt.
4. Explain the definition of racism, microaggressions, and other words, as is used by anti-racists.
5. Use analogies and logic.
6. Challenge them to live up to their highest selves.
7. Point them to resources.

Asians are positioned by the media narrative as superior outsiders and Blacks are positioned as inferior insiders. However, KADs are closer to superior insiders due to their white adjacency. If we choose the side of Blacks, then we make this pitting against one another less effective and we can use our privilege for good, but if we choose the side of whites then we are no better than them despite gender, as East Asian women have been known to make as much as white men, with Asian men making far more (U.S. Bureau of Labor Statistics).

I started writing this book in 2007, and in 2020 not much has changed, sadly, which also means that older books and resources that I cite are still relevant today. As I read the most important, most relevant, and most recent literature on anti-racism, I'm surprised by how the majority of blogs and websites I've been sent to had been abandoned at least five years ago. I can bet that most of the Black community gave up talking with the white community closer to 2007 than 2020, and particularly due to Trumpers around 2016 or soon after.

Adoptees often believe they have the option of "not rocking the boat" or "throwing the baby out with the bathwater" with both parts of the triad. It will be uncomfortable to have these discussions, but do not unfriend your white friends and do not disown your white family during this time. Make both a commitment to your white network and a commitment to Black Americans. It will be super uncomfortable at times, but part of anti-racism is embracing the discomfort in the knowledge that what you are doing is furthering the cause of Black Lives Matter. We occupy a super important position in the United States of America and around the world. You can do this. Black Lives Matter needs you.

You need to be having these conversations with not only white people, but Asian people too. You need to be having a deep conversation, though not in the first reunion meeting with a birthparent. Wait until a relationship has been built.

If you wonder why I include biological parents in this, then we might need to have a "come to Jesus" moment here. A lot of KADs want to think of themselves as anti-racist allies and do not see themselves as privileged, but don't actually know much about their country of origin. However, their own internalized positive and negative stereotypes play a role in the search and reunion process, in addition to the desire to just travel there.

If you think racism is bad in America, think again. Take what you know here and multiply it. Korean Koreans—I've been learning a lot about their way of thinking lately. Korea is a very homogenous, intolerant, and hierarchical society, filled with denial and secrecy. Koreans treat their own adopted-out offspring the way Americans treat Latinos/as and the Latinx community just because we don't speak Korean. When they don't want us, they'll have no qualm with calling us foreigners daily, and when they do want us (our money), they'll call us valuable assets. Their own language requires that one person is always above another in a group of two or more, so women always get the short end of the stick. And there's so much competition that kids study 24/7 and people are refusing to have kids because they wouldn't want their child to go through what they went through. I have even seen North Korean defectors in YouTube videos state how bad they feel for South Koreans because of the intense pressure to "keep up with the Joneses." They'll spit on Black people upon seeing them without provocation. They treat LGBTQ people with don't ask don't tell. And they are huge into fat shaming and colorism (with a major industry for skin whitening) against other Asians brought into the country through trafficking. It was the top country for suicides at least 18 years running. And there's a higher rate of domestic violence among Korean-Americans (60%) than any other Asian-American group (which ranges from 33-53%) (Chang, Shen and Takeuchi), which as a whole is larger (2 out of 3) than the rate for all women (1 out of 3) (Fuchs).

Due to our white adjacency, we have the challenging role of not only talking with the white community but even the right-leaning

Libertarians (including Anarchists), Republican community, Trumper community, Tea Party community, and the alt-right community, which will take more kid gloves than just talking with the regular white community.

I'm not saying you can move them from one extreme to another, but if you can just move the people around you even one tick, then that will still make a difference. And in between educational moments for or from you, also consider supporting the inclusion of adoptee-based and race-based trauma to be included into the DSM.

Not only can you try these ideas with right-leaning Libertarians (including Anarchists), Republicans, Trumpers, Tea Party followers, and the alt-right, but you can even try them with fellow adoptees. However, if the adoptee of color is an African or even an African-American adoptee raised in a predominantly white neighborhood, and you're an NBPOC, then the education must come from an anti-racist Black friend or acquaintance. I'm not saying to "whitesplain" to them about the things they should already know but don't, but to gently get them to see that they have bought into a way of thinking that isn't helping them.

Understand the Amygdala

Most of the anti-racist literature out there is from the focus of race for Blacks (not always *from* Blacks), not conflict resolution. So I feel that the reason why action is keeping people apart instead of bringing them together is the lack of understanding of how people—all people—function.

The conversations and judgments we have in current-day discourse implies that the amygdala does not hijack our brains, and that needs to change if we want any sort of compassion for our fellow human beings or ourselves. Anyone who is a practicing anti-racist knows that uncomfortable feelings of pain, anger, and guilt hinder discussion of race considerably. I recently heard someone tell me she heard that anger was holy and from God, as everyone has it, but that violence is from the Devil. However, it's not that simple and anger and violence are both on the same spectrum.

Even though everyone gets angry and afraid, understanding the amygdala is key to reducing domestic, sexual, and verbal violence; divorce; obsessive compulsive disorder (OCD); obsessive-compulsive personality disorder (OCPD); post-traumatic stress disorder (PTSD); etc. and using it for social justice work.

It's true that most of the work of anti-racism falls on white shoulders. Due to the more blatant racism that Black adoptees face, there is something that Black adoptees and the Black community can do besides validating attempts to sympathize, and this is to try to understand things from their parents' point of view.

It doesn't help to start a conversation you wish to be productive with a perceived insult. This is why conversations about race, without knowledge of the amygdala, can lead to losing friends, family, and jobs and why it's considered risky. Insults trigger anger, which triggers the amygdala (the reptilian brain, which is different from the lizard brain), which, according to brain scans, prevents the brain from accessing the frontal cortex, which is where a productive and respectful conversation would originate. Character assassination will do nothing to further the cause of anti-racism, but it will lead to denial, invalidation, and defending, which is exactly what anti-racists tell white people not to do without realizing that their actions will lead to "a shitty [amygdala] thought process" in white people most of the time (In). Always remember to be respectful when having conversations about race, otherwise the entire process is unproductive.

To explain, I'm going to make an analogy. The term "narcissism" has been thrown around quite a bit lately as interchangeable with narcissistic personality disorder, a disorder in the DSM. It's normally used toward exes or dislikable people as an insult. However, if someone is not a psychiatrist or psychologist with a specialty in that disorder or with the proper credentials, they do not have the credentials to diagnose others. There is a huge difference between the rare someone who has a diagnosable disorder and the average human being who has some degree of egocentricity. For example, people in physical pain have a certain degree of self-centeredness, only out of the necessity of wanting the pain to go away.

To use another analogy, it's like calling a Japanese an otaku, in their mind meaning "reclusive and potentially dangerous Japanese animation fan," when all you know is what an American otaku is, which is a "mostly harmless and quirky Japanese animation fan." Understanding how a culture uses a word is everything (Merriam-Webster).

Instead of tone policing (minimizing, derailing, changing topics, and invalidating), we need to return back to the acronym HALT (hungry, angry, lonely, or tired) because more often than not, anger will be driven by being hungry, tired, scared, hurt, etc.

Eryka Soleil, who is in poverty, said, "Not only is the elephant (the amygdala or emotions) still driving, but the less control you have over key things in your life, the harder it can be to coax that elephant due to lack of access to thing, etc. Being well-rested is also important for tackling the elephant. And fed. I've seen articles talking about how parents will come into, say, WIC offices being short-termpered, and it turns out they're just really hungry, because they've been feeding their kid(s) first. So their first step is to tell the parents that they're making that choice for a good reason, but they have to also eat. Maybe there is more going on than is obvious" (Soleil). She also taught me about the term "spoons," which refers to the level of one's energy for tackling mundane daily tasks.

Just as we say "person with disabilities" instead of "disabled person," so should we say "person with subconscious racial thinking and behavior" rather than insult someone's morality, particularly a white Christian. The reason why a Black trans woman was let go by L'Oreal was not because the company was racist, but because the woman said "all white people are racist" (which shames all white people) instead of "everyone should reflect on how they participate in racism" (which guilts white people so they won't do that related behavior and produces a completely different result). By the way, if you're talking with an adoptive parent who's not even at anti-racism 101, then I guess it's okay to call racism "racialized tension and prejudice" to make him/her more comfortable, as long as he/she doesn't stop there and realizes it's not about staying comfortable. I have more about the definition of racism in a future section.

Both Black and Korean communities have fallen prey to the victim part of the drama triangle. In addition to the amygdala, one must also understand the drama triangle. A drama triangle consists of a persecutor, victim, and rescuer. The ways to collapse a drama triangle are to be calm (e.g., deep breaths, meditation), validate BOTH sides (i.e., publicly), and/or refuse to participate.

When considering current events, the drama triangle includes persecutors (i.e., cops), victims (i.e., black community), and rescuers (i.e., the press and readers of the news). It's difficult to refuse to participate here because, unfortunately, those who refuse to participate are victims of judgers in their own drama triangle. The persecutor (i.e., dominant culture) tends to see things as not matching up to their expectations. When the persecutor escalates (e.g., full gear, standing in a horizontal line, declaring a protest illegal), then the victim escalates (e.g., riots). No one wants to be a persecutor, so they will break off to be a victim in a new triangle with the same or a different rescuer (i.e., Republican press).

So out of one drama triangle we now have other drama triangles either automatically or out of attempting to resolve the original triangle:

1. victim (cops), persecutor (Democrat press), and rescuer (Republican press)
2. victim (anyone willing to validate both sides), persecutor (judgers), and rescuer (non-judgers)
3. victim (non-participants of original drama triangle), persecutor (judgers), and rescuer (non-judgers)

It doesn't appear like this will go away easily until we all individually make the decision to collapse all drama triangles, which is difficult since every attempt to collapse the drama triangle results in a new drama triangle.

Understand Their Mindset

My father always quoted Stephen Covey when he would say, "seek first to understand, then be understood." The reason why the first three steps here start with the word "understand" is because it is the thinking part, not the doing part, that will make the most difference.

To help understand the mindset of the majority of adoptive parents who happen to be white, it's important to understand the mindset of a white person on the topic of anti-racism.

Upon reading multiple blog posts on anti-racism, I noticed that many were inundated with comments about affirmative action from white people, even though nothing in their post implied anything about affirmative action. This led me to asking Eryka Soleil about this because, even though I couldn't possibly fully understand the Black experience, I can't fully understand the white experience either. Even though she considers herself an anti-racist, she wanted to share insight on how white people think.

She said, "So I think people mention affirmative action because that's their personal experience with anti-racist measures. It's what they know and have direct experience with. It's that one thing that has directly impacted people. I got a letter from one of my prospective colleges that directly told me I was being turned down because they have to leave room for a minority. I had friends whose parents lost out on job applications because they were against an equally qualified Black candidate, and the employer cited that as a factor. When you are already in the mindset that racism is not a modern issue, and then you lose out on a job offer because of affirmative action, or a scholarship, or a college entry, that just feeds the fire of thinking that it's gone too far, that it's now a detriment for white people. My friends' parents really needed those jobs at the time. I was really crushed that the school told me I was qualified, but too white. The perception was that it was not fair to us, that it was punishing us. The reality wasn't clear at the time because none of us realized we had more overall chances than a POC in the same situations. And when you're desperately trying to pay rent, get scholarships, etc., it doesn't look fair from where you are when you've been raised in a racist system"

She also explained that, to a white person in poverty, it's like they're on an obstacle course. "The poor don't realize they're racist because their lives suck too, so clearly race is not the issue, right? And poor people who want to become rich often embrace the values of the rich: Those who work hard get ahead, and those who don't stay poor. In regards to the poor, think of it like this: Let's say you're competing against other people on an obstacle course, but each of you have a separate course, and you don't see each other's courses. You've been scoring good times and points on yours, and you worked hard to get them. But now you're being told that the other people are having their courses retooled so they have a better chance of placing closer to your numbers. You'd think it was unfair, right? You're told the other players have much more difficult courses than you, and show you some pictures. And they describe a couple of obstacles to you. And yeah, those things look and sound hard, but surely they must realize you're your course is also difficult? That's kind of how it feels to poor and middle class white people when you tell the that you're traying to make things more equal." (Soleil).

People who have these views on affirmative action will also mention Irish slavery, which was actually not chattel slavery but rather indentured servants.

If perchance you find a white adoptive parent who does not take the above stances on affirmative action, it's still very likely that the way they parent is without spanking. They allow their children to have time to be kids. White children are raised and taught to believe in themselves and for them to express themselves and for them to be upset in public. They do not realize that this in itself is a form of white privilege.

When asked how a KAD mother practiced anti-racism for her Black children, she said that she did not practice corporal punishment; she did not spank them. An unfortunate reality for Black parents is that they have to discipline their toddlers faster so teachers don't see their children as future criminals or see their parents as criminals either. That means they have less time to be children. Such a choice is really radical, rebellious, and revolutionary when taken out of the framework of white grandparents and inserted into the framework of a Black neighborhood. Sometimes their choices cost them a lot of judgment from the Black community.

I understand that this step can be challenging for a Korean adoptee. I'm not alone in finding it to be a lifelong challenge in trying to understand my parents myself. I have researched and worked very hard to try to understand them. The same KAD woman I mentioned also shared how she really wanted to understand white people. She came across *Let the Circle Be Unbroken* as a child, and even though she couldn't relate fully, she could relate to how Black people saw white people. It brought both validation and reassurance that she was not alone.

Prepare for Conversation

Prepare to have a deep conversation, first mentally. Make sure to not start in the red zone, being either hungry, angry, or tired. If you are triggered within the conversation and feel yourself moving into the yellow zone, let the other person know that you need a break so you can return to the conversation refreshed and ready also to *listen*. Give them a time estimate of when you'll be ready. Some people need a half hour and some people need a day. Getting to a state of anger or anxiety can "stop us from hearing things that need to be said" and "can stop us from saying what we really mean to say" (Oluo).

Remember your top priority and don't derail yourself. Be explicit in your intentions. Ijeoma Oluo says, "Very often, these attempts at conversation fail because two people are entering with two very incompatible agendas." It's important to do your research beforehand, even as a KAD, as it will go a long way in helping you be more persuasive. Always ask to have a discussion, but never demand to have a discussion. Some people have had too many of these discussions whereas some people have had not enough.

Another thing that Oluo says that I like is "victory will rarely look like your opponent conceding defeat [...] Because your opponent isn't a person" (Oluo). These ideas are modified from *So You Want to Talk About Race?* by Ijeoma Oluo.

Define Key Terms

Some of the key words I will be defining in this section are "racism," "white supremacy," and "microaggressions."

White people treat the word "racist" as offensive as the "n-word" is for Black people. Black people says there's no equivalent for the "n-word" in a white person's lexicon, but they also do not have the white experience. I know this analogy is true because I've never seen my father more angry than when I said he was a "racist," and I've seen him angry often. No one wants to be compared to Germany's "Nationalsozialismus" or white nationalism, euphemistically called "racial realism." Most white people believe that *any* acknowledgment of race is racist in itself and resent the fact that they are being forced to be more racist, by their definition of the term, and therefore less moral, by acknowledging it. That is why they may say things like, "You're racist for making this an issue of race." And they resent being literally shamed and told that their identity is an immoral one, from their perspective.

However, you can try "Did you know the definition of racism used by the Black community?" Explain that racism is not the ultimate insult, not punching someone in the stomach, not blaming, not the ultimate in immorality, and does not have to be extreme. Racism instead is a phenomenon of systemic advantage where the majority of the ruling class belongs to one race; the cultural messages, institutional practices, and beliefs of individuals support it; and people of that race have apathetic authority over another race, or other races of people, called "doing business as usual." Scott Woods once said, "Racism is a complex system of social and political levers and pulleys set up generations ago to continue working on the behalf of whites at other people's expense, whether whites know/like it or not" (Caracola). The definition of racism accepted by the Black community is an idea that makes the idea of reverse racism both implausible and impossible.

Korean adoption as an industry is the epitome of systemic racism and explains both the why and the how: how Korean adoption got started (mandated export of half-black Korean babies), why it continued (adoptive parents more willing to adopt Asians), and why it looks the way it does (higher rate of white-Korean marriages than the general population).

Another example of systemic racism is outsourcing. Rich white men outsourced their customer service to South Asian countries who speak Indian or Filipino English. What happens is that their voices have trained us like Pavlov's dogs to believe we will be dealing with either Mercury Retrograde challenges (meaning frustration) or a scam that will cost us thousands of dollars, in the case of the corrupt publishing system throughout the world replete with vanity publishing houses with bad editors. Do you think they enjoy being put in a situation where they need this job? I don't think so.

White people think that "racism" is an explicit conscious sin borne out of hatred and a desire to hurt, but do not realize that Black people have accepted that racism is often implicit, subconscious, and borne out of ingrained habits stuck in the brain, but, most importantly, of ingrained systems with white people in the ruling class. The former definition, closer to "prejudice," meaning a preconceived opinion based on limited information that came from our socialization, allows for the idea of "reverse racism" (Sommers), and the latter definition, closer to "white supremacy"[77] makes reverse racism impossible because, in the words of Beverly Daniel Tatum, "there is no systematic cultural and institutional support or sanction for the racial bigotry of people of color" (Tatum). The intentions, in the definition of racism embraced by the Black community and POCs, is mostly *irrelevant.* In the definition of racism accepted by the Black community and POCs, both everyone is implicated and no one is being singled out unless as an example, in the efforts of dismantling a system, not a person. In addition, it's neither about the person, nor the behavior, but about the system. A white intellectual could possibly understand the

[77] Not to be confused with just overt, and socially unacceptable, white supremacy, like the KKK and neo-Nazis.

definition of racism better as a Herrenvolk democracy. Herrenvolk is German for "master race," and we all know what happened in Germany. There is a large difference in interpretation, as one can see, but one can only communicate about racism effectively with one definition, not two conflicting definitions.

Perhaps the reason why white people see racism the way they do is because they were raised in and reenforce both a (false) belief in meritocracy and a punitive response to wrongs, whereas the Black community seeks transformative justice instead.

An example of this is with interpersonal violence[78]. A white person's response to interpersonal violence is to incarcerate the person who did harm. However, a transformative justice model seeks to teach the offender in the acknowledgment that fire (police violence) cannot fight fire (interpersonal violence). It is a much more life-affirming method that acknowledges everyone's humanity, even the offender's. It also acknowledges that the person who was harmed loved and still may love the person doing the abusing and that to choose a punitive model over a transformative one limits not just one person's freedom (the abuser), but the entire family's freedom to transform.

Transformative justice seeks not to ostracize, but to teach that they can choose another way besides the way in which they were raised. It teaches that interpersonal violence is not a personal family matter (via natural or created family), but a community problem. We must seek to use such a model also in efforts to teach about race. It is not that the Black community wants to replace the Black people in prison with white people; it is that the Black community wants us all to live in a better world where there is no need for a prison in the first place. A punitive model is very disempowering, but a transformative justice model reaffirms that we are all one. Racism is not a personal matter; it is a community problem. It is only a personal matter in the way that a community problem is personal.

[78] Preferred to the term domestic violence because not all violence is domestic

Most people don't want to see themselves as mean hatemongers or bad people, which is what white people think racism means even though it does not, so if you can explain that being "nice" (or colorblind) is actually mean, or, in the words of Michelle Alexander, "catastrophic" and "cruel," then they will change (Chilton). And white Christians, in particular, came from a 17th-19th century tradition where the highest compliments were regarding "the content of their character," in a way that could not be understood today (but which *Reverend* Martin Luther King Jr. would have understood). Words used in this time were "virtue," "goodness," and "nobility of heart" (Davenport). This is why even today white women have transformed the slang "basic" because their highest concern is their reputation.

However, most people will be familiar with Ibram X. Kendi's definition of racist: "someone who expresses racist ideas and/or supports racist policies through their action or inaction."

At this point it is okay if the person you are teaching this to still takes issue with the definition. The important thing here is that you are both using the same definition so that you can talk about the same issue at the same time without talking past each other on completely two different trains of thought.

It's even okay if you ask "Did you know the definition of racism used by the Black community?" and the person with whom you are speaking says, "No, and I don't want to know." It's okay if someone does not wish to know the definition of these terms; but they should know at least how you feel about these terms, because most likely they care more about you than people they only know conceptually.

Regarding white supremacy, most people think that the phrase white supremacy only applies to hate groups. However, the way it is used by the anti-racism community is to refer to anything that keeps white people the ruling class. It goes along with the (new) definition of racism.

As for the word "microaggression, "many white Americans do not realize that asking a Korean adoptee, "Are you from North Korea or South Korea?" is a microaggression, or unintentional racism.

In fact, it just might point to the stereotype of the geographically uneducated American.

In the KAD community, colorblindness in itself is considered microaggression. Common microaggressions from white adoptive parents include the following:

- "I am raising a German-American in an African-American body."
- "I don't think of you as Asian."
- "Stick to your own [white] culture."
- "You should feel grateful or lucky!"
- "But those aren't your REAL parents."
- "Aren't you glad you weren't aborted?"
- "If we can't have kids, we'll just adopt."
- "My son doesn't like _. If he doesn't change, I'll put him up for adoption."
- "You are as Korean as I am." - When I was 32, my father told me I was no more Korean than he was.
- "I didn't realize you paid attention to race." - My parents told me "I didn't realize race was a factor in choosing a college." I can count on one finger how often we discussed my race prior to college. And when I say discuss, I mean a comment or observation.

One cannot talk about colorblindness without also talking about the "I have a Black friend" fallacy. When discussing feminism, one does not say, "I have a wife." When discussing ageism, one does not say, "I have grandparents" or "I have grandkids." Claiming that an adoptive parent has a multicultural family is misleading because 1) the only culture in that family is most likely white culture and 2) any child of color in that family and his/her/their culture are in clear submission to the culture of the person in authority and must be granted permission to coexist.

They are left in a bubble because spaces where they could learn about race appears both unenjoyable and unwelcoming to them. In that aspect, I have even more privilege than a white person because I'm welcome to and able to move organically among both all-white communities and all-Black communities without fear. Elisha Marr, who wrote about transracial adoptees in the context of race, did a study to find exactly what I have known all along. I'm comfortable with it because I was raised to be comfortable with it; I've always been the "token" Asian. However, white people have rarely been a token anywhere.

Use Analogies And, Yes, Logic

What one can do to call people in is to use analogies and appeal to their logic, since if logic without emotion is a hallmark of white supremacy culture, then it's also the best way to reach them. One of the best examples of this is Beau the Fifth, a YouTuber, who has made an analogy of what it's like to fear the cops by using an analogy a rural white person would understand.

I will provide some examples.

If speaking to a progressive environmentalist: Cultural racism, according to Beverly Daniel Tatum, is like air filled with pollution. No one would call themselves a pollution-breather, but everyone who lives in a pollution-filled area, such as South Korea, cannot avoid breathing the air, and is partly why face masks were common prior to the pandemic. Though we may not even own cars, we still have a civic duty to actively reduce our carbon footprint and provide awareness so others may do their part. This analogy might work best with someone who is an environmentalist.

If speaking to a gamer: When you want to talk about white privilege, and you happen to be talking with a gamer, you can refer to it as the lowest difficulty setting in a game (Scalzi).

If speaking to a traveler: An analogy Beverly Daniel Tatum uses is a moving walkway. Active racism, also known as racism with a capital R (from the *Orange is the New Black* TV show), is walking fast on the moving walkway, but passive racism is just letting the walkway take you to your destination more slowly. Active anti-racism is getting off the walkway from the direction where you got on (Tatum).

If speaking to someone with disabilities or advanced age: Consider a deaf person. It does not help that person if you do not acknowledge his/her deafness, as lack of acknowledgment means lack of accessibility and lack of authenticity. Such lack of acknowledgment erases their lived experiences.

This might be a surprise to many white people, but according to Ibram X. Kendi, racial descrimination is not inherently racist because, for example, affirmative action seeks to remedy inequities, and that the only remedy to racist discrimination is antiracist discrimination. So, while white people may assume that acknowledgment of race is racist, it's actually destructive. As Ijeoma Oluo says, "it's the neglect of the specific needs of color [...] that necessitate it ["putting race in everything"] in the first place" (Oluo).

If speaking to a conservative: If speaking with someone who is far right, such as a Trumper, Tea Party member, or alt-right follower, then it is also imperative to emphasize that loving thy neighbor as thyself has nothing to do with Chairman Mao Zedong's Cultural Revolution. Here it helps to both understand the definition of "cultural Marxism" and to understand the history of China's Cultural Revolution. To train you on how anti-racism works, you can Google these things yourself.

If speaking to a critical thinker: Another thing to try is the "Did you know?" method. If you are speaking to someone who is very logical, you could say, "Did you know that after Germany granted reparations to the Jewish people, their GDP increased?"

If speaking to a Christian: Before introducing the next example, I need to provide a brief history lesson. The groundwork for both slavery and the Holocaust was laid as early as the Spanish Inquisition. During the Spanish Inquisition, warriors were sent out to kill the Jewish people and the Muslims. That was where we got the idea for one-drop rule, because if a Christian had one drop of Jewish or Moorish blood, they were to be executed as well. Since Christian hegemony got us in this mess, let's use Christianity to get us out of it.

Instead of telling people what to believe or do, Jesus invited people to parables, to see average things in a new way. If you're speaking to someone who believes in "What Would Jesus Do?," I have another analogy. If all people are inherently good, and all human brains are wired to see outsiders with suspicion because there was an evolutionary advantage, then even those who go to heaven could still have a measure of prejudice. The reason why Jesus was different was because he never saw any type of human as being an "other." He saw everyone as One.

From this conversation, you can go directly into challenging that person to be their best and highest self. Ask them if they could be treating those around them better and/or if they want to learn what their blindspots are in those areas (and I can tell you that most white people's blindspots also include Asian matters). This can open up the dialogue to teaching what you know about anti-racism practices. Of course, this would require that you too educate yourself on such practices.

Challenge Them To Grow

Challenge them to live up to their role models and their highest self (don't berate them for something their ancestors did, or something someone else's ancestors did, before they were born). I added the parenthetical remark since my parents did not have slaveholding ancestors but still participate in a society that is systemically racist.

The problem also with colorblindness is that it does not require adoptive parents to learn and expand their knowledge. For instance, my father still believes that the George Floyd incident was an isolated incident. He is only representative of many, many like him. Challenge them to learn. Challenge people to grow.

Challenge them to do more than the minimum. If MoveOn or Change.org asks you to sign a petition, send a Tweet, or buy a sticker, don't stop there. Take each opportunity to also send a letter to your senators and representatives.

In terms of growth, if, on the off chance that you are speaking to someone who is already practicing anti-racism 101, allow them to consider the possibility that the critical moments in their life that they considered to be "good luck" was actually someone giving them the benefit of the doubt due to their white privilege or white adjacency. These incidents could be chalked up to Law of Attraction too, but even the Law of Attraction was hoarded by majority white secret societies before it trickled down to the average person.

Create an Action Plan with Them

Ask Them to Observe

Challenge them to observe small acts of racism in their daily life first, before asking them to respond or call people out, just so they can see how prevalent it is in society.

One way to "actively observe" is to be a witness. Don't just watch bad things occur, do something that can help people down the line. Videotape what you're watching. Videotaping does not prevent you from speaking. Take active notes of what is going on so you can provide an accurate recounting to whoever is along the path that can provide justice.

Be Mindful of Your Money

Most people don't want to see themselves as ignorant either, so if you can explain that buying and consuming movies and literature related only to their field of interest keeps them ignorant, and that it is now a civic duty to get a liberal arts education to keep them well-rounded and to explore topics they wouldn't normally, then they will take you up on the challenge to read or watch at least one thing not in their field of study.

Many white liberals have no qualms about buying organic food for their health or recycled paper for the environment, yet some do not realize that buying from Black vendors helps those vendors economically. There's not yet a sticker to indicate such.

Ask them to consider where they put their money. Leave banks for credit unions that support communities. Buy Black media from Black businesses. Put your charitable donation budget toward NAACP and similar organizations. Don't support businesses that pay less than minimum wage.

Demand Racial Justice In Schools

Participate in the PTA for your child's school and demand diversity in universities.

Make Your Voice Heard

Recently the 19th Amendment hit a milestone; it has been a century since white women were allowed to vote. Let's honor the memory of all suffragettes and acknowledge how much work was put into allowing us to vote. Vote locally, vote for diverse representatives, vote for racial justice.

Speak up in union meetings or really any meetings when there's an opportunity to make a difference for racial justice. I recently heard someone share that she went to a local town hall meeting to decide if a gas station would be added to a rural area. The man on the committee asked an unrelated question "what size tree will you plant?," and when the man answered "whatever size is legal," the man on the committee said he would vote against the gas station because the size was too small. The only people in the audience were this one couple, and the woman's response to this situation was enough to change his vote to a yes. This is not a racial example, but an example that you will never know the extent of your influence. However, to keep realistic expectations, it doesn't always go that way. For example, I attended multiple meetings regarding the installation of biking paths in lieu of street parking when only a small fraction of the apartment dwellers could afford to pay or had been high enough on the waitlist to acquire a dedicated parking space. The situation was different because even though I represented everyone in my apartment, the majority of people invited to the meeting were non-residents hellbent on gentrification.

Whenever there is an opportunity to provide public comments, take full advantage of it. We have more power in numbers, and the numbers are not quite there yet. For example, when I provided public comments to something that affected me (the replacement of parking space with bicycle pathways), I was appalled that 1) the choice had been decided prior to my knowledge of it to satisfy white tourists, 2) the majority of people who called in were white bicyclists, and 3) I was the only representative in my diverse apartment complex and one of the very few representing people who actually lived in the area. If more people actually participated in public comments, they would have more power, and the people would not be bulldozed by the government.

Support Police Reform

Write to senators, representatives, mayors, the police department itself. Even community groups like churches and libraries can have sway. If you're not quite ready to "Defund the Police," at least you can encourage the use of bodycams (and vehicle cameras), community policing (with care packages for homeless people), social workers in response to a call, or getting rid of police unions.

Point Them To Resources

When they finally ask what they can do to improve, you can point them to some of the resources in the Resources section and/or you can tell them to make a point to read things for and by people who are different from them, kind of like a liberal arts education. The above list is a modification of the list from *So You Want to Talk About Race* (Oluo).

Most Importantly, Don't Give Up!

Ijeoma Oluo suggests not to keep trying to fix things when everyone's upset, keep the main thing the main thing, and remember that the road to hell is paved with good intentions (Oluo). If you're going to apologize, make sure to include not just "sorry," but the actions you'll take so it won't happen again and give them time to respond with how they feel. Understand that you will make (large) mistakes, but don't let that discourage you from continuing. Learn from your mistakes, grow, and get back on the horse.

Continue Studying: Take What You Need and Leave the Rest

I behoove you to continue to learn and study anti-racism with the caveat to use discernment. This section could appropriately be entitled, "Criticisms of Anti-Racism by an Anti-Racist," which is similar in concept to "Must I Be a Womanist?" by Monica A. Coleman. This may be the most controversial part of this book, but it's important and needs to be said.

First off, based on what someone has explained to me, anti-racism has a high barrier of entry as it requires people to seriously consider giving up those people who paid for their college bills, those who have helped them raise children, those who know the best and worst of themselves, those who've been there through thick and thin. Anti-racists are encouraged to be as willing to cut people out of their lives as Scientologists.

Anti-racism rules of conduct do not help upper middle class Blacks who grew up in white neighborhoods and Black adoptees who grew up in white families who may not be aware of the extent of racism but are forbidden from learning about it from a white person or NBPOC. The idea that it's a non-POC's responsibility to learn about racism is detrimental to the Black person because they don't know what to research if they don't know it's even a problem, and particularly if the Black person doesn't even know the extent of the problem either. Most people assume Black people all know the extent of the issue but never actually ask them how much exposure they've had to Black culture. If my ex had told me about his encounter with the police when it happened instead of hiding it for the first few years we dated, I could have researched and learned more and had set better expectations of our life together. If he had told me about racism back then, I would've fought longer to be his unemployment insurance, would have made a budget with him, would not have listened to my dad about his character, would not have compared his job application process with mine, would not have thought that he was using me, and would not think he had abandoned me like my birthmother. But he had trauma and fear of airing his dirty laundry. What we really need is for this to be taught to *everyone* in every school, however it may realistically take longer to get into schools than sex education. I address trauma in a later section.

Anti-racism teaches people to call others out on racist behavior. The idea here is not just to call people out on their behavior (which is terribly difficult on the neurodiverse[79]), but to call them in, like a prodigal son. And to also validate their personal experiences too if that is what you wish them to do for you. The neurodiverse comprise 53% of United States Americans as of September 2020 (Searing).

Anti-racism teaches one to avoid "tone policing." In the discussion of the brain, some may believe that there is a way to access the frontal cortex from the amygdala even though the brain scans don't bear it out, if speaking on the emotions of anger or fear. It's not just the work of the non-Black anti-racist to remain calm while allowing the other person to remain angry, while also not being triggered into a subset of anxiety or depression, but it's the work of the non-Black anti-racist to mirror, sympathize, and validate.

White Fragility teaches people to use white savior complex to eradicate white savior complex. *White Fragility* by Robin DiAngelo is a case study in what not to do. What not to do is to give someone "feedback." How many times has someone given you feedback, whether codependent or not, that you took as unconstructive criticism? Exactly. Because tearing down white savior complex with white savior complex while simultaneously diminishing Black people doesn't actually work (McWhorter, "The Dehumanizing Condescension of White Fragility"). If giving "feedback" to a person of color (POC) is not anti-racist, then why would you use it for the cause of anti-racism?

---

[79] See the section on adoptee trauma to learn more about how KADs are neurodiverse. Even though people with Black families can get a reprieve or time out from their anti-racist work, there is much less possibility of such reprieve or time out for adoptees of color.

But, in fact, the entire philosophy of anti-racism is white savior complex (codependency), for isn't the very idea of codependency encapsulated in the idea we are capable of changing people? I want you to consider, "How can we change society without changing people?" From a spiritual viewpoint, everyone and everything is already perfect; we just refuse to see it.

Even empathizing or sharing your own experience can be invalidating, even if that is what recovering codependents were taught to do in lieu of giving advice. From either side, saying one's personal experience with marginalization is apples to apples OR apples to oranges with someone else's experience with marginalization is participating in oppression olympics and is derailing, invalidating, and denies personal realities. However, the person with more privilege is encouraged to either not share personal experiences for showing sympathy or to understand that such sympathy might not always be appreciated. No one said this was going to be easy.

Anti-racism literature tells you to read more African-American literature. However, I would not stop there. I never would have considered racism a possibility of the troubles my ex and I had in 2007 despite the fact that African-American literature had been thrown to me left and right in a predominantly white liberal college.

The problem with anti-racist literature is that it oversimplifies things and was not founded by someone with both a psychology background and a worldly view. Despite its talk of intersectionality, it also does not consider the following:

- Gypsies (Roma etc.) who are still not accepted in much of Europe
- A higher likelihood that whites will die from drunk driving or drugs (including prescription) (Chilton)
- Jews (who also endured 400 years of slavery plus the Holocaust) and are still not accepted in certain parts of Europe

- That Black Lives Matter has the potential to shift racism to the Chinese by evoking the literary inquisition in which people were killed over homonyms
- The fact that any citizen should be well-informed of who they are voting for and be allowed to criticize anyone who is president or very possibly will be president within four years of taking oath
- The fact that Hispanics had the lowest educational attainment rates in high school and college in 2016, according to the Census Bureau and whites and Hispanics both have the highest literacy rates (35% and 34% respectively) (U.S. Department of Education National Center for Education Statistics).
- The fact that many people experience severe racism, not just African-Americans, for example, Indigenous Americans (Google "anti-racism," and I bet that the majority will be Black-centered.)

Some may think that anti-racism is part of the Democratic party's platform, which is not necessarily so. The Democrats are on the side of someone who was on the side of police. Anti-racism is not specific to a political party even if more people from one party may accept it. Anti-racists are well aware that even white liberals have racist practices, and white liberals do not always realize they need to embrace anti-racism more fully. Anti-racism is outside of party and is something that all people from either or any party should embrace, following their own intuition.

I want to share an opinion that I thought should be heard, but the interviewee did not want her name attached to this opinion, so I will paraphrase. KADs were mostly raised middle class and are well educated, but one cannot assume that educated people are more fair or less racist. Liberals can be classist at times, pretend to be authorities on something they don't have experience with, and created political correctness because they haven't done as much work on being civil with many different kinds of people as the working class has out of necessity. More can get done if they focus on concrete changes (the economy and prison system) over ideological changes.

Knowing all the above, is it still worth it to study anti-racist material? Absolutely. Just know that the discernment you apply to it could be seen as part of what white supremacy culture entails, according to Show Up for Racial Justice (SURJ).

Perhaps the best approach is to consider how each action you take affects other people and future generations.

WHEN THERE'S DRAMA, THERE'S TRAUMA

Disclaimer: Interview opinions do not necessarily represent my opinions. Matthew Durkee occasionally used pronouns interchangeably, not in an LGBTQ way, but in a way where "you" often means the objective "one."

PROFILE OF A TRAUMATOLOGIST STUDENT

Bio: Matthew Durkee is studying Community Counseling Care and Traumatology for his EDD (Educational Doctorate).

How do you feel that trauma is different for adoptees versus the traumas unique to the Black experience?

Matthew Durkee: That's a good question. For Korean adoptees, it's focused on loss of culture, but we're in a safe space. But there's still continuous trauma without resolution. The difference is that African-Americans have historical roots, but for Korean adoptees it's a new trauma so people are more in denial of it. I love using the term "I'm an insider on the outside looking inside." We are looking for that identity. What I've heard from other Korean adoptees is [...] we look Korean, but we don't have the Korean accent, and even our last names too. [At an interview,] when they saw my name, their first impression is that I must be a white guy. When I entered, you could see their faces change.

Are you familiar with adoption-based or identity-based trauma? An example would be loss, separation, stressful transition, and assimilation to a new culture.

Matthew Durkee: I'm very familiar. Adoption-based trauma focuses on loss of culture. When we're adopted from another country, we're taken and don't understand [why]. I was adopted when I was 5. I have vague episodical memories that will trigger a memory, but I can't place it. In America, we repress a lot of negative memories that we don't want to share. But it does surface every so often. An example for me is I have certain memories of a sound, and I'll remember running to a field in a uniform. When I went to Korea [near the orphanage], I saw a soccer field.

There are stages of grief and loss. There's no movement from there. We've lost ourselves. We've lost [our] culture. For me personally, I don't understand Korean culture 100%. There's little idiosyncrasies we don't understand.

Identity-based trauma is the sense of loss of identity. It's indicative of a lot of marginalized population groups to self-identify us as a person. I just recently did my DNA test and found that I'm 46% Mongolian and 1.6% Finnish, which I thought was interesting. What is the essence of me? When I was a child, I was very angry. "Why did my parents give me up? Was I that bad?" I have certain episodical memories.

Are you familiar with race-based traumatic stress injury or slavery-based trauma? An example would be experiencing a SWAT raid, being hurt by a police officer, or going to prison. It can also be accumulated from multiple smaller microaggressions.

Matthew Durkee: I am very familiar with microaggressions. The things that pop to mind are commercials with the dehumanization of Asian-Americans [during the time of] internment camps. [I remember] "ching chong ching." I remember wallball[80] as a kid, and when I'd win and get up on the wall, instead of ten people, fifty people would be throwing a ball at my butt. As a kid, I played it off as funny, but it was hurtful. I'd see different microaggressions in conversation. I never fit the model minority rule. There was a lot through my journey and through my education; I had to unpack my childhood and overt racial comments.

Are you familiar with inherited, secondhand, or vicarious trauma? This is also known as epigenetic PTSD, empathic strain, compassion fatigue, or burnout. Do you think it's controversial?

Matthew Durkee: No, it's not controversial. You can self-relate to other people's traumas by secondhand knowledge of it. A perfect

[80] Wallball is a schoolyard game similar to handball.

example I would say is 9/11 or the pandemic, COVID-19. I get really upset when Trump says the "China virus" because he's making fun of a culture. He's making fun of the Chinese. It hurts me vicariously being Asian because of certain things that happen to us.

One of the books I'm reading to get my doctorate is *Community Psychology: Foundations for Practice* by Victoria Chien Scott and Susan M. Wolfe.

Are you familiar with combat and operational stress reactions, or COSRs? Do you think that the pandemic is producing similar effects in people?

Matthew Durkee: I am a combat veteran from Desert Storm, and I have seen those stressors. It doesn't affect you in the moment, but out of those moments it affects you a lot. My master's was in military psychology. In a nutshell, yes, it's affecting everybody. Going back to the adoptee community, you can be on the sidelines but still in the context of that environment. I support Black Lives Matter. I support BIPOCs. I have been in these Black Lives Matter marches; I carry signs for "Veterans for Black Lives Matter."

Yes, people see the injustice that happens. The other side says, "This is the status quo." We need to change that narrative. Those narratives are community bias, and that needs to change.

Do you think that classic traumatic stressors as defined in the DSM are not all-inclusive? Do you realize that the DSM was created from a white lens?

Matthew Durkee: The DSM was created definitely from a white lens. However, it's very hard because you're taught what you're taught. There needs to be more DSM voices in the DSM V. I'm glad that "moral injury" is coming to the DSM. We believe in right vs. wrong. I always go back to the veteran perspective. We're taught not to kill, but veterans are [were] shouted at to kill. I do feel that more voices need to be part of the DSM. It shows a very white perspective on diagnoses. I remember attachment disorder and identity issues, but those are from a white lens. I know the APA association is trying to change that narrative and bring those voices to enrich the DSM VI. I do belong to the APA Association Division 19 and soon Division 27. I always get those emails about bringing more cultural awareness into the practices, literature, and policies. It's going to be continuous forever. It's not like, "We solved the race crisis; let's move forward." We can't. Even for myself, I learn every day about terminology and verbiage. Everybody's going to make mistakes, but those are learning growths [opportunities]. We were [My college was] the last college to talk about Black Lives Matter. It took Black people. There's gonna be definite major changes coming.

Are you familiar with the updates to the DSM regarding PTSD?

Matthew Durkee: Yes, I'm very well-versed in it. When we look at PTSD, particularly for veterans, it's lower than what most people want [it to be]. It's a catch-all term people want to use like "My child has ADHD." PTSD is also becoming a buzzword. PTSD came from "shellshock" to "PTS" to "PTSD". The prevalence is only 13% if you look at the criterion. The community is starting to look at that. That's why I'm part of a group of thinkers and educators.

Biopsychosocial spiritual model is [more appropriate] (I use a Venn diagram with yourself in the middle). Instead of using the term "PTSD" as a catchall phrase, we need to look at other terms that capture the essence. For instance, moral injury. Do we suffer from certain cognitive disorders?

The *social* model: What are the social stressors?

The *biological*: What are some biological factors that affect us? I have to take two pills to manage [my physical condition].

It can become *psychological* if I think, "Now I need to take this medication to help me." There has been a lot of hesitancy to use PTSD.

I have friends in the veterans and Korean adoptee community. I knew one vet who had never seen trauma, but when he got out, he says he has PTSD because he was military, but he had no combat. They now say, "I have PTSD because the military robbed me of this". It's a transition phase, not PTSD.

Have you seen *Deadpool*? Are you familiar with the term "trauma-lympics"? Do you think this can be invalidating?

Matthew Durkee: I think it can be invalidating, but I think people can use it to self-diagnose themselves to the point that they become disabled due to their own thought processes. I have to be careful about this one here; it reminds me of family members when they think they have this, this, this, and I will tell them, "You should seek medical help first. We're not medical experts." It can become true because of the psychocognitive ability of the brain to create things that might not be realistic. Going back to my biopsychosocial spiritual model, some people may think they are heavy even if they aren't, and they'll create pain, or they'll say they didn't sleep last night. It's kinda like "Seek help." They'd rather not listen to me because they thrive in that "trauma." It's a negative attention that people crave. We do want a certain amount of attention and will crave it. Babies crave that soft touch. They did the test with the monkey with the fur and the other one didn't have fur. The soft monkey created positive emotion[81]. I'm not an expert [yet]. I could be blowing a lot of smoke.

Do you think that people with trauma are more likely to buy guns?

Matthew Durkee: I've never thought of that because I see the people that buy, and I see the people that respect guns. I believe in the 2nd Amendment. I own a 9mm Beretta. The people that buy those AR-

[81] He is referring to the Harlow monkey experiments (Suomi, Collins and Harlow).

15s. Do you know what AR means? The term AR means assault rifle, which means to assault someone with a rifle. The 5.56 round is a high-yield grade. The AR-15 or AR-22 uses the low-density bullet. I think there's a higher percentage of people with trauma. They see that as a protective device for themselves, like a pacifier or blanket, something that makes them feel empowered. The 17-year-old kid that killed three people had an assault rifle.

Yes, a lot of people with trauma buy these rifles. I think it's funny in a grotesque way that these people have to buy guns and say, "All Lives Matter" and are shouting "America!" I served. I'm a veteran. Did you serve? No. I was in Lyndon, WA where there was a Black Lives Matter march. Lyndon is a very conservative town. They were all wearing their Trump hat and assault rifles. I would ask them, "Are you a veteran? Are you a veteran?" and they'd all say, "No." Right now Black Lives Matter is the narrative due to the historical trauma. I look at people [a person] my age carrying this rifle. He was white and screaming and yelling at an African-American girl. I was thinking, "You're in your 40s/50s swearing at a teenage girl. There's something wrong with that picture." I asked him, "Why are you screaming at this young kid? And why do you have a rifle if you believe in freedom of speech?" For me personally, I [physically] walked between Black Lives Matter and the other side. I do a lot of qualitative analysis. It's a protection.

Do you think we let too many things traumatize us?

Matthew Durkee: Yes, and no. I think sometimes we worry about ourselves, and we worry about how we see ourselves in our social network. We have a lot of self-doubt and give ourselves trauma.

At the college that I work at, we've been talking about equity and inclusiveness. I'm one of three men of color on the campus as a whole. There are more white people, more female vs. male. As a male POC, I also feel sometimes that in academia we talk about degrees being the road to success. I have a friend who says, "We need to change the narrative. Educate yourself. Get your degrees to move forward. Help yourself to help others. If you get your Bachelor's, Master's, Doctorate, you can grow and learn." I know people who don't even have an Associate's. In the military, I learned that you have to work your way up. I don't want anything on a silver platter; I want to earn it. It's a fine line. I do believe.

I have experienced specific examples within KAD organizations where one or more people act out from a place of trauma (e.g., feeling unworthy of love etc.). It is not a pretty picture, word gets around, and it's a (relatively) small community. To those who have witnessed enough KADs, we might even have the stereotype of inviting drama into our lives. I was certainly like that sometimes in my past. That's why there's a belief that dating another KAD can be either heaven or hell. Heaven because of deep understanding, and hell because of fear of abandonment. This is frustrating because, with all that drama, you're not really sure where you can be safe or where to find your sanctuary. I'm sure the same thing can be said of the Black experience.

It's apparent that we're not asking the right questions to understand how we can fix this country, and the problem is that we want quick and easy solutions, but it will require depth and compassion to understand and hear the depth of someone's pain. What we are actually dealing with is deep trauma, for both the transracial adoptee, the Black adoptee, and Blacks in general. In order to deal with trauma, what is important is for others to understand the magnitude of it without minimizing, belittling, or diminishing it.

I placed this chapter directly after the chapter of talking with adoptive parents because the amygdala is front and center to both discussions.

Adoption is a traumatic event in itself, the loss of culture, the stressful transition, but a lot of times adoptees are "sheltered and abused," enslaved, or they lose their adoptive parents to suicide or other types of deaths. Some adoptees have the added challenges of being persons with disabilities, disfigurations, or cleft lips. Sometimes adoptees get deported because their parents never bothered to naturalize them[82]. Even if they have citizenship, they are denied their driver's license (Lopez).

Adoptees are four times as likely (54 out of 100,000) to commit suicide than the average United States American (13.7 out of 100,000) (Leininger). In 2002, international adoptees in Sweden were found to be "three to four times more likely to have serious mental issues, including suicide and suicide attempts" than native Swedes (E. Kim). This is even a higher rate than in South Korea, which had the 4th highest suicide rate in the world in 2016, at 26.9 out of 100,000. This was much improved over 28.5 out of 100,000 in 2014. South Korea was not only a world leader in baby exportation but also in suicides for 18 years straight, with Mapo Bridge nicknamed the "Suicide Bridge" (World Health Organization). Taking an epigenetic look at this, one could even conclude that it's in our blood. (Epigenetics, literally "above," "on top of," or "in addition to", is the study of the biological mechanisms that will switch genes on or off but do not change the DNA sequence, leaving behind a heritable signature.) The subject of suicide in the adoptee community is controversial.

There are two cases I would like to mention here. One involved suicide and the other is as recent as January 2019. Philip Clay, 42, allegedly jumped from a 14th-floor window from an Ilsan apartment

---

[82] However, for those adoptees facing that issue, I heard there is a way to get a certificate of citizenship without going through the naturalization process. Naturalization was reserved only for whites who had lived in the U.S. for two years with the 1790 Naturalization Act, Mexicans could be naturalized in 1848, birthright citizenship was established in 1898 via the 14th Amendment and *Wong Kim Ark v. United States*, people could petition to be white in 1922, Indians can be naturalized via the 1924 Indian Citizenship Act, and Asians were eligible via the 1954 McCarran-Walter Act, probably since Asian adoption began in 1952, but Koreans had to wait until 1965 to immigrate en masse (PBS). The Child Citizenship Act of 2000 created automatic naturalization for those under 18 by February 27, 2007, but many US KADs without US citizenship were over that age at that time.

building after being deported to South Korea from the United States of America in 2012 (Soo-sun). Adam Crasper, 43, who had attended Philip Clay's funeral and ceremony, attempted to sue South Korea and Holt Children Services after being deported in 2016, partially also due to his criminal convictions, and being separated from his wife and child (Randall). Crasper was not only abandoned by his biological family but was abandoned twice by two different adoptive families.

Just as there is a grieving process, there is a process for processing the experience of adoption that also begins with denial and ends in acceptance. It is a 5-step process called the Adoption-Reconstruction Phase Theory, which includes denying awareness, emerging awareness, drowning in awareness, reemerging from awareness, then finding peace (Woolston). However, many adoptees criticize this for being dangerous because it is not clear that these phases may be in different orders for different people. I believe that I'm in the drowning in awareness phase.

There has been some forward movement in getting psychologists to clinically recognize adoption as a trauma in and of itself and recommend that adoptees should only frequent trauma-centered therapists.

TRAUMA FROM PAST SLAVERY

Slavery goes back generations and should be categorized as trauma first. There have been epigenetic studies done that shows that people who have never been exposed to a trauma but are descendants of those with trauma will retain their parents' trauma, which I kind of mentioned in the previous section regarding suicide (DeGruy). For example, during an alternative healing energy session, my adopted friend was able to uncover my inherited emotion of being taken for granted on my birthfather's side that went back 230 years, even though I don't even know my birthfather's name.

There's even such thing as secondhand or vicarious trauma, which can affect both African adoptees, African immigrants, or NBPOCs. It can also be called empathic strain, compassion fatigue, or burnout. In addition, scientists are finding that PTSD can be inherited, as in children of those in Khmer Rouge, the Vietnam War, or the Holocaust, which should be no surprise to those who lived it. However, the theory has even been tested with rats, where the children of rats exposed to a smell before electric shock would also have a fight or flight response to that smell, despite not having witnessed that event. It's possible the theory is controversial due to implications that white people don't want to admit. It's theorized that epigenetic PTSD markers travel via the small RNA, but scientists have yet to make further studies (Lennon).

Racial discrimination is a factor that makes racial minorities more likely to have PTSD, referred to as "race-based traumatic stress injury," but not yet accepted into the DSM, despite the 2012 correlation between racial discrimination and increased mental disorders (Wortham). Such incidents of race-based traumatic stress injury range from classic traumatic stressors to "cultural paranoia" to cumulative daily microaggressions, but only classic traumatic stressors are offically recognized, though that may change (VA's National Center for PTSD - Executive Division). This is problematic because, since racism is not included as a listed option under "qualifying trauma," it is not being tracked, studied, and taken seriously by professionals. The effects of racism also mirror what is seen in rape victims or victims of interpersonal abuse, particularly due to victim shaming. The new changes to the PTSD definition in the DSM include the symptoms of self-destructive behavior, distorted self-blame or blame of others, and a persistent negative emotional state, all of which can apply to race-based traumatic stress injury (D. T. Williams).Therapists even used to believe that a client's comments on race were a defensive and resistant change of topic away from "important" issues, thus leading to further traumatization (Williams).

Trauma also gets compounded when those who are supposed to honor, defend, and protect are those who oppress, as is the case with the occasional-to-frequent animosity and antagonism between adoptees and adoptive parents or Blacks and the police.

Fifty percent of women and sixty percent of men experience trauma at some point in their lives, and 8 million adults in the United States have PTSD. The loss of social activity for many during the pandemic exacerbated PTSD symptoms as it gave them more time to think about traumatic incidents. The George Floyd incident was the needle that broke the camel's back, both further exacerbating PTSD and increasing the likelihood of developing it. "Holly O'Reilly, a clinical psychologist [...] added, 'So repeated trauma exposure will increase the likelihood of developing post-traumatic symptoms.'" (Military Health System Communications Office).

Trauma can expose itself as a daily mental health challenge. It is well-known that addiction, attention deficit hyperactive disorder (ADHD), OCD, PTSD, and other mental health issues relate to or stem from trauma. Poor coping skills and the lack of ability to self-regulate are connected to trauma. Loss of control at one point in life can manifest as a need to control everything, internally or externally, as is the case with OCPD, which is rooted in childhood PTSD. Trauma can put a person on guard and create a situation where one is easily triggered. Certain kinds of trauma can affect the amygdala, making one more fearful or more irritable or impatient, and, therefore, not having enough energy to explain things one more time or more likely to destroy things and relationships that are of value. Learning is connected to trauma. It can affect the hippocampus, making it difficult to learn and retain knowledge and memories. It can damage the prefrontal cortex, making it more difficult to have good judgment. It can even affect the medulla oblongata, which controls autonomic, or involuntary, functions of the sleep-wake cycle, blood pressure, heart rate, breathing, vomiting, sneezing, and even the habitual prejudiced response in all humans. It can cause avoidance and constant bad moods and hopelessness. It can kill brain cells and prevent the production of brain cells. Trauma can result in seeking constant escapism, lack of trust, feeling on guard, not caring for personal safety, feelings of emptiness, agreeing to keep the peace or to keep security, craving control, and feeling responsible for other's happiness. Do you recognize any of these things in yourself or in people you know?

Stress can cause your brain to seize up during exams and job interviews. Stress can cause nightmares, which can lead to insomnia, which can lead to depression of all kinds, which can lead to suicide. It is also well-known for being the leading cause of all types of medical issues, like dementia, Alzheimer's, etc. It can also create excessive suspicion or defensiveness (Alban and Allebeck and Hjern).

During the COVID-19 pandemic, trauma can resemble combat and operational stress reactions (COSRs), due to the witnessing of death and dangerous working conditions. COSRs can result in anxiety, isolation, hypervigilance, fatigue, insomnia, and decreased attention (Evans, MA, MDiv and Case, MS).

For men in particular, trauma gets compounded by wearing oneself out to fit into a culture of toxic masculinity. Toxic masculinity can increase violence, both physical, verbal, and sexual. Studies have shown that it is not only tiresome to put on a tough façade, but also takes away brain power from other brain functions. Too much self-control is bad for your physical and mental health. Pretending reduces focus and executive function, increases stress and anxiety, increases the odds of overreactivity or aggression, causes one to overeat, and encourages one to engage in risky behavior (McGonigal). The same things that apply to men putting up a front can also apply to anyone who is in a "closet." Trauma is also what makes a grown man who rarely ever cries cry.

Trauma affects the ability to have healthy interpersonal relationships with others. That is why it is so important for others to do the work of understanding those with trauma from the comfort of their own home. Several step-by-step guides already exist and are available to those who seek them out.

Resources for family and friends:

Trauma Recovery:
https://trauma-recovery.ca/recovery/supporting-family-and-friends-affected-by-trauma/

National Center for PTSD:
https://www.ptsd.va.gov/publications/print/

TAKEAWAY

Korean adoptees are in a unique place in history where we have a vital role to play to help our Black brothers and sisters, whether literal or figurative. In the hope that we're still connected to our adoptive parents (or even our biological parents), we can have their undivided attention. Even if they disregard the first, second, or third attempts, we still have the best chance of reaching them. Since at least some of us live our Korean adoptee lives as figurative nomads, we have the opportunity of bridging the gap between the communities we're in. We can stand by like complicit bystanders, or we can make an actual change right where we're at—in our homes, in our jobs, and in our community.

What Korean or Black adoptees can do is support putting both adoption-based trauma and race-based traumatic stress injury into the DSM so it can be recognized, studied, assessed, diagnosed, and treated officially with publications in peer-reviewed journals. In addition, have compassion for those who possibly have it and learn about and practice anti-racism in their everyday lives.

We have a very important role inherent in our being born and our being placed into adoptive homes. I hope that with the understanding of how the Korean adoptee community is tied with the Black community, the understanding of trauma, and the understanding of how to talk with adoptive parents, you can take away how important your role is and what you can do to help the Black community by educating the white community, and, thereby, helping yourself.

In closing, we have to remember that "grief and love live in the same bed." Pain has a gift in it. If people use pain as a catalyst for conversational or policy change, or even a motivator to invest time into therapeutic art, we will all be able to move through the pain and come out the other side far improved.

APPENDIX A

EXTENDED TIMELINE

300 B.C.E.: Aristotle stated that some are born to be slaves, or barbarians (Pate, "How Asian Adoptees Can Support Black Lives Matter").

1501-1619: 500,000 Africans are enslaved in America (Hogan).

1636: Boston created the first police in America, called "Night Watch," after the creation of indentured servitude and prior to the first slave. In the following century, "slave patrols" were created to return runaway slaves to their owners.

March 5, 1770: The first protest against police brutality results in Crispus Attucks' death during the Boston Massacre (Harriot).

1785: Thomas Jefferson states in *Notes on Virginia* that he suspected that Black people were inferior because he only saw them as slaves and concludes that some are born to be ruled (Pate, "How Asian Adoptees Can Support Black Lives Matter").

December 1791: The 2nd Amendment was created to protect against slave uprisings, not to protect them against the British.

1845: The white race included only Northern European descendants and excluded the Irish, Jewish, and Romani, among other groups we consider white today. The hatred against Catholics had its roots in hatred against the Irish.

1879-1918: The Carlisle Indian Industrial School was the first federally funded off-reservation boarding school to contain only Indigenous children. Ten thousand children attended from 140 tribes.

February 19, 1942-March 20, 1946: The Japanese internment camps incarcerated 120,000 Japanese whether US citizens or not.

1945: Irish people are accepted as white because they fought in WWII (Hogan). However, Black people are not even though they fought too.

1948-1962: 3,000 Japanese children and 840 Chinese children were adopted by white parents, starting two years after the Japanese internment camps ended, making the the first adoptees in the United States of America. This is not related to adoption from China, which comes later.

1950-1953: The Korean War, or "isan kajok," took place and never completely ended.

1950s-Present: About 1,000 Latino children are adopted each year.

1953-1981: 38,000 Korean children were adopted (Silverman).

1958-1967: The Bureau of Indian Affairs and the Child Welfare League of America, among others, placed 395-696 Indigenous children in 84-97% white homes through the Indian Adoption Project.

August 11, 1965: The five-day Watts Rebellion took place in Watts, Los Angeles, CA and was the largest urban rebellion in the '60s in the United States even though anger over racial discrimination had been boiling for twenty years. It was a result of two brothers and a mother being arrested. After an officer drew a gun after a traffic speeding incident, the brothers' mother jumped onto the officer's back. The rebellion ended when 4,000 National Guard troops were called. Sadly, not much changed as a result of the protest (Nichols).

Late 1960s-1976: The Open Door Society in Minnesota recorded that about 12,000 Black children were placed into white homes.

1972: NABSW opposed transracial adoption (Silverman).

1978: The Indian Child Welfare Act slowed transracial adoption of Indigenous children.

1986-1990: 83 excessive force lawsuits against the LAPD resulted in a minimum of a $15,000 settlement (McKennett).

March 3, 1991: Four police officers (three who were white) clubbed Rodney Glen King Jr. more than 50 times with batons after stunning him with a taser, leaving him with facial nerve damage, a broken eye socket, and 11 skull fractures. This was witnessed by officers from the LAPD, the California Highway Patrol, and the Los Angeles School Police without anyone making a single report of misconduct[83] (Newton). Rodney King was days away from a job interview for a construction job. George Holliday, a plumber, made one of the first viral videos showing police brutality from the balcony of his apartment with a 35mm Sony Handycam SLR camera (Nevett).

March 15, 1991: The four officers who clubbed Rodney King were charged with assault (McKennett).

March 16, 1991: 51-year-old Soon Ja Du shot 15-year-old Latasha Harlins, an unarmed Black female adolescent, in her Empire Liquor Market Deli store in South Central LA with a 0.38-caliber altered handgun after accusing her of shoplifting orange juice[84] (Fang).

---

[83] Officers' shorthand for Blacks were "NHI," meaning "no humans involved."

[84] Things haven't changed much, after Sung Ho Lim, owner of Missha Beauty, was caught on video putting a Black female customer in a chokehold as late as 2017 after accusing her of shoplifting (Fang). And it's not just Koreans. In 2019, Kiyomi Brewer had been involved in three hate crimes and had met with Identity Evropa with her husband, but it was Kiyomi who was tried (Gorcenski).

November 15, 1991: Mrs. Du was sentenced to five years probation instead of the maximum of 16 years for voluntary manslaughter.

April 21, 1992: A state appeals court upheld the sentencing decision for Mrs. Du.

April 29, 1992: The 1992 Los Angeles uprising took place a week later, and lasted for six days, after the Simi Valley jury acquitted those four police officers who beat Rodney King. The uprising, which wouldn't have occurred without video evidence aired on the news, disproportionately affecting Koreatown. The Insurrection Act of 1807 was used, and George Bush deployed 4,000 Marines and soldiers and 1,000 federal troops trained in urban policing to supplement the 4,000 California National Guard members. Famous African-American poet Lucille Clifton wrote "officer powell whispers to himself" in response (Jenkins). The violent protests over the acquittal of the police officers that hurt Rodney King finally ended with 63 deaths (including two Asians); more than 2,000 injuries; 2,300 Korean liquor stores destroyed (including Empire Liquor); and $1 billion in property damage in LA (Kim and Yu 373 and Nguyen). This was especially devastating for those Koreans who owned up to 30 stores per person (KFSN-TV). Hong thinks that so many stores were burned that day because the TV and radio advised Koreans owners to stay away from their stores. Some say that this might not have occurred had they stayed in their stores because rioters do have hearts even though they're in a rage. However, Koreans with many stores would need at least one person to be working at each one. After the uprising, two of the officers who clubbed Rodney King served 30 months in prison.

April 1992: The first adoption law was created in China. "To international adopters and Western adoption agencies, this law heralded the 'opening' of Chinese adoption to the world," says Johnson, "but from the perspective of domestic[85] adoption it represented the final legal codification of severe restrictions and the closing down of spontaneous and customary adoption practices" (Volkman 17 and 124).

1992: Karen Bass helped to pass a City Charter measure to create a civilian review of officer misconduct and to change LAPD's structure (Haberkorn and Wire).

May 1992: May became the official month for Asian Pacific American Heritage Month by law.

July 1992: The Harlins family received $300,000 in a settlement from Mrs. Du's insurance company as a result of pressure from the Latasha Harlins Justice Committee (Feder-Haugabook).

May of 1993: Renford Reese, Rodney King's mentor and interviewee Hayley Hoffman's dear friend, was selected for a Presidential Fellowship program where he created the "Colorful Flags Human Relations Module," and app, which teaches implicit bias, cultural sensitivity, cultural competency, and the most important human relations statements in 26 languages in an attempt to reconcile the African-American and Korean-American community, as well as the Black community with the police department. He brought his work to businesses, schools, social service agencies, and police departments (Reese).

1993: Tupac Shakur released the first of many songs dedicated to and making mention of Latasha Harlins.

---

[85] I learned while writing this book that the meaning of this is not readily apparent to non-adoptees. The word "domestic," in this context refers to adoption and adoptees born in the United States of America, as opposed to those born outside of the country.

Late 1990s-early 2000s: More than 5,000 Chinese adoptees were placed in American homes.

July 27, 1998: National Korean War Veterans Armistice Day was established to commemorate the 45th anniversary of the signing of the armistice at Panmunjom that returned Korea to the post-WWII status quo but never ended the Korean War and is celebrated in both the United States and South Korea even though North Korea has not honored the armistice three times. The Korean War was in "thanks" to the United States allowing Russia to declare war against Japan. Japan, also an oppressor, released what is now North Korea to Russian control, thinking it had the power to do so as the colonizer. South Korea is the way it is now due to the American attitude of implementing "police action" to fend off communism (Wallace).

2015: Jamar Clark was shot by two police officers in Minneapolis. Twin Cities Coalition for Justice 4 Jamar was created in response (Bates and Villa).

2016: Philando Castile was killed by a police officer in a suburb of Minneapolis. The police officer was acquitted.

2017: A Black police officer killed a white woman and was sentenced to 12.5 years in prison (Hinton).

May 25, 2020: the Korean Consulate sent out 370,000 face masks to 14 countries, sending 25-50 masks to each KAD or Korean War veterans who requested them (Kim and Dobson). The Korean Consulate sent a total of 35,000 to Korean war vets in Canada (CBC).

May 26, 2020: The George Floyd protests took place, one day after four police officers were widely seen in a video asphyxiating George Floyd, whose charge in no way justified the treatment, disproportionately affecting Minneapolis, the city that hosts the most KADs in America.

June 11, 2020: U.S. Senator Rand Paul introduced the Justice for Breonna Taylor Act, which will ban no-knock raids.

June 12, 2020: A South Korean court ruled that Kara Bos (Kang Mee-sook), a KAD, had the right to be part of her biological father's family registry, which acts as a cross between a genealogical record and a legal system akin to an American social security number (Choe).

June 25, 2020: Karen Bass, Chairwoman of the Congressional Black Caucus, passed The Justice in Policing Act[86] in Congress. Her interest in police reform began during her time living in South LA in 1973 when the chokehold was common. LA police had also vandalized her car and broke into her house multiple times. Her name has often come up as to who will replace Nancy Pelosi when Pelosi retires (Haberkorn and Wire). This would affect all 12,000 police departments in the United States (Cory).

June 25, 2020: This was the 70th anniversary of the Korean War, which is still officially going on to this day.

[86] This Act would require bias training and more data sharing regarding use of force, would ban "no-knock" search warrants and chokeholds throughout the nation, would make it easier for victims to sue police, and would roll back "qualified immunity" protections for police (Nadler).

APPENDIX B

CURATED ANTI-RACIST RESOURCES

This is not and never will be a complete list. There are many, many anti-racist resources available. I've only highlighted a very few that I think are exceptionally noteworthy.

Apps

Stand Up to Racism: https://apps.apple.com/us/story/id1516334642

Here are multiple apps you can look into to help you in your anti-racist journey.

Apple News: If you just want to start with something really easy, check out the Racial Justice section in Apple News, then look under Resources.

Articles

Shutack, Corinne. "75 Things White People Can Do for Racial Justice." *Medium*. 13 August 2017. https://medium.com/equality-includes-you/what-white-people-can-do-for-racial-justice-f2d18b0e0234

Asante-Muhammad, Dedrick; Collins, Chuck; Hamilton, Darrick; Hoxie, Josh. "Ten Solutions to Bridge the Racial Wealth Divide." Inequality.org. 15 April 2019. https://inequality.org/great-divide/ten-solutions-bridge-racial-wealth-divide/

Books and Movies

Alexander, Michelle. *The New Jim Crow*. 2010. Book.

Chilton, Karen. Alexander, Michelle. *The New Jim Crow: 10th Anniversary Edition*. 2020. Audio Book.

Jarecki, Eugene. *The House I Live In*. 5 October 2012.

John, Jaiya. *Black Baby White Hands: A View from the Crib*. 5 May 2005.

Tillman Jr., George. *The Hate U Give*. 19 October 2018.

Organization

Hollaback! https://www.ihollaback.org/

Teaches bystander training to prevent harassment of all kinds.

WORKS CITED

Abadi, Mark. "'The blacks,' 'the gays,' 'the Muslims' — linguists explain one of Donald Trump's most unusual speech tics." *Business Insider* 17 Oct 2016.

ACLU Foundation. *War Comes Home: The Excessive Militarization of American Policing*. New York, NY: American Civil Liberties Union, 2014.

Alban, Deane. "12 Traumatic Effects of Stress on Your Brain." *Be Brain Fit* 12 December 2018.

Allebeck, Peter and Anders Hjern. "Suicide in First- and Second-Generation Immigrants in Sweden: A Comparative Study." *Soc Psychiatry Psychiatric Epidemics* 10 April 2002: 423-429.

Baldwin, Rachel Kavanagh. *Facebook Messenger Interview with Rachel Kavanagh Baldwin* Woo Ae Yi. 2020.

Barker, Kim. "The Black Officer Who Detained George Floyd Had Pledged to Fix the Police." *The New York Times* 27 June 2020.

Bates, Josiah and Lissandra Villa. "A City Mobilized." *TIME* 15 June 2020.

Bishoff, Tonya and Jo Rankin. *Seeds from a Silent Tree: An Anthology By Korean Adoptees*. San Diego: Pandal Press, 1997.

Caracola, Ola. "A Quick Read for White People Who Don't Consider Themselves Racist." *Medium* 5 June 2020.

Carlson, J. "Adoption and criminal behavior." *Workshop American Adoption Congress*. Calgary, Alberta, 1988.

CBC. "A gift with Seoul: Korean War vet thrilled with gift of masks to recognize service." *CBC News* 1 July 2020.

Cha, Steph. *Your House Will Pay: A Novel*. Los Angeles, CA: Ecco, 2019.

Chang, Doris F., Biing-Jiun Shen and David T. Takeuchi. "Prevalence and demographic correlates of intimate partner violence in Asian Americans." *Int J Law Psychiatry* (2009): 167-175.

Chilton, Karen. *The New Jim Crow*. By Michelle Alexander. Audible, 2012. Audiobook.

Choe, Sang-Hun. "Korean Adoptee Wins Landmark Case in Search for Birth Parents." *The New York Times* 12 June 2020.

Clement, Thomas Park. *Telephone Interview* Woo Ae Yi. 8 February 2007.

Collins, Ben, Brandy Zadrozny and Emmanuelle Saliba. "White nationalist group posing as antifa called for violence on Twitter." *NBC News* 1 June 2020.

Community Marketing & Insights. "CMI's 13th Annual LGBTQ Community Survey." June 2019. *Community Marketing Inc.* 11 July 2020.

Cory, Eli. *Community Policing Discussion* Ed. Burke, VA, 21 July 2020. Zoom.

Cox, Susan Soon-Keum. *Voices from Another Place: A Collection of Works from a Generation Born in Korea and Adopted to Other Countries.* St. Paul, MN: Yeong & Yeong, 1999.

Davenport, Barrie. "25 Good Character Traits List Essential for Happiness." 12 October 2014. *Live Bold and Bloom.* 11 July 2020.

DeGruy, Dr. Joy . *Post-Traumatic Slave Syndrome: America's Legacy of Enduring Injury and Healing.* New York, NY: Joy DeGruy Publications Inc., 2017.

Dunbar, Joy. "Korea's reggae bands keep busy releasing new music." *Korea Times* 9 March 2019.

Enyclopædia Brittancia. "Africa: Continent." 7 November 2019. *Encyclopædia Brittanica.* 22 June 2020.

Essence. "Letters [to the Editor]." *Essence* May 2007: 28.

Evans, MA, MDiv, Christian and Spencer Case, MS. "The Physiology of Combat Stress Reactions." *Psychological Health Center of Excellence (formerly Deployment Health Clinical Center)* 12 July 2020.

Faiola, Anthony. "Japanese Women Catch the 'Korean Wave': Male Celebrities Just Latest Twist in Asia-Wide Craze." *The Washington Post* 31 August 2006.

Fang, Jenn. "26 Years After the Murder of Latasha Harlins, Asian Americans Still Have a Lot of Work to do Around Anti-Blackness." 15 March 2017. *Reappropriate.* 26 June 2020.

Feder-Haugabook, Ayala. "Latasha Harlins (1975-1991)." 14 September 2017. *Black Past.* 29 July 2020.

FindLaw for the Public. *Glossary of Adoption Terms.* 2007. 2 April 2007.

Fletcher, Steve. "Why We Must Disband the Minneapolis Police." *TIME* 22-29 June 2020: 35.

Fox, Nancy and Dr. Sook Wilkinson. *After the Morning Calm: Reflections of Korean Adoptees.* Detroit, MI: Sunrise Ventures, 2002.

Freundlich, Madelyn and Joy Kim Lieberthal. *The Gathering of the First Generation of Adult Korean Adoptees: Adoptees' Perceptions of International Adoption.* New York: The Evan B. Donaldson Adoption Institute, 1999.

Fuchs, Chris. "Asian-American Advocates Work to End Stigma of Domestic Violence." *NBC News* 21 October 2015.

GHFP. "Trauma of slavery and epigenetics." 15 October 2018. *Healing the Wounds of Slavery.* 22 June 2020.

Gook. Dir. Justin Chon. Perf. Justin Chon. 2017. Movie.

Gorcenski, Emily. "Ben Shapiro and the Conservative Chorus." 3 June 2020. *Political Research Associates.* 10 July 2020.

Haberkorn, Jennifer and Sarah D. Wire. "Rep. Karen Bass saw police reforms fizzle after Rodney King. She doesn't plan to let that happen again." *Los Angeles Times* 10 June 2020.

Harjo, Suzan Shown. "Washington 'Redskins' is a racist name: US pro football must disavow it." *The Guardian* 17 January 2013.

Harriot, Michael. "A Timeline of Events That Led to the 2020 'Fed Up'-rising." *The Root* 30 May 2020.

Hinton, Elizabeth. "The Minneapolis Uprising in Context." *Boston Review* 29 May 2020.

Hjern, Anders, Frank Lindblad and Bo Vinnerljung. "Suicide Attempts and Severe Psychiatric Morbidity Among Former Child Welfare Clients--A National Cohort Study." *Journal of Child Psychology & Psychiatry. Association for Child and Adolescent Mental Health.* Blackwell Publishing, 2005.

Hogan, Liam. "Were Irish people the "first slaves in America"?" *Medium* (2020).

Holt International Children's Services. *The Gathering.* 25 January 2007.

Honda, Rep. Michael M. "H. Res. 121." *A resolution expressing the sense of the House of Representatives that the Government of Japan should formally acknowledge, apologize, and accept historical responsibility in a clear and unequivocal manner for its Imperial Armed Forces' coercion of young* . Washington, DC: 110th Congress, 30 July 2007. House resolution.

In, Saroful. "So you think you know a thing: Feministing 201." 24 January 2017. *CrossKnit ~ Gauge as Rx'ed.* 10 July 2020.

International Adoptee Congress. "Memberships." *The International Adoptee Voice.* International Adoptee Congress 1.1, February 2007.

—. "What was the best connection you made at the 2006 IAC gathering in Washington, DC?" February 2007. *The International Adoptee Voice.*

Jenkins, Megan. "Literary Treasures: Lucille Clifton reading her poems in the Montpelier Room, Library of Congress, Dec. 2, 1999." 26 June 2020. *From the Catbird Seat: Poetry & Literature at the Library of Congress - blogs.loc.gov.* 30 June 2020.

Jones, Zoë. "Los Angeles-area Social Justice Program Announces Community Racial Justice Education Effort." *Colorful Flags.* Pomona, CA: Colorful Flags, 6 August 2020. Press Release.

Juvenile Law Center. "What is the Foster Care-to-Prison Pipeline?" 26 May 2018. *Juvenile Law Center.* 25 June 2020.

Kendi, Ibram X. "The American Nightmare." *The Atlantic* 1 June 2020.

KFSN-TV. "Former LAPD Chief Daryl Gates dies at 83." *ABC30* 11 November 2010.

—. "Rodney King, who beating led to LA riots, dies." *ABC30* 17 June 2012.

Kim, Elaine H. and Eui-Young Yu. *East to America: Korean-American Life Stories.* New York, NY: The New Press, 1996.

Kim, Eleana. "Our Adoptee, Our Alien: Transnational Adoptees as Specters of Foreignness and Family in South Korea." *Anthropological Quarterly* (2007): 497-531.

Kim, Monica. *Zoom interview* Woo Ae Yi. 27 June 2020.

Kim, Stella and Mahalia Dobson. "South Korea to send masks to Korean adoptees living abroad." *NBC News* 25 May 2020.

Lee, J. S. "Adoption & Slavery." 2020. *JS Lee: Author. Cat Pillow. Maker of Things.* 29 July 2020.

Lee, Marie Myung-Ok. *Somebody's Daughter: A Novel.* Boston: Beacon Press, 2005.

Leininger, Tim. "New foundation focuses on helping Korean American adoptees and families find out where they fit in." *Journal Inquirer* 24 June 2020.

Lennon, Annie. "Can We Inherit PTSD from Our Parents?" 16 June 2019. *Lab Roots.* 30 July 2020.

Lifton, B.J., Ph.D. *Lost and found: the adoption experience. 2nd Ed.* New York City, 1988.

Lin, Alvin. "Study Finds Disturbing STD Rates Among Asian Americans." *Hyphen Magazine* 6 May 2010.

Linguistic Society of America. "The political power of 'the': A linguistic analysis." *AAAS* (2019). Press Release.

Lopez, Elwyn. "Naturalized citizen says state was unable to verify her citizenship when she applied for a driver's license." *11Alive* 20 February 2020.

Mapes, Diane. "It takes more than love: What happens when adoption fails." 1 August 2012. *Today.* 11 July 2020.

Marr, Elisha. ""I'll Have the Melting Pot Soup with a Side of Black.": Transracial Adoption and the Racial-Ethnic Color Line." *Michigan Sociological Review* (2011): 33-52.

McGinnis, Hollee. *Interview with Hollee McGinnis* Yi Woo Ae. 2007.

McGonigal, PhD, Kelly. *The Willpower Instinct.* New York, NY: Avery, 2011.

McKennett, Hannah. "How 15-Year-Old Latasha Harlins' Murder Over a Bottle of Orange Juice Helped Spark The L.A. Riots." *All That's Interesting* 30 September 2019.

McWhorter, John. "The Dehumanizing Condescension of White Fragility." *The Atlantic* 15 July 2020.

—. "Why Latinx Can't Catch On." *The Atlantic* 27 May 2020: 1-4.

Menakem, Resmaa. *My Mother's Hands: Racialized Trauma and the Pathway to Mending.* Las Vegas, NV: Central Recovery Press, 2017.

Merriam-Webster. "What does 'otaku' really mean?" 23 June 2020. *Merriam-Webster.* 23 June 2020.

Military Health System Communications Office. "Invisible wounds: understanding PTSD." 26 June 2020. *Health.mil.* 30 June 2020.

Minnesota Department of Health. *Populations of Color and American Indians.* 2012. 18 June 2020.

Mitchell, J., M.D. "Anorexia nervose and bulimia." *U of Minnesota P* (1985).

Mo. "The Mongolian Spot--The Article." 16 February 2006. *Korean Adoption Blog.* 16 February 2006.

Nabiya. *Telephone interview* Woo Ae Yi. 14 February 2007.

Nadler, Jerrold. "Amendment in the Nature of a Substitute to H.R. 7120." *George Floyd Justice in Policing Act of 2020.* New York, NY: House Committee on the Judiciary, 15 June 2020. Congressional Bill.

NAPAWF. "APA Women and Abortion: A Fact Sheet." 8 April 2007. *National Asian Pacific American Women's Forum.* 8 April 2007. <http://www.napawf.org>.

—. "APA Women and Proposition 73." 8 April 2007. *National Asian Pacific American Women's Forum.* 8 April 2007. <http://www.napawf.org>.

—. "Medicaid and Asian Pacific American Women." 8 April 2007. *National Asian Pacific American Women's Forum.* 8 April 2007.

—. "Reproductive Health Care and APA Women: A Fact Sheet." 8 April 2007. *National Asian Pacific American Women's Forum.* 18 June 2020.

—. "Sex Selection: A Fact Sheet." 8 April 2007. *National Asian Pacific American Women's Forum.* 18 June 2020.

—. "Violence Against Women Act of 2005." 8 April 2007. *National Asian Pacific American Women's Forum.*

—. "Vote NO on Proposition 85!: Talking Points." 8 April 2007. *National Asian Pacific American Women's Forum.*

National Center for PTSD. *Understanding PTSD: A Guide for Family and Friends.* National Center for PTSD, 2019.

Nelson, Kim Park. "Korean Transracial Adoption in Minnesota." *MNOPEDIA* 23 July 2018: 1-6.

Nevett, Joshua. "George Floyd: The personal cost of filming police brutality." *BBC* 11 June 2020.

Newton, Jim. "Op-Ed: Rodney King's beating provides a road map for investigating police misconduct." *Los Angeles Times* 11 June 2020.

Nguyen, Viet Thanh. "The Model Minority Trap." *Time* 6-13 July 2020: 59.

Nichols, Casey. "Watts Riot (August 1965)." 23 October 2007. *Black Past.* 29 July 2020.

NowThis News. "This PSA Is Making Sure Asian Americans GOTV." *YouTube.* NowThis News, 8 September 2020. YouTube video.

Olitzky, Rabbi Avi S. "Why I, a Minneapolis Rabbi, Changed My Mind About 'Black Lives Matter'." *The New York Jewish Week* 2 June 2020.

Oluo, Ijeoma. *So You Want to Talk About Race.* New York City, NY: Seal Press, 2019.

Oparah, Julia Chinyere, Sun Yung Shin and Jane Jeong Trenka. *Outsiders Within: Writing on Transracial Adoption.* Cambridge, MA: South End Press, 2006.

Ostroff, R. "A look inside America's hidden system of teen control." *Rolling Stone* 20 November 1986.

Pate, SooJin. "How Asian Adoptees Can Support Black Lives Matter." *How Asian Adoptees Can Support Black Lives Matter.* Minneapolis, MN: AK Connection, 23 August 2020. Zoom Meeting.

Pate, SooJin. *Telephone interview* Woo Ae Yi. 22 June 2020.

Pate, SooJin. *Telephone interview* Woo Ae Yi. 19 January 2007.

PBS. *RACE - The Power of an Illusion*. 2020. 17 July 2020.

Radar Staff. "BREAKING NEWS: Ex-LA Police Chief Daryl Gates Dies At 83." *RadarOnline* 16 April 2010.

Randall. "Deported Korean American Adoptee Sues South Korea and Adoption Agency." *AsAm News* 24 January 2020.

Reese, Renford. *Colorful Flags*. 2020. 11 July 2020.

Register, Cheri. *Beyond Good Intentions: A Mother Reflects on Raising Internationally Adopted Children*. St. Paul, MN: Yeong & Yeong Book Company, 2005.

Robinson, Katy. *A Single Square Picture: a Korean Adoptee's Search for Her Roots*. New York: Berkley Books, 2002.

Roorda, Rhonda M. and Rita J. Simon. *In Their Own Voices: Transracial Adoptees Tell Their Stories*. New York, NY: Columbia University Press, 2000.

Roorda, Rhonda M. *Phone interview* Woo Ae Yi. 27 March 2007.

Sack, Kevin. "Door-Busting Drug Raids Leave a Trail of Blood." *New York Times* 18 March 2017.

Sambou, Tawanda Scott. *The First Time I Realized I Was Black*. 2020. Video.

Saslow, Eli. "The white flight of Derek Black." *Washington Post* 15 October 2016.

Scalzi, John. "Straight White Male: The Lowest Difficulty Setting There Is." 15 May 2012. *Whatever.* 11 July 2020.

Schecter, M., Ph.D. "Lecture." *American Adoption Congress*. 1981.

Searing, Linda. "During pandemic, growth of U.S. adults with mental health issues jumps to 53 percent." *The Washington Post* 6 September 2020.

Show Up for Racial Justice. "History of the Race Construct." June 2020. *Dr. Works Book*. 16 July 2020.

Silverman, Arnold R. "Outcomes of Transracial Adoption." *The Future of Children* (1993): 104-118.

Simmons, Ann M. "African immigrants are more educated than most -- including people born in US." *Los Angeles Times* 12 January 2018.

Smith-Morris, Carolyn. "Addressing the Epidemic of Missing & Murdered Indigenous Women." *Cultural Survival* 6 March 2020.

Soleil, Erykah. *Interview with Erykah Soleil* Woo Ae Yi. 14 July 2020.

Sommers, Sam. "Whites Believe They are Victims of Racism More Often Than Blacks." *TuftsNow* 23 May 2011.

Soo-sun, You. "A sad ending for deported adoptee." *The Korea Times* 5 June 2017.

Starr, Terrell Jermaine. "Words Matter: How the Language Used to Describe the Unrest in Baltimore Supports White Supremacy." *AlterNet* 29 April 2015.

Stransky, Llyn. "In the matter of Latasha Harlins: A Regrettably Late Apology." 20 May 2020. *For Latasha*. 29 July 2020.

Suomi, Stephen J., et al. "EFFECTS OF MATERNAL AND PEER SEPARATIONS ON YOUNG MONKEYS." *The Association for Child and Adolescent Mental Health* (1976).

Swanson, Kirsten. "Minnesota nonprofit to help reunite Korean adoptees with birth families." *KSTP TV - Minneapolis* 2 November 2019: 1.

Tatum, Beverly Daniel. "Defining Racism: "Can We Talk?"." Tatum, Beverly Daniels. *Why Are All the Black Kids Sitting Together in the Cafeteria? and Other Conversations About Race*. New York City, NY: Perseus Books, LLC, 1997. 3-13.

Taylor, David. *Phone interview* Woo Ae Yi. 19 June 2020.

Taylor, Marisa. "Rodney King Case Changed Perceptions of Police Brutality." *ABC News* 17 June 2012.

The Gide Foundation. "KTsq Leadership Team Meeting." 3 August 2020. Meeting Minutes.

The International Adoptee Voice. "IAC Mission." February 2007. *International Adoptee Congress*. February 2007.

There Is No Me Without You: One Woman's Odyssey to Rescue Africa's Children. Dir. Amazon Shorts. 2006. Short film.

Treisman, Rachel. "Minneapolis Police Reportedly Identify Viral 'Umbrella Man' As White Supremacist." *NPR* 28 July 2020.

U.S. Bureau of Labor Statistics. "Highlights of women's earnings in 2017." Report 1075. 2018.

U.S. Census Bureau. "65 and Older Population Grows Rapidly as Baby Boomers Age: U.S. Census Bureau Releases 2019 Population Estimates by Demographic Characteristics." 25 June 2020. *United States Census Bureau.* 30 June 2020.

U.S. Department of Education National Center for Education Statistics. "Adult Literacy in the United States." *Data Point* July 2019.

Unicef. "Orphans." 2020. *Unicef.* 9 September 2020.

University of Minnesota. *Adoption Medicine Clinic.* 2020. 6 October 2020.

VA's National Center for PTSD - Executive Division. *June is PTSD Awareness Month - PTSD Monthly Update, June 2020.* 26 June 2020. Email.

Vickery, Martha. "Multicolor Dream Becomes Reality: Here project finds a partner in Rainbow World." *Korean Quarterly: Second Section 9.1* Fall 2005: 49 and 71.

Volkman, Toby Alice. *Cultures of Transnational Adoption.* London, UK: Duke University Press, 2005.

Wallace, Joe. "National Korean War Veterans Armistice Day." 27 July 2020. *Military Benefits.* 29 July 2020.

Wanshel, Elise. "Black Man Gets KKK members to Disavow by Befriending Them." *Huffington Post* 22 December 2016.

Wilkinson, Ph.D., Hei Sook Park. *Birth is More Than Once: The Inner World of Adopted Korean Children.* Detroit, MI: Sunrise Ventures, 1985.

Williams, Dr. Monnica T. "Can Racism Cause PTSD? Implications for DSM-5." *Psychology Today* 20 May 2013.

—. "Colorblind Ideology Is a Form of Racism." 27 December 2011. *Psychology Today.* 11 July 2020.

Wilson, Cindy. *Too Much Soul: The Journey of an Asian Southern Belle*. Jackson, MS: Too Much Soul, LLC, 2018.

Wing, Nick. "When The Media Treats White Suspects And Killers Better Than Black Victims." *Huffington Post* 6 December 2017.

Woolston, Amanda. "A Discussion of Adoption-Reconstruction Phase Theory with Dr. L. DiAnne Borders." 23 April 2013. *Declassified Adoptee*. 21 August 2020.

World Health Organization. "Suicide Rate by Country 2020." n.d. *World Population Review*. 25 June 2020.

Wortham, Jenna. "Racism's Psychological Toll." *The New York Times Magazine* 24 June 2015.

Yam, Kimmy. "Kelly Chauvin and a history of Asian women being judged for whom they marry." *NBC News* 22 June 2020.

Zara. "Narratives of White Women Used to Uphold Racism and Patriarchy: A Partial Timeline." 11 May 2011. *Conspire for Change*. 10 July 2020.

ACKNOWLEDGMENTS

I would like to thank the many friends, relatives, and supporters who have made this happen. All the people I interviewed helped me with my research. I am indebted to all the participants I interviewed for helping me with my project, in 2007 and in 2020: Amy Elizabeth, Bree Davis, David Taylor, Hayley Hoffman, Helsen Valdes, Holly Choon Hyang Bachman, JaeHee Melanie Chung-Sherman, Jessica Farrell, Jordan Davis, Lisa A. Quaites, Matthew Goodman, Milton Washington, Monica Kim, Renford Reese, Rhonda Roorda, Rutledge, SooJin Pate, Thomas Park-Clement, Yoon-Sook Kim, and Young-wha. I'm also thankful to Renford Reese, Professor E. Ethelbert Miller, Yun-Sook Kim Navare, Erell Reeves, Hayley Hoffman, Helsen Valdes, Jordan Davis, Monica Kim, and many of the previously named interviewees, for reviewing my manuscript, despite busy schedules and to Janine Vance for creating the cover image. I'm honored to have had open, deep, nonjudgmental conversations about race, a privilege that not everyone has. I am thankful to my spouse for understanding the importance of this project to me and letting me work many hours, days, and weeks on it without distraction. Finally, I thank God for leading me down the path that resulted in this project.

ABOUT THE AUTHOR

Yi Woo Ae is an author, poet, lyricist, playwright, and unofficial anthropologist who was born in a suburb of Seoul, South Korea, and is an U.S. citizen. She has published twelve books, including this one, on the topic of Korean adoptees, Goths, romance and sex, spirituality, and prison. She was raised in the white-populated area of Little Korea, the Koreatown of the metropolitan DC area, and lived in the Korean-populated area of Little Korea for more than 10 years. She volunteers at Adoptee Hub as a copywriter to help stand up a birth search portal, among other adult adoptee services.

A COMPLETE LIST OF BOOKS[87]

[87] Most are still under the former name of Ame Ai

1. *Best Hits of Yi Woo Ae* (2020), a free lyrics book available on OurBoox during the pandemic, https://www.ourboox.com/books/best-hits-of-ame-ai/. Please ask for permission before using lyrics.
2. *Imprisoned Love Without a Home in the North vs. the South (and Other Directions)* (2020), a free poetry book available on OurBoox during the pandemic, https://www.ourboox.com/books/north-vs-south-and-other-directions/
3. *What Is This, Art Exhibitionistella* (2018), a poetry book available on Amazon and Kindle
4. *Ebb and Flow: Anthology of Korean-American Poets 2017* (2017), a poetry anthology I edited, available on Amazon
5. *Enlightenment without a Home* (2013 and 2020), a free poetry book available on OurBoox during the pandemic, https://www.ourboox.com/books/enlightenment-without-a-home/#
6. *Prison, Poetry, and Purpose-Full Songs* (2011), a poetry and lyrics book available on Amazon
7. *Fringe and Frivolity* (2010 and 2019), a poetry book available on Amazon and Kindle
8. *Cheating on Someone* (2010), a novel available on Amazon
9. *Escape from Crystal City* (2010 and 2018), a play available on Amazon and Kindle
10. *Lyrics and Verses* (2009), a poetry and lyrics book available on Amazon, Kindle, and Audible, as well as large print
11. *Valley of the Mind's Shadow* (2009 and 2019), a poetry book available on Amazon and Kindle
12. *Love, Not Love* (2008 and 2019), a poetry book available on Amazon and Kindle

www.ingramcontent.com/pod-product-compliance
Lightning Source LLC
Chambersburg PA
CBHW021307190726
48288CB00003B/738

* 9 7 8 1 9 5 3 3 9 7 2 1 8 *